The Reference Shelf

Representative American Speeches 1996–1997

Editors

Calvin McLeod Logue
Josiah Meigs Professor of Speech
University of Georgia

and

Jean DeHart
Assistant Professor of Communication Arts
Appalachian State University

The Reference Shelf
Volume 69 • Number 6

The H. W. Wilson Company
New York • Dublin
1997

The Reference Shelf

The books in this series contain reprints of articles, excerpts from books, addresses on current issues, and studies of social trends in the United States and other countries. There are six separately bound numbers in each volume, all of which are usually published in the same calendar year. Numbers one through five are each devoted to a single subject, providing background information and discussion from various points of view and concluding with a subject index, and a comprehensive bibliography that lists books, pamphlets and abstracts of additional articles on the subject. The final number of each volume is a collection of recent speeches. This number also contains a cumulative speaker index. Books in the series may be purchased individually or on subscription.

Visit H.W. Wilson's web site: http://www.hwwilson.com

Library of Congress has cataloged this serial title as follows:

Representative American speeches. 1937 / 38–
    New York, H. W. Wilson Co.
        v. 21 cm.—(The Reference shelf)
    Annual.
    Indexes:
        Author index: 1937/38–1959/60, with 1959/60;
        1960/61–1969/70, with 1969/70; 1970/71–1979/80,
        with 1979/80; 1980/81–1989/90, 1990.
      Editors: 1937/38–1958/59, A. C. Baird.—1959/60–1969/70, L.
    Thonssen.—1970/71–1979/80, W. W. Braden.—1980/81–1994/95,
      O. Peterson.—1995/96– , C. M. Logue and J. DeHart.
    ISSN 0197-6923 Representative American speeches.
      1. Speeches, addresses, etc., American. 2. Speeches, addresses, etc.
      I. Baird, Albert Craig, 1883–1979 ed. II. Thonssen,
    Lester, 1904– ed. III. Braden, Waldo Warder, 1911–1991 ed.
    IV. Peterson, Owen, 1924– ed. V. Logue, Calvin McLeod, 1935– and
    DeHart, Jean. eds. VI. Series.
PS668.B3   815.5082   38-27962
                                     MARC-S

Library of Congress [8503r85]rev4

Cover: President Clinton campaigns for reelection in New York City.
Photo: AP/Wide World Photos

Printed in the United States of America

Contents

Preface vii

I. The Human Community

1) Janet Reno. You Can Make a Difference...1

2) Billy O. Wireman. Productive Careers & Noble Lives: A New Mandate for Liberal Arts Education 8

3) Hillary Rodham Clinton. Our Global Family 17

4) Jeanne Tessier Barone. The Sky's No Limit at All 23

5) William J. Clinton. Remarks to the American Legion Boys and Girls Nation 32

II. Religion and Prejudice

1) William J. Clinton. Dedication of the Mt. Zion African Methodist Episcopal Church...43

2) Carol Moseley-Braun. Church Burnings...48

3) Edward M. Kennedy. The Issue of Prejudice 51

4) Sam Nunn. The Whole World Is Watching...56

5) M. Craig Barnes. Choosing Good Government..................................62

III. Race

1) Paul Simon. Social Dynamite..67

2) Vernon E. Jordan, Jr. A Different Melody 70

3) Myron H. Wahls. The Moral Decay of America: Racism—Putting the American Dream Out of Reach 76

4) Johnnetta B. Cole. A House Divided 83

IV. Arts and the Humanities

1) Jane Alexander. Identity Through Art 89

2) Kenneth Lauren Burns. Worth Defending...94

3) Claudia Hopkins. Learning Styles...100

4) Ingrid Saunders Jones. Custodians of Our Culture...........................106

V. Government

1) William J. Clinton. Second Inaugural Address 111

2) Balint Vazsonyi. Four Points of the Compass: Restoring America's Sense of Direction 116

3) Patricia Schroeder. Proud of Liberal Accomplishments 123

4) George Anastaplo. "Private" Gambling and Public Morality 126

VI. Foreign Policy

1) William J. Perry. Completing Marshall's Plan in Europe 137

2) Jeffrey Davidow. U.S. Policy Toward Latin America and the Caribbean: Building Upon a Solid Foundation 145

3) Robert H. Pelletreau. U.S. Policy Toward the Middle East: Steering a Steady Course 150

4) Strobe Talbott. Ukraine at Five: A Progress Report on U.S. Policy 159

5) Warren Christopher. The U.S. and China: Building a New Era of Cooperation for a New Century 166

Cumulative Speaker Index: 1990–1997 175

Index 179

Preface

The tradition of the First Amendment has been envied by other countries on the presumption that free speech encourages both self-actualization and a lively democracy. From the debates on framing the Constitution to street protests, a recurring theme in American social discourse has been to what extent should citizens be free to express their views. In a commencement address at Rutgers University on May 18, 1995, professor Richard D. Heffner, television host and former chairman of the motion picture industry's voluntary film classification system, argued that "we no longer can afford the unquestioned and voluptuous pleasures of absolute, untrammeled speech, even as the language and pictures of violence and hate provoke, often invite, the hateful deeds that so often follow hateful words, even as such words themselves become such deeds." Several sections in this compilation contain speeches which attempt to both define the limit of free speech and action and describe the particular arenas in which First Amendment rights are most often called into question.

In addition to discussions on the limits of free speech, public address in the United States throughout 1996 and 1997 reflected a concern for what kind of community, both at home and abroad, people hope to establish. In Section I, The Human Community, speakers recognize the tumultuous times in which we live, and relay signs of progress in efforts to focus on education, career, and a faith in the future. According to these speakers, strengthening the community entails avoiding the pitfalls of hatred and bigotry, while continually preparing children to provide effective leadership in the future.

Section II of this compilation addresses religion and a recent outbreak of church burnings in the South. Recently, two former members of the Ku Klux Klan, both having pleaded guilty to burning two churches in South Carolina, were given lengthy prison terms. In August 1995, two other individuals pleaded guilty to violating federal civil rights and arson laws in the 1995 burning of the Mt. Zion A.M.E. Church in Greeleyville, South Carolina. They have also been incarcerated for an extended period of time. According to Rene Josey, U.S. attorney in South Carolina, the sentences should serve as a wake-up call for those who may contemplate the illegal use of force and violence to intimidate people because of their race or religious beliefs.

The subject of race relations is also discussed in Section III, in which speakers counsel against the reinforcement of ethnic or religious differences. Reflecting this quest to minimize the differences between individuals, the Clinton administration has recently recommended that people be allowed to select more than one racial category when filling out federal forms. This section also discusses other measures taken to bridge the racial divide, and provides assessments of America's overall racial climate.

In Section IV, Arts and the Humanities, speakers lament cuts in public, private, and corporate spending on the arts and humanities. They feel that such cuts are undermining U.S. cultural and educational institutions. Next year, little if any increase in the National Endowment for the Arts' (NEA) budget appropriations seems likely for a number of reasons: concern over balancing the federal budget, uncertainty about nondefense discretionary expenditures, and ambivalence among many members of Congress regarding direct federal support of the arts. The NEA will, however, remain in operation because of the emergence of a more forceful Senate that tends to support the NEA, and the increased influence of moderate House Republicans.

Section V, Government, contains speeches that both discuss past accomplishments of American government, and anticipate the future course of our political system. In his second Inaugural Address, President Clinton recalled the victories won during his first term, and outlined those areas he would concentrate upon during his second term. As the 104th Congress ended, fourteen representatives announced plans to retire, and this section includes Patricia Schroeder's retirement speech, which relays her praise of the goals the nation has been able to accomplish during her tenure in office. On a more current note, George Anastaplo questions government's increasing role in the gambling industry, and whether gambling is entertainment or immoral.

In the final section of the book, Section VI, Foreign Policy, America's role in the more turbulent areas of the world is discussed. Before retiring in 1996, Secretary of Defense William J. Perry defended the expansion of NATO into Eastern Europe, while assuring Russians leaders that their security was not threatened. The following speeches discuss strategies and agendas to unite other areas of the world, including Latin America, the Middle East, the Ukraine, and China. Common to all of these speeches is the belief that with common interests at heart, the United States can aid these areas in achieving a lasting and stable peace.

In compiling our second volume of *Representative American Speeches*, the editors received invaluable assistance locating information about speakers, speeches, audiences, and occasions from Doyle Srader and Joseph Bellon. The editors also appreciate the support provided by John Campbell and Don Rubin. Finally, the editors wish to thank the speech communication departments and the library staffs at the University of Georgia and Appalachian State University, and the staff of the H.W. Wilson Company.

Calvin M. Logue
Jean DeHart
November 1997

I. The Human Community

You Can Make a Difference[1]

Janet Reno

U.S. attorney general, 1993– ; born Miami, FL, 1938; A.B., Cornell University, 1960; LL.B., Harvard University, 1963; associate partner, Brigham and Brigham, 1963–67; partner, Lewis and Reno, 1967–71; staff director, Judiciary Committee of the Florida House of Representatives, 1971–72; attorney, Steel, Hector & Davis, 1976–78; attorney general, Dade County, FL, 1978–93.

Editors' introduction: Approximately one month after the year anniversary of the bombing of the Alfred P. Murrah Federal Building in Oklahoma City. U.S. Attorney General Janet Reno urged graduates to guard against extremism, cynicism, and defeatism. In this speech, Reno refers to the bombing and asks people to speak out against violence and continue to hope for a better future. Reno, the first woman to serve as U.S. attorney general, addressed some 1,200 graduates from the University of South Carolina, and expressed to them the importance of making choices based on reason and a sense of morality, rather than unchecked fanaticism.

Janet Reno's speech: Thank you very, very much. I am honored to share this day with you. And it is so wonderful to look out to see so many who have worked so hard to obtain their diploma today.

I especially want to say hello to my fellow chemistry majors. In 1960, I earned my Chemistry degree from Cornell University. So to you parents who worry that your graduating sons and daughters still lack a clear career goal, I suggest give them a little more time. You never know what might happen.

Since my graduation in 1960, so many things in America have changed for the better. in 1960, the Iron Curtain divided the world between freedom and dictatorship. Just two weeks ago, I walked the streets of Budapest, alongside the free people of Hungary, and I talked with western Europeans and eastern Europeans alike about our common fight against crime.

In 1960, even after the Supreme Court outlawed racial segregation, much of America was still divided into two nations, black and white. But in the civil rights efforts that soon followed, our

---

[1] Delivered at the University of South Carolina commencement exercises, in Columbia, South Carolina, on May 3, 1996.

nation kept the promises the founding fathers made, and finally made equality the law of the land.

In 1960, when I graduated from college, people told me a woman couldn't go to law school. And when I graduated from law school, people told me, "Law firms won't hire you." Thirty years later, no one has ever told me I couldn't be Attorney General.

You are graduating into an amazing era. In 1960, nobody had ever heard of the Internet. No one had been to the moon. The CAT scan was not invented until 1973. But even though our world is more safe, our country is more just, and new technologies are changing our lives, nobody would say that we are a nation without serious, serious challenges.

"Each generation looks to its children to keep our society moving and to make life better."

Many of these challenges seem so stubborn and unyielding, such as violent crime, homelessness, and poverty. Others seem complex and inscrutable, like the international economy and the spread of AIDS. And others seem overwhelming, like the fear of terrorism and environmental catastrophe. But America is a nation of optimists and problem-solvers. Each generation looks to its children to keep our society moving and to make life better. After the parties and the vacations and the graduate degrees yet to come, America will look to you for help. For no matter where you go, and what you do, you can make a difference.

That's what I would like to talk about today. For in these last thirty years, too many people of good will have looked at these very hard problems and started throwing up their hands and turning away. They are getting caught up in the three deadly sins of our public life: extremism, cynicism, and defeatism.

The first great threat to our optimistic spirit is extremism. For it blinds us to the tough, tough choices we all confront when we wrestle with the difficult problems of today.

The historian Arthur Schlesinger once observed that America's progress and freedom were fueled by what he called the "vital center" in American politics. He meant a place where men and women of reason and good will could meet, regardless of their political party affiliation, a place to hash out their differences and debate the problems of the day. A lively debate, to be sure, sometimes even unruly. But one carried out on common terms with respect for the other person.

The vital center has always been a place where people might be divided in their approach to solving a problem, but where they were united as Americans in their determination to act reasonably and to see the virtue in other points of view. In short, the politics of the vital center means using democracy as a process of working together, to find solutions that attack problems with progress, slow sometimes, terribly slow, and exhausting, to be sure. But always in the American tradition of reforms that are not perfect, but taken one step forward, one important step forward.

Today I fear many Americans are forgetting about the vital center. Too often, in today's politics, on all sides, people are confronting tough problems, and retreating to extremes and simple solutions, instead of embracing the complexity that problem-solving always demands, and that democracy requires.

You may not like everything that government does; I know I don't. But the alternative is not to throw up your hands or turn to violence. What we must do is to sit down together as reasonable people and make our government do what is right, and stop doing what may be wrong-headed or wasteful.

Extremism wants to spread, when the race is really a marathon. Extremism wants to escape the complexity of democracy, and the staggering diversity of human nature, but it never can. Extremism argues that problems are easy to solve, but if they were, we would have licked them a long, long time ago.

As Attorney General, I deal with problems that frustrated previous Attorney Generals for years, such as crime, terrorism, and domestic violence. There is no vaccination for crime, as there is for polio. The only thing we have is hard work, seven days a week. Parents raising children right, police walking the beat every single night, and prosecutors putting criminals behind bars, one by one.

"We're not a bumper sticker away from solving terrorism."

We're not a bumper sticker away from solving terrorism. We have to be eternally vigilant, close our borders to those who threaten us, and work slowly and patiently for peace in the lands where foreign terrorists come from. Just as we must fight the hatred and the paranoia that fuels domestic terrorism.

There is no sound byte that can make domestic violence go away. You have to stop abusers, one by one, and let them know that there is never an excuse for hitting someone you love. We have to build shelters one at a time to give victims a safe place away from the abuse, and we have to help victims rebuild their lives slowly and steadily.

The vital center knows that problems are complicated, and that answers are rarely simple. I hope that in your lives you will choose the course of leadership, not partisanship. Think twice when someone has a simple answer. Remember that so many of our problems took decades to get where they are. That no amount of sloganeering can fix them overnight.

And don't ever forget to listen. For I have learned so much when I have listened to the people with whom I have disagreed. Sometimes I have changed my mind, and sometimes I have changed theirs.

The second great threat to our nation's optimistic spirit is cynicism. Maybe you have faced it already. The cynic knows so much about what is wrong, and why it can't be fixed. He can tell you which baseball players strike out the most, and why planes and stock markets crash. She can tell you which public figures were caught doing something wrong, why the current peace negotiations are doomed, and why so many marriages end in divorce. It may be a beautiful South Carolina day, but the cynic knows it's going to rain again someday.

Of course, cynicism never happens by itself. It always builds on genuine problems and disasters. Watergate and other scandals convinced millions of Americans that government was permanently broken, and that everyone in public life was some sort of alien from ordinary American life, that they might as well have landed in a spaceship.

In fact, you can look at any of our institutions, and you can find a scandal, and cynics told you so. Sports heroes, police officers, business leaders, doctors, ministers, teachers and politicians; everyone can point to people in all walks of life who have fallen below society's standards.

We can use a funny line to dismiss politicians or teachers or Wall Street bankers, but that's the easy way out. And after we do, what's different? Nothing, except that fewer people are willing to work to make our government better, care for the helpless amongst us, or build a business that puts its customers' needs first. At the very least, if you're finding yourself falling prey to cynicism, consider its' cousin, skepticism.

At least the skeptic has an open mind. The skeptic sees all the same problems, and asks all the same questions, but is willing to let the answer be good or bad. If you're a recovering cynic, and you have made it back to skepticism, why not just take the final step, and become an idealist in the best American tradition?

And I don't mean for a minute that you should be naive. The Reverend Martin Luther King, Jr. talked about the need for all of us to have a tough mind and a tender heart. I can tell you that no one can come to Washington and ever hope to do well, if they don't start the morning by asking tough questions, and end the day getting real answers. But this nation was founded by idealists with tough minds, and with tender hearts, and they formed a government designed to check the worst in human nature, just as they risked their lives to found a country that cherished freedom and liberty over oppression. They took the hard way, and they made a difference.

A month ago, as the sun was setting, before it rose again on Easter morning, I was in Dover, Delaware, listening to President Clinton honor Commerce Secretary Ron Brown, and 32 other Americans who died in the plane crash in Bosnia. They were young and old, men and women, government workers and business leaders, but they were all there because they believed they could help a ravaged country heal from civil war. These 33 lives, said the President, show us the best of America. They are a stern rebuke to the cynicism that is all too familiar these days. He talked about how family after family told him how their loved ones were proud of their work, and believed in what they were doing, and believed they could make a difference.

Finally, I want to talk to you about the brother of extremism and cynicism: defeatism. Not everyone faces hopelessness, but no one is far away from someone who does. It may be across town, where a family can't afford to pay the rent, or take the child to the doctor, because they don't have a job. It may be in the next classroom, where a student is convinced that he will never succeed, that no one cares, and that street crime will be the only way out of a hard life. It might be next door, where a wife or child faces terror every night, at the hands of an abusive spouse or parent.

You may never find yourself at the bottom of life's pit, and if you do, I pray that you have the energy and the courage to get up and out. But you may know someone who has fallen, someone who doesn't even want to try, because they are sure it won't make a difference if they do.

Defeatism isn't always dramatic. When more people stay at home on Election Day, it means that they don't see how voting can make their lives any better. When good people hear the screams outside or next door, and shut their windows, they have given up hope that they can work with the police and the community to make our streets safer.

"When more people stay at home on Election Day, it means that they don't see how voting can make their lives any better."

And worst of all, what about the children who never learn to hope? Their bright faces have fallen by age 12. Perhaps they are ignored or abused. Maybe they can find their first real family in a gang. But what if there is a police officer who spends time with that child, to get him off on the right path? What if a neighbor or counselor takes the time to make a difference? What if defeatism is met head-on by the apostles of the American dream, people who know in their hearts that we can all do better?

One of your greatest challenges in this world will be to learn how to deal with extremism, cynicism, and defeatism. But the more I travel around America, the more I see we can. I see what the alternative to these evils are. It's right in front of our face, if we will just lift up our eyes and see it.

Nobody can choose the problems they face, but everybody has the power to choose how they will respond to them, and the Americans past and the Americans present are filled with people who have faced up to their choice, and who have chosen the path of action, and who have chosen to stand for what is right and good in the world.

Ten minutes east of here is the W. A. Perry Middle School. Eight years ago, like a lot of schools, it faced so many tough problems, like teen pregnancy, drugs and violence. And a woman named Mary Solomon made a choice. She's not a politician, or a generous millionaire, or a Rhodes scholar. She could have just let the problem be, and closed her doors, and even moved somewhere else.

But Mary Solomon made her choice, and took a stand. She organized forty of her neighbors. None of them had children in the school, but all of them remembered better days. They formed the Perry Middle School Task Force. Together, they got the school board to fix up the school. Then they heard there was no money in the budget for a nurse, so they got grant money to pay for one.

They identified more resources to fight drugs, got the city police to work with students, and worked with social workers to turn things around.

Mary Solomon and the Perry Middle School Task Force made a choice. And they made a difference. Teen pregnancies fell nearly ninety percent. Students had more extracurricular activities to keep them on the right path. A whole school of young people is being taught to reject extremism, cynicism, and defeatism in their life. Mary Solomon is here today with us, and I'd like her to stand and be recognized for taking the stand she has. (Pause).

In my own hometown in August of 1992, I watched the people of Miami respond to Hurricane Andrew, as you watched people respond to Hurricane Hugo. In the first two or three days, the world seems to fall apart from you. There was no cohesion, there was no community, there was no society. People looked stunned and adrift. But then people came together. They started directing traffic on their own, and delivering materials, and bringing water, and reaching out and caring and helping. And that community is stronger and better for it today.

"My faith in the American people, and their ability to deal with adversity, has never been so strong."

And then, almost a year ago, on the Sunday that followed the terrible tragedy in Oklahoma City, I went to a memorial service in that town, and watched the people of that city come together, to speak out against the violence that had spawned that blast, to work with law enforcement to hold those who had done it accountable, and to reach out to the survivors, to help them begin to heal.

I have been Attorney General now for three years. My faith in the American people, and their ability to deal with adversity, has never been so strong. I have never been so sure that we can prevail against the causes of wrong in this world. I know we can defeat extremism, and reclaim the vital center. I know we can defeat cynicism, and seek what is good amidst all that is bad. I know we can defeat defeatism, and teach those who have fallen to get up and hope again.

It won't be easy, and it will take a lot more than any speech can ever do, but I come here today because you are the future of this country. I know you have the energy. I know you have the commitment. I know you can make the choice to stand for what is right and good in this world. If you choose public service, you will be choosing one of the most rewarding and fulfilling careers our society can offer. But whether you are running a business, or teaching a class, prosecuting criminals, or raising a family, you can make a difference.

In another springtime, 33 years ago, the Reverend Martin Luther King, Jr. sat in a Birmingham jail, exhausted from years of seeking justice for all. He was dispirited, and now even some of his fellow ministers were saying he should back off and wait for progress to happen on its own. He must have struggled to keep cynicism out of his every thought, and sitting in that jail cell day after day, with progress coming slowly or not at all, he had to wonder why any man had a right to hope.

But Reverend King made his choice. He began writing until his words filled the margins of a secondhand newspaper. The power of his choice flowed out of the pen, and into the conscience of America.

Today, as you prepare to make your choices in life, I would like to close with a few of those words from Dr. King's letter from that Birmingham jail:

> We must come to see that human progress never rolls in on wheels of inevitability. It comes through the tireless efforts and persistent work of men, willing to be co-workers with God, and without this hard work, time itself becomes an ally of the forces of social stagnation. We must use time creatively, and forever realize that the time is always right to do right.

I hope and pray that you will make your choice the choice of standing for what is right and good in this world. Thank you, congratulations, good luck, and God bless you.

Productive Careers & Noble Lives:
A New Mandate for
Liberal Arts Education[2]

Billy O. Wireman

President, Queens College, Charlotte, NC, 1977– ; born Jackson, KY, 1932; B.A., 1954, Georgetown College (KY); M.A., University of Kentucky, 1957; Ed.D., Vanderbilt University, 1960; faculty, 1960-63, vice-president, 1963-68, president, 1968-77, Eckerd College; U.S. Marine Corps, 1973; educational consultant to South Korea, China, and Philippines, 1982, 1988-89.

Editors' introduction: On Han Nam University's (South Korea) 40th anniversary celebration, Billy O. Wireman, president of Queens College, in Charlotte, N.C., gave this keynote address. Wireman described the liberal arts program at Queens College, which has a strong Presbyterian affiliation. Dr. Wireman asserted that a liberal arts program in a religious context leads students to productive careers and noble lives. According to Wireman, the best place for the values of future leaders to be shaped is in college. Wireman further remarked that his goal as an educator was "to lay out a new vision for church-related, liberal arts education in the 21st century." To achieve that goal, Wireman drew upon his "personal journey of 40 years…to keep the Christian presence alive in higher education in America and throughout the world." In this speech, he sought to relay this message to all colleges with religious affiliations, irrespective of their surrounding culture or language.

Billy O. Wireman's speech: Mr. Chairman, Mr. President, Han Nam University trustees, faculty, students and staff. Distinguished guests.

I am truly honored to be here on this splendid occasion. We have been friends now for many years—you and I, Han Nam University and Queens College.

During the past forty years, as you have worked to create this fine Presbyterian institution, I too have worked, on the other side of the world, with your sister Presbyterian colleges.

Only four years after Han Nam was founded in 1956, I joined the faculty of the brand-new Florida Presbyterian College—now Eckerd College—in St. Petersburg, Florida. I served there as professor, dean, vice-president, and, from 1968–1977, as President.

---

[2] Delivered at Han Nam University, Taejon, South Korea, on October 17, 1996. Reprinted with permission of Billy O. Wireman.

Early in 1978, 1 assumed the Presidency of Queens College.

The forty years since 1956 have been among the most tumultuous in human history. We have experienced the end of the Industrial Era and the beginning of the Information Age. After spending trillions of dollars on military defense, we have watched Communism collapse under its own weight. We all witnessed the symbolic end of the twentieth century on November 9, 1989, when the Berlin Wall fell and the Cold War turned into a street dance overnight. Quickly, however, that euphoric moment was vaporized by harsh realities and we moved from "poetic promise to accounting." Indeed, we now are challenged to do the "rough work of freedom," as former U.S. president George Bush says, insure that "freedom's time does not turn into a nightmare."

Last fall, after speaking at Soong Sil University in Seoul, I boarded a plane and flew directly to Beijing. I marvelled that such a flight, all but impossible and unthinkable only a few years ago, has become a routine occurrence.

In America, the last forty years have been exceedingly turbulent. The heroic Civil Rights and Women's movements, the tragic war in Vietnam, the violent deaths of John Kennedy, Robert Kennedy, Martin Luther King, and Malcolm X, the political turmoil surrounding Presidents Johnson and Nixon, the dramatic transformation of our economy—all of these events punctuated a tumultuous time.

"From three million students in 1960, America now has nearly 15 million college students."

Since 1960, American higher education has experienced explosive growth. From three million students in 1960, America now has nearly 15 million college students. We have done a splendid job in opening access to higher education. But now we must turn to the focus, quality and substance of what students are learning. Here, we have some work to do.

In Korea, as in America, the last four decades have been dramatic. You have recovered from a devastating war. You have created and preserved democracy, in spite of storms of controversies and dangers. You have become masters of commerce and an economic model to the world. You have been faithful stewards of the church. As I'm sure you know, there are more Presbyterians in Korea than in America. Perhaps it's time you sent missionaries to us.

This is my twenty-fifth trip to Asia. Each time I come I see more evidence of the "Asian economic miracle." And for me, coming to Han Nam University is like coming home. Your generous hospitality and your beautiful campus evoke fond and rich memories in my spirit.

I think of the sister college relationship between Han Nam and Queens. I want to thank your American colleague, Dr. John Somerville, in particular for making this possible.

I remember my friendship with your former president, Dr. Won Sul Lee—now a writer for *The Korean Herald*—and your Board Chairman, Dr. O-Bong Kim. I recall their visits to Queens and the awards we were honored to bestow upon them. Then there is the lively International Symposium we held at Queens in 1989, at which time your then president was one of our distinguished speakers.

And I remember the wonderful experience my family and I had as your guests during the 1988 Olympic Games. Your country's pageantry and hospitality proved that South Korea and the city of Seoul were, and continue to be, truly mature citizens of the world community. I wear your Han Nam University Medal of Honor with pride and respect.

When I recall the hospitality of Presbyterian College and Seminary and Soong Sil University in Seoul, and the warmth of Korea's religious, economic, and political leaders, I am very grateful. I remember especially the interesting interview I had with Kim Dae Jung, one of your long time political leaders.

In America, I have tried, in numerous talks and articles, to share my admiration for my Korean and Asian friends with others.

Now, strengthened by these memories, let us turn to the future. In particular, I want to examine the work we will have before us, in the next millennium, as scholars at church-related colleges.

Two concepts are keys to the future of the human race: productive careers and noble lives. We must design academic programs and institutions which unite these two powerful ideas and use them to transform our students' lives. Either concept, alone, is an orphan. Together, the two can become a forceful theme for liberal education in the twenty-first century.

First, let me describe where I think we are today. Second, let me suggest where we should be going. Third, let me explain concretely what I mean by productive careers and noble lives.

Let's define where we are today.

Our time is marked, above all, by the universal failure of ideology. With this collapse of ideology has come the opportunity for a sustained, world-wide economic expansion; a development that could raise the living standards of millions of now impoverished people throughout the world. Managing this economic explosion will require morally-based leadership skills unprecedented in human history. And where will these leaders' values be shaped? Where better than in the world's colleges and universities, especially those related to the church?

Earlier this week in Seoul, I met with the U.S. Ambassador to South Korea, Dr. James Laney, a long standing friend whom I knew when he was president of Emory University. We also worked together through the United Board for Christian Higher Education in Asia. During our meeting, we talked about Emory economics professor Jeffrey Rosensweig's contention that the world is on the brink of "the greatest era of economic growth in history." And most of that growth, Rosensweig contends, will be in the developing countries.

Now, by the demise of ideology, I do not mean *the demise of ideas*. Quite the contrary. Ideas have never been more important.

But ideas now must be connected to harnessing this vast engine of growth and development.

By ideology, I mean those closed, rigid, and dogmatic fantasies of secular utopias which festered through the twentieth century. Ideology haunted our planet for much of the twentieth century; fascism, communism, racism, imperialism, and militaristic nationalism enslaved the bodies and minds of millions. Hatreds fueled by ideology left much of the world in blood and ashes.

But, at least for now, ideology is waning. Fascism as an organized system is dead; communism as a viable social system is dying. I remember visiting the office of now Czech President Vaclav Havel in Prague in 1990, and seeing a sign which read: "We want Democracy, Market Economics, and Pluralism." For millions throughout the world, this will be the motto of the next century.

Democracy, the free market, and cultural and political pluralism are the very opposite of ideology. They represent individual freedom, choice, diversity, and mobility. Democracy, the free market, and pluralism are all rooted in an intense respect for people, a commitment to popular sovereignty and to the rule of law. And around the world, this is what is in people's hearts.

In 1991, the American political scientist Francis Fukuyama advanced the controversial notion that we were somehow at "the end of history." What he meant was that we had come to a genuine turning point in the human experience, from which there was no going back. The ideologies which had terrorized the twentieth century were gone or fading. From South Africa to Eastern Europe to the great cities of America and Asia, the cry is for democracy, free markets, and respect for diversity.

Visit any area in the world—Asia, America, Russia, Latin America, Africa—and you see bright, young women and men entrepreneurs, cellular phone in hand, working on a project.

Their task is to make things work. We have moved from utopian, wild speculation to cautious planning, from fanaticism to prudence, from fantasy to the burdens and joys of daily life. It is this idea of making things better that challenges us now. Around the world, the great job before us is creating the conditions of a civil, prosperous society and living responsible, rewarding lives. And this is all right. We have moved from *words* to *work*. Creating the conditions of a decent life is no small task, particularly in a world in which poverty, and even famine, is a daily reality for millions.

Economics has become, in many ways, the new master science. In America, on almost every college campus, more and more students are studying business and economics. And I find that students, no matter what academic discipline they study, are concerned, above all, with preparing themselves for the world of work and decent living.

Connecting productive careers with the life of the mind and good citizenship is a dignified and even heroic act. It encourages

"Around the world, the great job before us is creating the conditions of a civil, prosperous society and living responsible, rewarding lives."

modesty, care and values. Why? Because each generation must remember that it is heir to a great legacy. Many of our forebears cared deeply about civic and political integrity. As Scripture tells us, "we live in cities we did not build." Each generation is not an owner but a steward of its inheritance. And the duty of each generation is to pass on to its children cities and a world that are safer, cleaner, and healthier.

To create nourishing foods, safer streets, potent medicines, better houses, great cities, stimulating schools, jobs and opportunities for the young and safety and security for the old, are tasks of great importance. And Asia has shown the world the way. In the last forty years, in Asia, nearly two billion people have arisen from poverty; terrible illnesses have receded; minds crippled by illiteracy and ignorance have been cured by education. The achievements of Korea in particular fill the rest of the world with awe.

But yet, even as our young people are learning marketable skills, I sense an uneasiness about them and their lives. While denouncing the failed ideologies of the past, they search at the same time for meaning which will enrich and enhance their lives.

Like you, I work with young people every day, and I am struck by their genuine hunger for *meaning*. They realize that democracy and markets and pluralism without moral vision are hollow shells. They are not cynics; nor are they materialists. Instead, they yearn for truth, and direction, and purpose. And they realize, like Dostoyevsky, that "without God, any horror is possible."

And here, a profound change in thinking is needed. What people in general, and young people in particular, yearn for is not therapy.

What they really yearn for is *wisdom*. We need a great revival of the wisdom traditions of the world. We need institutions which speak to life and its purposes, death and its meaning, work and its values. As Believers, especially, we need to remember that what we preach is not simply dry abstract assertions, and that what we offer is not simply another form of social organization. Rather, what we should try to live by example is a wisdom about a just, enlightened, and humane society.

If what I have said is true, what, then, are we as scholars at church-related colleges to do? I believe that we ought to create an education that will lead to productive careers and noble lives.

We have to insure that the ballot and market—the two major forces that will drive us—are shaped by humane values and thus do not leave the public square naked.

Let us recall that the liberal arts—those abilities to speak and act thoughtfully and coherently—first evolved, in ancient times, not as academic specialties but as the practical tools of the citizen. The liberal arts were designed not as aides in speculation, but as means for action. Thus, we must recognize that helping students achieve productive and noble lives has become, again, a central theme of the liberal arts.

Is it wrong for students to wish to learn to work productively and well, with skill and dignity? I think not. Rather, to be concerned with work, with craft, with competence, is something to applaud. Vaclav Havel often condemned communist regimes for their disdain for the realities of people's daily lives. The communist rulers, so obsessed by ideology and dogma, had contempt for the real concerns of real people living real lives. To return to reality from propaganda and lies is a step toward recovering humanity.

Scholars should have no fear of the world of work. To the contrary—who better could help guide students in the ways of this world? Scholarly theory, research, and speculation will continue to be essential to the life of the mind. But this connection must have roots; it must be accountable to today, and it must have a home in a creative interaction between thought and action, between work and citizenship. Havel again gives us insight:

> The only real hope of people today is a renewal of the certainty that we are rooted in the Earth and, at the same time, the cosmos. This awareness endows us with the capacity for self-transcendence. Politicians at international forums may reiterate a thousand times that the basis of the new world order must be universal respect for human rights, but it will mean nothing as long as this imperative does not derive from the respect of the miracle of being, the miracle of the universe, the miracle of nature, the miracle of our own existence.

As scholars and intellectuals, we should have no fear of finding connections between the life of the mind, these impenetrable miracles, and the work-place. Ancient Scripture tells us these miracles are Divinely created and given to us to cherish and pass on.

As scholars, then, we are obliged to help our students develop productive careers, a task rooted both in the liberal arts tradition and in our faith.

But there is another task as well.

I mentioned before that our young people have a genuine hunger and thirst for wisdom. From history, they are acutely aware that force and strength without humane direction are too terrible to contemplate. We need but to look at Hitler or the savagery in Cambodia and parts of Africa to be reminded that productive careers must be wedded to noble lives. In my country, we have work to do in lowering crime rates and drug abuse. Recent "ethnic cleansing" episodes are painful reminders of how far we have to go. And students will turn for counsel to those of us who are committed to finding connections and relevancy between intellectual inquiry and the correction of these social injustices.

When I speak of noble lives I mean three things: character, conscience, and community.

By character, I mean those personal qualities or virtues which

"Scholarly theory, research, and speculation will continue to be essential to the life of the mind."

mold us as human beings. I have yet to find a society in which cowardice was praised over courage, selfishness was prized instead of generosity, or ignorance was preferred to wisdom. Expressions of courage, generosity, and wisdom take many and differing forms; customs and cultures are very different. But, as human beings, we ought to praise courage and generosity and wisdom whether we find them in America, or Korea, or Africa, or anywhere, and we ought to repudiate cowardice, selfishness, and ignorance wherever they are found.

Character needs to be grown and nurtured. It needs to be strengthened daily. We need to recover the world's great wisdom traditions, the world's ancient schools of virtue. We can still learn from Aristotle and Confucius and the other ancient sages. But ultimately we ought to return to the virtues of justice and mercy identified in our Judeo-Christian heritage.

Noble lives also mean conscience, that spark of Divinity within each of us, which we recognize as the Spirit who prompts and corrects us always. It is an old and hallowed tradition that calls us, above all other things, to be true to our conscience. To act against our conscience is always illicit. But we also must work to have an informed and correct conscience. We must be sure that we do not mistake our own voice, or some other human voice, for the voice of the Spirit. We must learn to discern the voice of the Spirit within us, and where better can one learn to discern the Spirit than in academies founded by the church?

Noble lives also include a deep concern for Community. Character and conscience flourish only in communities which value them. To be a member of a community is to be a citizen, a participant in the life, and suffering, and triumphs of the community. Indeed, without a civil society, character and conscience wither.

The heroes of our time, from Havel to Nelson Mandela, have called on us to rebuild and restore communities of harmony and trust so that character and conscience may flourish. When Nelson Mandela was released from prison after 27 years, for example, he was asked whether he intended to take revenge on his persecutors. Mandela responded that he had no time for revenge because he would be too busy rebuilding his nation. Francis Fukuyama has written that mutual trust is the essential social capital without which nations perish. To be an active and vigorous citizen within a community which honors character and conscience is central to living a noble life.

In our new world of markets, we turn increasingly to Scottish economist Adam Smith. We should recall Smith's assertion that the end and purpose of free economics, as he said in *The Wealth of Nations,* is the "general wealth" of all.

Markets are means to this end, but, unfortunately, all too often this end is not achieved. For example, from 1960 to 1991 the gap between the richest 20 percent of the world's population and the poorest 20 percent has doubled. We know that the wealthiest 20 percent of the world's population now receives over 80 percent of the world's wealth, while the poorest 20 percent of the world's population receives less than two percent of the world's wealth.

If our end is "general wealth" for all, we have not achieved it; and because of this our church and colleges must continue to look carefully and critically at our means. We must teach our students to value three characteristics above all others: COMPETENCE, COMPASSION and TRUST. Competence is the embodiment of a productive career, and compassion and trust are the end result of a noble life.

We must encourage growth and achievement for all, but our success must not come at the expense of another's failure. And we can no longer rely on governments to correct all of society's inequities. In America, we have learned the sad lesson that a more intrusive government leads to bureaucracy, mistrust, and a less efficient society. In a recent poll, 60 percent of Americans said that the private sector can have the most impact in helping solve social problems; only 10 percent believed that the government can.

It is clear that a private, creative, entrepreneurial spirit must guide our "global village" towards economic expansion with a humane foundation.

Our task, again I emphasize, is to prepare students to link the mutually enriching notions of productive careers and noble lives.

Building such an education on these tenets will not be easy. All of us involved in education know how difficult and time-consuming it is to structure programs, raise funds, build buildings, and simultaneously deal with the many distractions and temptations which come our way.

At Queens College, we have worked to construct a program which, we hope, will nurture productive careers and noble lives. Our program is based upon a five-semester, inter-disciplinary, core curriculum that we call Liberal Learning, required of all students. Its motto is "only connect," and Liberal Learning works to connect the academic disciplines, the academy and the work place, the individual and the community, and above all, the world of worldly action to the world of the Spirit.

The academic major is the second part of our program; the major permits the student to study topics in depth and prepare for a specific career.

Our third component is an enhanced internship program, which is designed to place 100 per cent of our students out into the world of work for at least part of their third year of study.

Our fourth component is our international experience program, which, through international study tours, provides 95 per cent of Queens students with a lively encounter with a foreign culture.

At the same time, we have actively reached out to older students and working adults who wish to further their education for career advancement and personal fulfillment. To them, as well as to our more traditional undergraduates, we work to provide the opportunity to link work with citizenship.

As I reflect on the work that both Queens and Han Nam have done, I believe that we are both moving ahead and coming home. We are going ahead into the twenty-first century, developing an education for students yet unborn. Each season has its unique dangers and opportunities; what worked a generation ago may not work well for the next. We must be able to change, adapt, reform, and re-create.

And yet, it seems that as we move forward, we are also moving deeper into our heritage. We are becoming more and more who we should be by returning to the ancient calling of scholars and recognizing work as worthy of respect.

"We are going ahead into the twenty-first century, developing an education for students yet unborn."

In 2036, Han Nam University will celebrate its 80th birthday. Another celebration will no doubt be held here on this beautiful campus on a crisp fall day.

The audience that day will represent a prosperous, united, democratic Korea, in an Asia on the move. China will be a world superpower. And the speakers will be asked to reflect on the 80 year history of Han Nam University, especially our stewardship of the last 40 years. And I wonder what our heirs will say of us?

I hope that they will say that we responded to the challenges of our time with care and humility.

I hope they will realize that, even as we constructed new and innovative educational programs for them, we preserved the intimate relationship between reason and faith which is the heart of our kind of education.

I hope that they will say that we continued the ancient work of spreading wisdom throughout the world by both precept and example.

I hope our heirs honestly can say that we were good stewards and that we left the world better than we found it.

I hope they will say that we worked diligently to find new insights into the crucial relation between productive, rewarding work and responsible citizenship grounded in noble living.

I hope they say that we shaped the 21st century economic expansion to moral ends, and that we remembered the Scriptural Injunction: "If you have done it to the least of these, you have done it to me."

If our successors can honestly say these things, then we will be worthy of the ultimate Scriptural tributes:

You fought the good fight...you kept the faith.
Well done, thy good and faithful servants.

Thank you.

Our Global Family[3]

Hillary Rodham Clinton

First Lady of the United States, 1992– ; born Chicago, IL, 1947; B.A., Wellesley College, 1969; J.D., Yale University, 1973; attorney, Children's Defense Fund, 1973–74; assistant professor of law, University of Arkansas, 1974–77; partner, Rose Law Firm, 1977– ; lecturer, University of Arkansas Law School, 1979–80; leader, Rural Health Advisory Committee, 1979–80; author, It Takes a Village and Other Lessons Children Teach Us *(1996).*

Editors' introduction: On March 9, 1996, First Lady Hillary Rodham Clinton gave this speech at a luncheon during the National Council of Jewish Women's 40th national convention. Upon receiving the group's Faith and Humanity Award, Clinton told 800 cheering delegates that the United States is a committed member of a global community that must necessarily view the protection of children as a top priority. Nan Rich, council president, described Clinton as "genuine in her concern for all of the children of America and the world." In the speech, Clinton contended that, "it not only takes a village to raise a child...it takes a village to come together to stand against violence, intolerance, and hatred and bigotry."

Hillary Rodham Clinton's speech: Thank you very much, and it gives me such an enormous personal pleasure to be here when Nan becomes your incoming president. As she told you, we have known one another for now more than 10 years. I have always felt very close to her, even though we have not been able to spend a lot of time together, with her living in Southern Florida and my living elsewhere.

But we've not only been able to work together, principally on behalf of HIPPIE over the years, but she has been a very warm and supportive friend to me personally. And I think it's difficult when you get older, number one, but when you get into positions like the one I find myself in now, to make new close friends it's hard. And I will never forget at one point in the past year, when Nan and a friend of hers came to see me at the White House just to say they were there as my friends. That meant so much to me, and I think that this organization is extremely lucky to have a new leader who follows in the tradition of the other extraordinary leaders you have had, who understands not only the public issues that we need to confront, but the personal needs that peo-

---

[3] Delivered to the National Council of Jewish Women, in Detroit, Michigan, on March 9, 1996.

ple face. And on behalf of myself personally, I want to thank you, Nan, and congratulate you on this new position.

I am also very honored—I cannot imagine any honor that I have been more moved by—to receive this from an organization I have so much respect for. To receive an award that is called the Faith and Humanity Award is overwhelming, and I want to thank you. But I particularly came here today not to thank you for this honor, but to join with old and new friends in thanking you for your leadership on behalf of faith and humanity.

The work that you have done, are doing, and will continue to do makes such a difference in so many lives, and it could not be done without the personal commitment of time, energy, and resources that each of you bring to it. I wish all of you could have been with me over the years as I watched the HIPPIE program in Arkansas literally change lives, awaken in mothers what many of us took for granted—that we would have such an enormous impact on our own children, that we would be our child's first teacher. But as a woman told me, "I always know I was supposed to keep him safe, and feed him, and send him to school, but I never knew before HIPPIE I had anything to teach my son." The kind of life-changing experiences that you have helped to bring about, not only with HIPPIE, but with so many of the projects you have sponsored, are ones that I hope you understand the significance of.

There are few organizations in the world that do as much as the National Council of Jewish Women to brighten the futures of children and families. Your efforts on behalf of parents, whether through HIPPIE or your Day of the Working Parent events that Susan mentioned, or the exciting new Parents as School Partners project that you have undertaken recently reflect your faith in our common humanity and our ability to move forward together as a society, not just in our own country, but around the globe into the new millennium.

Your original motto, "Faith and Humanity," certainly is timely today. Today our faith in our world and in each other has been put to the test. Our ability to feel that we are part of a common humanity is often under attack by those who would attempt to divide us.

We know as we meet here in Detroit that across an ocean, the people of Israel are responding to unspeakable acts of terror. When young men are willing to strap bombs to their bodies and to sow destruction that kills innocent children and people on the streets of Tel Aviv and Jerusalem, we can only shake our heads and feel the pain in our hearts. Logic does not apply, reason cannot explain, and our own faith in humanity is tested. Which requires us all to dig deep within our hearts and souls to understand why such hatred and violence is happening and what we can do individually and collectively to stand against it and stop it.

In the past week, the President has made it clear that the United States will stand behind Israel through good times and bad. As Americans, we must do everything we can to help ease the grief of the Israeli people and to permit peace to take hold in the Middle East. Just a few days ago, the President attended the memorial service at the Israeli Embassy in Washington. I want to repeat part of what he said because it is a message not only for that very sad occasion, but for us as we move into the future. He said, "Our faith may be shaken, but we must persevere. These fanatical acts are aimed, not just at killing innocent people, but at killing the promise of peace. We must not allow these forces of hate to derail our historic journey. The best way to defeat them is to bolster the peace they fear."

The President has pledged to the Prime Minister that the United States will work with Israel and our friends in the Middle East to stop the killing, to bring the criminals to justice, and to permit the peace process to continue. Earlier this week, he announced the transfer to Israel of sophisticated equipment for detecting explosives, he dispatched American specialists in counterterrorism, and provided other technical assistance to help Israel root out violence and to find the perpetrators.

This coming week, the President will travel to Egypt to take part in an anti-terrorism summit hosted by President Mubarak. As King Hussein of Jordan said when he met with the President in the White House on Thursday, the latest terrorist bombings are the work of, and I quote, "a small group against an overwhelming majority in our region who are seeking peace."

I think that the challenge we face in the Middle East is certainly an extreme and horrific example of what we face in other parts of the world today. When I went to Northern Ireland, I met with Protestants and Catholics who are attempting to bridge the differences between then to find their common humanity. I had an extraordinary meeting with a group of women who themselves had lost husbands and brothers—a group that was led by a remarkable woman named Joyce McCartan who had seen her 17-year-old son killed before her very eyes. These women knew the wages of hatred and violence and were determined to stand against that small group in their society who want to change the course of history by sowing hatred instead of working with each other to create a better future. We see the same thing at work in the former Yugoslavia, where people are tired of the killing, tired of the ethnic violence and hatred, and struggling against great odds to find their common humanity.

Despite these examples of violence that occur that still bring such terror to innocent people, we are seeing signs of progress as well. About 10 days ago, I met with a group of Israeli and Palestinian teenagers at the White House. They were traveling through the United States—sponsored by Peace Now as part of the Israeli-Palestinian youth dialogue program—and each of them told me what had drawn them to the peace movement and what their hopes were. It was impossible not to be moved by their courage and not to feel in some ways their young wisdom because they knew what would make for the best possible future for themselves.

One 16-year-old Israeli boy talked about the devastation he felt after the assassination of Prime Minister Rabin. And yet he said after that tragedy he felt a new resolve to work for peace. He told me, "I think it is the only way of living that is really worth fighting for." A young Palestinian boy talked about the fear he felt during the Intifada and the pain he endured when a classmate was killed in that violence. His own hopes were that his people, too, would understand how important dialogue and negotiations were for progress for both Israelis and Palestinians. He said, "my main concept is blood brings more blood."

If you look in the faces of young people from Belfast to Sarajevo to Jerusalem to Tel Aviv and Gaza, you can see what our challenge is, but also what our hope has to be. These young people are showing great faith in themselves by standing up for peace. They are standing against the siren songs of easy answers of how violence solves problems and taking their stand instead in favor of the long, slow, and sometimes discouraging work of bringing peace and reasserting a positive future.

"These young people are showing great faith in themselves by standing up for peace."

Speaking to all of you, I am reminded how much you have invested in the American family and in our global family. HIPPIE is not only in Israel and the United States, it's in other countries as well. Your example and your work serves to inspire people who are inclined sometimes to give up on the brighter future that you're determined to help create.

You also remind me that we are part of a village today, maybe more than we have since we used to live in small places that were physical villages. We know none of us can meet the challenges of today's world alone. Certainly young Israelis and Palestinians need each other to work for peace. Young mothers in America need the help that is provided through programs like HIPPIE so that they feel they're not alone and they learn what they can do to be better parents.

When I think about all of the challenges we confront in America, I am not pessimistic, I am not fearful, and I am not negative. I'm, in fact, quite optimistic and hopeful. Does this mean I think it will be easy for us even in this most stable and pluralistic and certainly relatively tolerant of countries to meet our challenges? No, I don't. I think we are living in a time of insecurity and transition when, as we work our way through, we will see many examples of people who would rather derail progress than contribute to it. But I think that history is on our side. I believe that the opportunities we have now to work together in pursuit of our common humanity far outweigh the difficulties we are confronted with.

It not only takes a village to raise a child and to give that child hope in his or her future. It takes a village to come together to stand against violence, intolerance, and hatred and bigotry. It takes people joining hands and hearts, even when they disagree with one another, but putting those disagreements into a proper perspective, minimizing them in order to make progress.

Much of what you do by reaching out to those in need is to search for the integrity of what it means to be a human being today, and particularly to a woman in today's world. The work you have done is an example of what happens when women join together and make their voices heard, particularly on behalf of those who would otherwise remain voiceless.

Each of you, as you know, has a stake in what kind of country and world we build. I believe that in the days and months ahead when we are confronted with new and unpredictable challenges at home and abroad, in times that are risky and pose dangers to our hopes, that we can look to many of the things NCJW has done and to the organization itself as an example of a positive vision, of a village, if you will, at work.

Our entire human family depends upon all of us to help secure a lasting peace with security in the Middle East, but so does our entire human family. If we look at our country today, we can see two stark views of the future.

One which wants more and more of us to basically make it on our own, to withdraw help for education and health care from all of us, but with particular impact on the most vulnerable among us. A view of the world in which security is only what you can make for yourself, with very little of the sense of obligation that knits us together as a society. I've heard it described this point of view really believes that people are a crowd, not a community.

The opposing view to that is that we owe each other more than that. That we owe each other respect, that we owe each other a helping hand when that hand is needed. That, yes, we intend for people to be responsible for themselves, but we have a little different, and I would argue broader, view of what life brings to all of us. There but for the grace of God go many of us. We've all had friends who fall on hard times through no fault of their own. We look at the statistics and we see that the poorest group of people in our country now are our children. We look at the income of our elderly and we see that the median income for the majority of women over the age of 65 in America is $9,000 or less. We see people not as statistics, but as individuals with their own particular needs and wants.

And so I hope that as we work to achieve what faith and humanity means to NCJW, we do so in our own lives and the lives of our broader communities. Every single day, our entire human family will be affecting how my daughter lives in the future. There is no place to hide in the global village. We are knit together now in ways that through communications and transportation and all of the other technological developments that have occurred make what happens elsewhere directly affect what happens here at home.

I don't think we have any choice as to which side of the vision we choose if we want to live in a society that honors the values

"Every single day, our entire human family will be affecting how my daughter lives in the future."

that you stand for. That for what you have done I am personally grateful, but more than that. I think your standing for what makes a difference in children's and families' lives is in a direct way standing up for the kind of society we all want to live in. So, on behalf of the President and many others who are grateful for your work, I say thank you. But I also ask you now, when we know it will be difficult, redouble your efforts to remain committed to the vision you hold and what kind of society you want to leave to our children.

Thank you very much.

The Sky's No Limit at All[4]

Jeanne Tessier Barone

Instructor, Indiana University-Purdue University, 1988– ; born Sycamore, IL, 1947; B.S., Northwestern University, 1969; M.A., Northern Illinois University, 1983; co-author, Interviewing Art and Skill *(1995).*

Editors' introduction: In this speech, Jeanne Tessier Barone discussed the quote from poet Rita Dove, "When the sky's the limit, how can you tell you've gone too far?" Barone examined whether such a limit exists, how a limit can be recognized as a limit, whether it is not just as important for people to know when they have not gone far enough, and what it means to go beyond so-called limits. Barone tried to encourage and inspire staff and volunteers at the start of a new year for Girl Scout activities. To reach that goal, she employed poetic language and cadences, as well as inspiring quotations. She also challenged participants to think and move beyond their own perceived personal and institutional limitations.

Jeanne Tessier Barone's speech: I had already agreed to deliver and was looking forward to this keynote speech when I received a note from one of the planners suggesting that my topic be based on this quote from the poet Rita Dove: "when the sky's the limit, how can you tell you've gone too far?" I confess that—at first—this suggestion somewhat dampened my enthusiasm, and I'll tell you why. My hope and plan, which was already stirring in the back of my mind, was to somehow find the words and images with which to affirm, motivate, uplift, and encourage you, whose work I admire. I wanted to bathe you in words so rich you would be nearly lifted out of your seats and floating on air by the time I was done.

And here, in the midst of my positive ruminations, came this request, which seemed at first glance to speak, and to ask me to speak, of limits and of going too far. There I was, with a head full of far-flung metaphors, when in came Dove's quote, and suddenly my planning fantasies felt a bit hemmed in, contained, constrained by what struck me at first as a somewhat negative statement or idea: "When the sky's the limit, how can you tell you've gone too far?"

But I have come to believe in my own life that all perceived challenges or burdens are really gifts in disguise, so I pondered

---

[4] Delivered to the Limberlost Girl Scout Council 1996–1997 Service Team Kickoff, at South Side High School, in Fort Wayne, Indiana, on July 20, 1996. Reprinted with permission of Jeanne Tessier Barone.

the quote awhile. You should know, by the way, that I have spent most of my life testing the edges of limits, my own and those imposed limits I've encountered along my rocky path. I am a born questioner and limit-tester, so much so that when I was the age of your Cadette and Senior Girl Scouts, my mother despaired, both of surviving my journey to adulthood herself, and of my surviving getting there. I can tell you it was touch and go at times, for both of us.

So, faced with this new wrinkle in my assignment, I responded as any good questioner and limit-tester would. I said to myself,

"Who said the sky's the limit anyway?"

And, "Is it really the limit, or do we just think so?"

"And how can we know a limit is truly a limit unless we test its edges with all our might?"

"And isn't it just as important—or more so—to know when we haven't gone far enough?"

"And what does it mean to go too far anyway?"

And so, like any good questioner and limit-tester, I went looking for answers to the questions Dove's quote stirred up in me, for the gift wrapped up in the topic I had been provided. And, sure enough, by the time I was done, I found myself grateful for the question, because it became the framework for my words for you today.

One by one, then, we will address these questions, inspired by Rita Dove:

First: Who says the sky's the limit anyway?
Second: Is it really the limit, or do we just think so?
Third: How can we know our limits unless we test them?
Fourth: How do we know we haven't gone far enough?
and Fifth: What does it mean to go too far?

Being as I am a lover of words and books, and an avid reader of dictionaries—yes, dictionaries—and books of quotations, I started off first in search of a literal answer to the question: "Who says the sky's the limit anyway?" My guess was that I would find the original creator of the phrase was Shakespeare. Pick any phrase in common use in the English language and the odds are good he said it first. This phrase did not come from Shakespeare, however, but from one of his contemporaries, a Spaniard named Miguel de Cervantes. Do you know his name? I was cheered to discover that the phrase came from Cervantes, because the source of the phrase revealed to me that it was not a saying meant to impose limits, but to challenge and push against them.

The original phrase by Cervantes was this: "No limits but the sky." I find that an oddly more positive phrase than how it now appears in modem usage: "The sky's the limit." The phrase appeared in a novel called *Don Quixote* which was first published about 1605. The timeless story of Don Quixote was made into a Broadway musical called *Man of La Mancha* about 30 years ago, with a song, famous at the time, called "To Dream the Impossible Dream." Maybe some of you remember it.

Don Quixote was a man who saw a world beyond the limits the world itself sought to impose. In himself, an aging eccentric, he saw a brave knight errant seeking to rid the world of that which caused others harm. In a foolish and ignorant barber, he saw a brave companion for his quest. In a despised and self-despising prostitute, he saw a beautiful woman waiting to be cherished. Don Quixote was a man without limits, who looked beyond what others called impossible and found rich and joyous possibilities. All those he encountered thought him mad.

So, in answer to the question: Who said the sky's the limit anyway? The answer is: a writer who sought to create a world seen through kinder and more redeeming eyes, almost 400 years ago. At the time he wrote, of course, the sky had not yet been pierced through by rocket ships, probed by satellites, traveled across in metal birds by you and I, and studied in all its glorious and infinite detail by a massive Hubble telescope traveling through space. Cervantes could not have known it at the time, but the sky is no limit at all; it only appeared so from the limits of one whose feet were firmly rooted on the earth.

"...human beings tend to enact or make real what they believe about themselves and others."

The sky, rather, is limitless in possibilities. *The American Heritage College Dictionary* defines the sky as: "The expanse of air over a given point on Earth; the upper atmosphere as seen from Earth's surface." The sky, in other words, is nothing more than the air we breathe, and an illusion created by a certain landlocked point of view. So the dictionary agrees: the sky is not about limits, but about possibilities.

Another writer, Arthur Schopenhauer, writing in the 1800s, had this to say about limits (I have corrected his masculine language): "Everyone takes the limits of her own field of vision for the limits of the world." We see blue above and nothing beyond and we assume the sky's the limit. We see a structure, an institution, an attitude, a habit of being, and we assume it must ever and always be so. A little Christian girl solemnly assures a little Jewish girl that the Jewish child will go to hell when she dies because she has not been saved. A child growing up in Belfast, Ireland sees nothing but hatred and strife between Catholics and Protestants, and assumes that Catholics and Protestants everywhere must greet each other with screams and hurled stones and other acts of rage. An adolescent girl looks at herself in the mirror and sees a being hopelessly ugly and unacceptable, and then assumes the whole world sees her this way, too. Each of these limits, thanks to you, are ones that Girl Scouts are encouraged to see through.

In my field of study, communication, we teach about the power of self-fulfilling prophecies: that human beings tend to enact or make real what they believe about themselves and others. I believe in a God who loves me and I pray to her... or him... and I believe my life offers evidence of her...or his...replies. A colleague of mine believes there is nothing, God or otherwise, beyond this life, and lives for the things of this world only, and day to day.

One woman believes that, discrimination or not, gender and cultural barriers or not, there is still no limit to what she can attain if she pursues her goals with all her heart.

Another believes her world is a closed system in which women are hopelessly shut out and disenfranchised, and so have always been. The first woman builds a life of accomplishment with dignity and grace; the second woman builds a life of bitterness, recrimination, narrowness. The first woman, by the way, is much more likely to have been a Girl Scout, because your work mentors and empowers girls to move beyond the limits their cultures impose.

"We had best build worlds for ourselves that have few walls, and many windows and doors."

So now we have an answer to our second question: Is the sky really the limit, or do we just think it so? We think it so. We are bound at every turn by the limits of our beliefs. They define what we think is real and what we ourselves will become. So: we had best be careful, then, about what we believe. We had best create and hold beliefs that leave as much room as possible for us to be wrong, for us to expand and grow. We had best build worlds for ourselves that have *few* walls, and *many* windows and doors. In 1902 William James wrote, "We can act *as if* there were a God; feel *as if* we were free; consider Nature *as if* she were full of special designs; lay plans *as if* we were to be immortal; and we find then that these words do make a genuine difference in our moral life."

There is much in James' words that both echoes and speaks to the power of the Girl Scout Law: "to be honest...to be fair...to help where needed...to respect myself and others through words and actions...." These are words that can and do make a difference in the moral lives of the girls who learn and try to live them.

Are there no real limits in our lives, then? Aren't there limits we cannot change simply by believing? Of course there are. Some persons struggle with terrible poverty. Some are differently abled in ways that make everyday life tasks difficult. Some carry burdens of abuse and experience that others will never know. Limits abound, but it is more how we think about them than what they are that will determine the quality of our lives. Writers Dominguez and Robin have said, "Once we're above survival level, the difference between prosperity and poverty lies simply in our degree of gratitude."

The third question facing us, then, is: How can we know our limits unless we test them? Here the answer is straightforward and simple: We can't. It is only through testing and pushing against the limits of our perceptions, experiences and culture that we can be a force for change. The Girl Scouts *is* a force for change, and has been since its creation. The Girl Scouts of

America would not exist if Juliette Gordon Low had not seen a need for change, for American girls to have new opportunities to test their limits and grow.

You as members of this organization seek a world in which all persons possess and are accorded the dignity, equality and respect that they deserve. The great strides made toward full equality for women in our culture could not have been made without powerful individuals pushing against the existing limits of our world. Many powerful women came before you in this effort.

On March 31, 1776, Abigail Adams wrote to her husband John while he and the other men who helped form the nation were writing the Declaration of Independence, and this is what she said: "If particular care and attention is not paid to the Ladies we are determined to foment a Rebellion, and will not hold our-selves bound by any Laws in which we have no voice or Representation." Too bad her husband didn't listen to Abigail's advice at the time—in fact, he promptly replied, "As to your extraordinary Code of Laws, I cannot but laugh." But, if the writ-ers of the Declaration of Independence had not been pushing against limits, our nation based on the ideal of human equality would not have been formed.

The great Sojourner Truth made pushing against the limits of slavery, evil, and sexism her life's work. In 1850, speaking to the Ohio Women's Rights Convention, her words won thunderous applause with a speech that included these famous lines: "That man over there says that women need to be helped into car-riages, and lifted over ditches, and to have the best place every-where. Nobody ever helps me into carriages, or over mud-pud-dles, or gives me any best place! And ain't I a woman? Look at me! Look at my arm. I have ploughed and planted and gathered into barns, and no man could head me! And ain't I a woman? I could work as much and eat as much as a man—when I could get it—and bear the lash as well! And ain't I a woman? I have borne thirteen children and seen most all sold off to slavery, and when I cried out with my mother's grief, none but Jesus heard me! And ain't I a woman?"

Earlier in this century, the crusader Margaret Sanger wrote: "Woman must not accept; she must challenge. She must not be awed by that which has been built up around her; she must rev-erence that within her which struggles for expression. Her eyes must be less upon what is and more clearly upon what should be."

And Margaret Chase Smith, the only woman in the U.S. Senate during the period when Senator Joe McCarthy was terrorizing citizens into silence with the threat of the label "communist," said this before the Senate in 1950: "Those of us who shout the loudest about Americanism in making character assassinations are all too frequently those who, by our own words and acts, ignore some of the basic principles of Americanism—

The right to criticize.
The right to hold unpopular beliefs.
The right to protest.
The right of independent thought."

If we didn't test our limits, we would never walk, we would never grow, we would never fly.

So: the sky is not limits but endless possibilities, and it is we who perceive and impose limits where none exist, and if we do not test the limits of our perceptions and our abilities and our worlds, we will never know what lies beyond.

But now we have arrived at our fourth question: How do we know when we haven't gone far enough? Most of us are committed, hard-working people, aren't we? Isn't that far enough to go? Isn't that *more than* far enough? No. How do we know, then, if we need to go farther? Here are some conclusions I've come to in my own search for an answer to this question:

> If we do not engage in work for which we have real passion and pursue our work passionately, we have not gone far enough.

> If we do not have a clear sense of direction and meaning in our lives, we have not gone far enough.

> If we do not understand that our actions and words can have a lasting impact on the quality of human life, we have not gone far enough.

> If we don't hope and strive to make a positive difference in our world, if we are content with what we do and don't continually look to how we can be better persons, we are not going far enough.

> If we haven't wholly loved another human being, if we don't at least try to recognize the good in everyone we meet, if we don't have times of real joy in our lives, then we have not gone far enough.

"Life is too short and too precious not to live it with passion and pursue it with zeal."

Life is too short and too precious not to live it with passion and pursue it with zeal. And your work is much too important to pursue with anything less than your total commitment.

As you know, these are very hard times in which to grow up female in the USA. Despite all the strides made in pursuit of equality for women in this country, there are many social and cultural forces at work right now that counteract the good that has been done. You know about these forces as well as I do—film and television bombard young girls with highly sexualized and unattainable ideals of female beauty. At the same time as girls are told they can be anything they want to be, deep cultural patterns still work to convince them they're incomplete without a man, and that, to win a man, they must be willing to sacrifice even their dreams. A multi-billion dollar cosmetics industry is built upon and encourages the fragility and vulnerability of female self-esteem.

There is so much work yet to be done in order to teach our daughters to love themselves, and to test and move beyond the limits of their image of the sky. The girls you serve need nothing less than your full commitment to their empowerment and growth. They need to feel your passion and to witness your zeal.

Georgie Anne Geyer, author and columnist, in a commencement address at St. Mary's College in South Bend in 1988, said, "I believe that women have a double moral and ethical burden, which is also a blessing; I believe that women are more open to understanding the new and more ambiguous issues in the world: resource exhaustion, the massive movements of peoples, over-population, the destruction of the earth and of culture." There is much we can do to make a better world for our children, so that they, especially our daughters, are empowered and secure enough to make a better world for children yet to come. Passion, direction, impact, change, love, and joy—when we have these things, we have begun to go far enough.

And now we come to our last question: "What does it mean to go too far?" I'm sure we all remember when "going too far" meant having sex before marriage—and I think we all know it doesn't mean that anymore. So what does it mean?

Have we gone too far if we try something new that fails? No. On the contrary, if we never fail, we can be sure we *aren't* going far enough. Have we gone too far if we try to re-envision our work, our organizations, our goals, our dreams? No. All change, all innovation, begins with re-imagining. Is it going too far to take important risks? No. We have to be willing to risk for the sake of movement and growth. Is it going too far to stand up for and speak out about what you believe, even if your ideas are unpopular? No. The human story would be a slow and sad one if there had not been individuals all along the way who spoke out against the status quo and called their peers to be better than they were. Is it going too far to remain a committed idealist in a world that invites pessimism? Never. Without ideals we die. The Girl Scout organization is *about* ideals.

Can we ever really go too far? This question is a tough one for me, because I am, as I said at the start, a lifelong edge-tester, and there's a part of me that always wants to say it can never happen. Even my current rapid descent into deep middle age hasn't deterred me from, often, heading out on metaphorical tightwires without benefit of nets. But I have also sometimes fallen—hard— onto the floor below. So, with the exhilarating experiences and occasional bruises to show for it, here is what I would say about going too far:

> First, take big risks and important actions, but give them careful thought. Also, make sure a part of the thinking process includes sharing your ideas with someone

whose opinion on these matters you respect, because we human beings are expertly capable of having blind spots in our thinking and of deceiving ourselves.

Second, try not to go so far that, when you arrive at your destination, you find yourself utterly alone. It is hard to be a limit-tester, a risk-taker, a traveller into new terrain. Seek and maintain the support of someone who loves you, even if, as is sometimes the case, the only one who seems to support you is one to whom you pray.

Third, be aware that change involves loss as well as opportunity. You can't leave one job for another without surrendering the comforts and sometimes the friendships of where you were. You can't take on new responsibilities without letting go of old—not for long, anyway, or you will soon be of no use to anyone, including yourself. You can't launch new programs without sacrificing some aspects of what's already being done. You have to make enough room in your life and work for growth to occur.

Fourth, be ready to feel afraid. All change is scary. It is human to love a rut; ruts are comfortable and safe. There are many ways in which most of us would prefer the predictable to the uncertain or unknown. This is why, for example, when change occurs in organizations, it is often met with resentment or anger. This is why "That *isn't* how it's done" and "But we've *always* done it this way" are such well-known phrases. Change requires that we rethink old ideas, and there is nothing scarier than giving up what we were convinced were truths about our work, ourselves, our world. But, you know, fear is also enlivening— this is why people skydive and bungee jump and scale sheer mountain cliffs. And it is good to feel fully alive.

Fifth, and this is advice without which I would never have lived to speak to you today: pray without ceasing, to whoever your God may be. And sixth, dare to dream. Let your mind wander. Rita Dove has a poem called "Daystar" in which she describes a woman who takes a chair out behind her garage to stare at an empty field while her children are napping. When her daughter finds her and demands to know what her mother has been doing out there, the mother responds, "Why, building a palace." We should build palaces in our minds.

Can we go too far? Maybe, but there are things to learn from it that we can't learn any other way, and even when I've sometimes thought I'd done it, gone too far, I've never regretted it for long.

I have no idea what Rita Dove had in mind when she uttered the words we began with:

"When the sky's the limit, how can you tell you've gone too far?" But I do know where my attempt to address her question has taken me. By way of conclusion, and in *humble* tribute to her poetry, let me end this way:

The sky is infinite.

> *"Change requires that we rethink old ideas, and there is nothing scarier than giving up what we were convinced were truths about our work, ourselves, our world."*

It is we who make of it a wall.
The only way to know is: go.
Standing still is death.
And far is never where you are,
but where you dream to be.
Everything good in life was born in dreams.
Be a dreamer.

Remarks to the American Legion
Boys and Girls Nation[5]

William J. Clinton

*President of the United States, 1992– ; born Hope, AR, 1946; B.S.,
Georgetown University, 1968; Rhodes Scholar, Oxford University,
1968–70; J.D., Yale University, 1973; professor, University of
Arkansas Law School, 1973-76; attorney general, Arkansas, 1976-
77; governor of Arkansas, 1979–81, 1983-92.*

Editors' introduction: In this speech, President Clinton spoke to
nearly 200 high school juniors attending the 50th anniversary of
the American Legion Boys and Girls Nation. Prior to the speech
two Boys and Girls Nation members were selected from each
state to spend a week in Washington, D.C. learning how government functions, and participating in mock legislative assemblies.
In contemplating their future careers, the President recommended that the students ask themselves, "What kind of country do I
want to live in? What do I want America to look like when my
children are my age?"

President Clinton's speech: Thank you very, very much. I want
to welcome all of you here. And before I begin the program let me
say I'm sorry I'm a little late today, but we have been working, as
I'm sure you understand, all day long on the plane crash last
night [TWA Flight 800]. I want to talk to you about your future,
but before I do I'd like to say just a word about the people that
were on that plane.

I'm determined that we will find out what happened, but I
want to urge all the American people not to jump to any unwar-
ranted conclusions about the tragedy. We should focus today,
our thoughts and our prayers, on the families of the victims of
that terrible, terrible tragedy last night. And you should know
that everybody in our country that we believe can make a contribution to finding out what happened is on the job, working
overtime.

I want you to know if you haven't heard that there were 16
high school students from Pennsylvania on that flight. Any
tragedy like this is made deeper if young people's lives are lost,
people who haven't yet had their chance to live up to their God-
given promise. These young people were from the Montoursville
High School french club in Pennsylvania. They were young, com-

---

[5] Delivered in the East Room of the White House, in Washington, D.C., on July
18, 1996.

mitted, filled with excitement about the prospect of visiting France. Our country will be poorer for their absence. And the rest of you will have to work a little harder to live up to your promise and to theirs as well.

The mayor of that small community was just on television, and I had a visit with him a few moments ago. And he said, you know, this is a big hurt that's going to last a while. I'm sure that's true. So I'd like to ask you before we begin the formal program today to join me in a moment of silent prayer for those students, for the other victims, and for their families. Amen.

I would like to welcome our leaders here from the American Legion, Joe Caouette, Lawrence Sperry, Judge Pete Johnson, a member of my Boys Nation class back in the Dark Ages. [*Laughter*] I welcome Peggy Sappenfield; Katherine Morris, the director of Girls Nation; Ron Engel, the director of Boys Nation; Jack Mercier, the director of activities who was also there and was a counselor to my class; George Blume, the legislative director.

I'm sure all of you know this is always a special day for me. It's the 50th anniversary of Boys Nation, almost my 50th anniversary on Earth here in a few weeks. [*Laughter*] This is only the second time ever, the first being the Bicentennial, when Boys Nation and Girls Nation have come to the White House together.

I remember a lot of things about my visit here in 1963, not only my much-heralded shake of hands with President Kennedy and the meetings we had with other leaders, but I remember very vividly the young men I was with from other states, the conversations that we had about the kind of world we would inherit and about what we had to do about it. Our obligations were focused, I think, especially on the issues that dominated our Nation more than 30 years ago now. We talked a lot about the struggle for civil rights and equal opportunities for all Americans. We talked a lot about the struggle against communism and the cold war.

To be sure, we weren't the first generation of Americans to have those conversations. They have been constant in our history. And we know that many of those who founded our Nation more than 200 years ago were themselves very young.

I'd like to ask you to think, because we are now on the verge of a new century, about what it was like the last time we stood on the edge of a new century. There's a magnificent portrait right over there in the corner of Theodore Roosevelt by the great American artist John Singer Sargent. Teddy Roosevelt became Vice President in the election of 1900 and was soon elevated to the Presidency when President McKinley was assassinated. He was our President for 7 years, in the beginning of what became known as the Progressive Era. He was the youngest person ever to become President of the United States. And as we stood at the dawn of a new century, he was infectious with his optimism and absolutely contagious in his determination to take on the problems of America and to make the new era we were then entering work for all Americans.

That was a time, like this, of enormous change. We were around the turn of the century moving from being primarily an agricultural country to being primarily an industrial country. We were moving from being primarily a people who lived on farms, in small, isolated rural areas, or in small communities to being a people who lived primarily in towns and in cities. And it changed dramatically the way we work, the way we live, the way we related to each other. There were enormously good things happening, but a lot of things that weren't so good, that required a vigorous response by our Nation and so Teddy Roosevelt led our Nation in that response and started, as I said, what became known as the Progressive Era. He and Woodrow Wilson—one a Republican, one a Democrat, both former Governors—were instrumental in kind of breaking out of the pattern of past thinking that had dominated our political life and taking America in a new direction.

"...we're now moving into an information age where every form of human endeavor will be dominated by the profound computer chip."

It falls to your generation to do something like that now, because we are changing in ways that are, to some extent, more profound than we changed a hundred years ago. Instead of moving from the agricultural to the industrial age, we're now moving into an information age where every form of human endeavor will be dominated by the profound computer chip.

Bill Gates said in his book "The Road From Here" that the digital chip was the most profound revolution in the way human beings communicate with each other since Gutenberg printed the first Bible in Europe 500 years ago. It won't be very long, especially if we succeed in hooking up every classroom and library to the information superhighway, before people in remote mountain communities or the poorest urban neighborhoods of America can go to school, hook into a computer, and do research on volcanoes in Australian libraries, for example. This is going to have enormous implications for the whole nature of work, how we learn, how we relate to each other. And it is a fascinating thing.

We're also moving—as people then moved from rural areas into the cities, we now are primarily an urban and suburban people. But people will be able to live in rural areas more easily than they used to because of the computer, and to do different things. And no matter whether we live in rural or urban areas, we will have to identify ourselves more and more as citizens of the world as well as Americans.

We're not dominated by a cold war world anymore where every country is either in the camp of democracy or the camp of communism, where we worry about the imminence of a nuclear war that could take the lives of the whole country away. But we do have a whole set of new problems in the world that directly relate to the fact that the cold war is over and things are more open now, and it's easier for people and ideas and money and technology to move around and cross national boundaries.

And when people become more open to new ideas and new

information it means that there are also more opportunities for the organized forces of destruction to take advantage of that openness. That's why terrorists can put poison gas on a subway in Tokyo or blow the World Trade Center up or the Federal building in Oklahoma City or set bombs in London or the Holy Land or do all the other things that you've read about in the last few years. The more open we are to moving around and working with each other, the more we'll have to be vigilant in dealing with these problems. It's why we're all more vulnerable to organized crime and drug running that crosses national lines. It's why we have to be more vigilant in dealing with the problems of the proliferation of small-scale nuclear weapons or biological or chemical weapons.

All of these things are the new security threats. And interestingly enough, there's also a very old problem that's rearing its head all over the world as the big threat of communism recedes. And that is the tendency of people everywhere to look down on each other, ultimately hate each other, and maybe even kill each other because of their racial, ethnic, or religious differences. That is at the heart of what is going on in the Middle East. That is at the heart of what is going on in Northern Ireland. That is the heart of what is going on in Bosnia.

"No country in history has ever lasted so long as a free country, a free people, with so many different kinds of people in it."

We have the most vigorous, vibrant, multiethnic democracy in human history, but that is at the heart of what is going on in these church burnings and that is at the heart of what led some mean-spirited people to paint swastikas on the doors of African-American Special Forces personnel at Fort Bragg in the last couple of days. The most patriotic members of a minority you could imagine still being subject to that.

Why is that? Because all throughout human history you see people being told that they should evaluate themselves not based on who they are, what they stand for, and what their values are, what's in the Constitution, the Bill of Rights, the Declaration of Independence, but on who they're not, what color they're not, what religion they aren't.

So you have to fight all that. Your generation will have more opportunities than any generation in human history. You will have more chances to live out your dreams in more different ways than any group of people who have ever lived. We have a chance to extend opportunities to people who would have automatically been left in the backwater of history without a second thought, just a few decades ago, because of their gender or their race or because of their disabilities. Things that now we wouldn't think of doing used to be the ordinary run-of-the-mill thing just a few decades ago.

So, on balance, as I look to the 21st century, I think this is going to be a great time for you. It is going to be a great time for America if we meet our challenges and protect our basic values. No country in history has ever lasted so long as a free country, a free people, with so many different kinds of people in it. And the world is coming our way. But there are still these dark forces of destruction that we have to stand against. And you have to speak against it when you see it in a big horrible way, in a manifestation of terrorism. But you also have to stand and speak against it when you see it in subtle ways, in your neighborhoods, on your street, in your schools. We've got to be able to treat each other with respect based on our shared values, not our essentially superficial differences.

Very interesting, don't you think that this movie "Independence Day" is becoming the most successful movie ever? Some say it's because they blew up the White House and the Congress—[laughter]—that may be. But, you know, you see story after story after story about how the movie audiences leap up and cheer at the end of the movie when we vanquish the alien invaders, right? I mean, what happened? The country was flat on its back, the rest of the world was threatened, and you see all over the world all these people have all of a sudden put aside the differences that seem so trivial once their existence was threatened, and they're working together all over the world to defeat a common adversary.

Why can't we work together to achieve common dreams? What is it about people that they need to adopt creeds that will enable them to demean other people and look on them as subhuman and take their lives away? We have to fight that. You're living in a time where, literally, you're going to be able to do things that have not been invented yet. A lot of you will be in jobs within a decade that have not been invented yet. The patterns of work and life, of travel and learning will be unbelievable. And no nation is as well-positioned as the United States if we seize our opportunities, meet our challenges, and protect our values.

You have to ask yourself—and I hope you'll take the time before you leave here, before you leave the White House, before you leave the Capital City—the whole history of our country is here—and say, what kind of country do I want to live in? What do I want America to look like when my children are my age? And what should I do to help America look like that? A simple question. Those are the questions I asked myself before I ran for President, because I knew that it's a rather rigorous enterprise and you have to have a high pain threshold today to do this sort of thing. [Laughter]

And to me, there are three simple answers. When my daughter is my age and I have grandchildren, I want America to be a place where the American dream is alive for every person who's willing to work for it, no matter where they start out in life. I want America to be a place that is coming together, not being split apart; that really appreciates all the differences that are in this country and binds us together by the things that have held this time. Just go back and read the Declaration of Independence, the Constitution, and the Bill of Rights. And I want this country to continue to be the world's strongest force for peace and freedom and prosperity, because we are doing something in this country that needs to be done in the rest of the world. People have to be able to bridge their differences and find a way to work together.

Now, that's what I want—fairly simple things; three things. And I work for it up here every day with a simple strategy: I think we have to create more opportunity for everybody, demand more responsibility from everybody, and do everything we can to build a community and make America stronger, and our families, our towns, and our national community as well.

There are some very specific things that we've tried to do. Four years ago, our economic house was out of order. We quadrupled our debt in 4 years. We had a $290 billion deficit. We had the slowest job growth rate since the Great Depression so we had to do some basic things just to put the house back in order.

And we had a very simple strategy: Drive down the deficit to reduce the burden of debt on future generations; lower interest rates and get investment back to put people to work; expand the trade in American products and services around the world because that creates more high-wage jobs here at home; and invest in education, technology, research, and the preservation of the environment.

"This is the first time in every year of a President's term that the deficit has been reduced since the 1840's."

Four years later, it's obvious to me that that strategy is working. Our deficit is less than half of what it was. It was $290 billion; it's going to be $117 billion this year. This is the first time in every year of a President's term that the deficit has been reduced since the 1840's. But we had to do it because we have never had a time in history when we built up so much debt so quickly. And the American people have responded. Our economy's created over 10 million jobs. So we're moving in the right direction. But that had to be done. It is not enough, but it's an important first step.

In terms of our leadership for peace and freedom, in many parts of the world we're better off today than we were 4 years ago, and there are no nuclear weapons pointed at any one of the United States for the first time since nuclear weapons were developed. So we're moving in the right direction. We're finally beginning to build compacts and partnerships all around the world to combat terrorism and the other problems that I mentioned.

We've worked hard to give you cleaner air and cleaner water and to preserve the natural resources of the land. I think one of the essential ideas that has to dominate the thinking of both parties and all Americans as we move into the 21st century is that you can develop the economy without destroying the environment. In fact, you can enhance the development of the economy with the right sort of environmental strategy. And if we continue to believe that the only way we can grow our economy is by destroying our environment, some day there won't be any economy to develop. And we have got to do that now. We have to make that commitment now.

You know, it's amazing how many science fiction books and

movies are all predicated on the fact that one day we won't have any environment left in America, we won't have any trees left, the air won't be fit to breathe. I'm amazed—we've now got with this new sci-fi channel on one of our cables here—it's amazing the percentage of movies that come on that thing that are predicated on the fact that we are determined to destroy our environment. We must not do it.

I also believe that we must not continue to tolerate the levels of crime and violence we have in our country. We have a crime rate coming down 4 years in a row now. We've got 100,000 police we're putting on the street in community policing. We've finally done something about putting guns into the hands of young people; we have a zero tolerance strategy for guns in schools. We've abolished a few assault weapons, 19 kinds, and passed the Brady bill. And I want to point out that a lot of people said some bad things when we did it. There's not a single hunter that's lost a rifle since we abolished the assault weapons and passed the Brady bill. But there are 60,000 felons, fugitives, and stalkers who could not get handguns because they were checked and their criminal record was found out and they did not get the guns. And America is safer as a result of that.

So we have to continue to work on the crime problem. And I want to make a personal plea to you. Citizens have a role to play in this. Yesterday the Vice President and I had representatives from citizens patrol groups all over America here at the White House, and we announced that the cellular telephone association is going to give 50,000 phones to these citizens patrol groups, so that when people are out here walking the streets and they find something wrong, they can immediately call the police department or the hospital, or the emergency room, or the fire department.

But in spite of all of our progress, the crime rate among people under 18 and the violence rate among people under 18 is still going up in most communities in America. That's because there are too many young people out there on the street that are raising themselves, that are joining gangs doing bad things because they're not in good gangs doing good things. We all want to be part of something. I mean, look, you've got the same shirt on; you're in a gang today. [Laughter] It's an important thing to know. And you can do that. You can have more influence on a lot of young people than I can. So I urge you to deal with that issue.

And finally, and most importantly, if we want to see everybody do well in the 21st century, we've to give everybody the tools to do well. And more important, more than ever before, that means education. We've worked hard to improve educational opportunities here, but we have more to do. And I want to encourage all of you to do what you can to support increasing access to high-quality education, from our initiatives to hook up all the classrooms to the Internet, to help the school districts that are hardest pressed in the country get some money to do rebuilding and repairs, to opening the doors of college education to everyone.

I hope that Congress will agree with me to give a tax deduction for the cost of tuition for college. I hope the Congress will agree with me to give a tax credit that will enable everybody to at least get a community college diploma, because we need to make at least 2 years after high school as universal for education as high school is today.

If you look at the economy, if you look at the census figures, if you look at the people that are doing well and the people that aren't, it is absolutely clear that in the information age the gains to education are far more profound than at any time in our history. And we have simply got to do more to make it universal if we want America to grow together instead of drift apart. We can do it. You can do it if you demand that it be done.

Finally, let me say that I believe we've got to do something more than we have done—many things more—to help strengthen the American family. And we have to recognize that families are in a different position than they used to be. I heard—someone made a funny joke last night, making fun of, to some extent, the Congress, to some extent, me—saying, you listen to people talk in Washington and they say the problem with people on welfare is that they want to stay home with their kids instead of going to work. And then they say give a speech and the problem with middle-class families is the mothers want to go to work instead of staying home with their kids. You know, and it's funny—you think about it. [*Laughter*]

What's the real issue? What's the real issue? The real issue is most people who are parents work; most people who are parents who work have to work. So what should our goal be? Our goal should be to help Americans succeed at home and at work.

I look at all of you—and if you want to make a contribution to our future, I want you to be able to make it. But I also think the most important contribution you can ever make is to have children and raise them right and make them good and strong and good citizens and good people, like you are. So what we should be doing is to think about instead of making it an either-or we ought to ask ourselves over and over and over again, what can we do to help people succeed at home and at work?

There's what the family leave law was all about. That's what my efforts, which have been very controversial, to try to help schools with experiments that they want to adopt, including curfews, or even in some school districts, school uniform policy, that's what that was all about. You may think it sounds bad but you're all here in one. [*Laughter*] And we haven't sought to impose them, we just sought to give schools the opportunity to adopt them if they wanted. That's what our controversial efforts to prevent the advertising and distribution and sales illegally of tobacco to teenagers is all about, trying to help parents deal with the implications of being away from their kids a lot, working, but also trying to do a good job raising their children.

It's also a large part of what the Vice President and I have worked on in the area of television. You know, we passed a law, the telecommunications law, which will create hundreds of thousands of jobs, but it also required in new television sets that a V-chip be placed that would give parents more control over the programming their young children watch. And all the entertainment industry agreed to set up a ratings system for television, which we thought was a very, very good thing. And we're working on that, they're working on it.

The television today is very different than it was when I was 10 or 11 years old, or 6 or 7. We have hundreds of studies, literally hundreds of studies showing the staggering number of hours that young people have spent watching people get killed by the time they're 16 or 17, and showing clearly that it makes people more numb to violence, less sensitive to the impact of their behavior on others.

So we've worked hard on that. But I don't think that is enough. And I just want to mention this issue, because I think it's very important. We have been working very hard not only to have a ratings system and a V-chip, which is sort of a negative thing, but also to try to bring more positive educational programming for children to television. This month we're challenging members of the entertainment industry who have done a great job on this rating to come to the White House to talk about improving the quality and quantity of children's programming. So the industry is doing its part.

The truth is that what we need now is for the Government to do its part. The Federal Communications Commission has had before it for a long time now a measure that would require broadcasters to put a minimum of 3 hours a week of quality educational children's programming on. If you think about all the hours the television is on a week, 3 hours a week doesn't seem like too much, at least doesn't seem to me. It's less than 2 percent of the Nation's air time. The initiative is stalled, and some people have opposed it. But the airwaves clearly, under our law, are designed to promote the public interest. I can't imagine anything we could do that would better promote it than to put more quality educational programming for children on television. So I'd like to ask all of you to support that. And I hope very much that the Federal Communications Commission will finally act on it.

Well, these are some of the things that I think we're facing as we move into the 21st century. We've got a responsibility, those of us in my generation, particularly those of us like me that had extraordinary opportunities to be in places like where you are over 30 years ago, to try to create opportunity—to try to create a framework within which everybody will be expected to be responsible and to try to bring this country together as a community.

But most of your lives are still ahead of you. And every one of you, if for no other reason than you're a part of this program, will have a disproportionate opportunity—a disproportionate opportunity to exercise leadership. And therefore you have a disproportionate responsibility to do a good job with it, every one of you.

When you go back home, your friends will look at you a little differently. They'll listen to you a little more closely. They'll want to know what you saw up here. They'll want to know what your opinion is. And I am telling you, you have got to be thinking now in this rapidly changing world, what do you want the country to look like when your kids are your age? What do you want your work years to be like? How do you want to feel about your country? And what do you have to do to get there?

And I leave you with this. It's very fashionable for people today to say, "Well, it doesn't really matter what's going on in Washington. Nobody can make a difference. Why should I vote; it's all a bunch of bull." I'm telling you, in the 4 years I have been President, I now am more optimistic than I was the day I got here. I believe more strongly than I did the day I got here about the potential of all of us working together to make good things happen.

"There are 10 million more people working than there were 4 years ago..."

And this country is a very great country. There are 10 million more people working than there were 4 years ago; 8 million people have refinanced their homes; 3.7 million people have homes who didn't have them; hundreds of thousands of people have better college loans than they did; 45,000 young people are working to rescue their communities in our national service programs and earning money to go to college. Don't let anybody ever tell you that you can't make a difference in a democracy, that you can't change the course of the country, that you can't lift people up or pull people together. That is not true.

And the most important thing maybe you can do in the short run when you go home is tell people this country works. That's why we have been around for 220 years. This country works. This is a great country. And you have to pull your weight and challenge your friends and family members to do the same. But I will say that if you do it, the best days of this country are still ahead.

Thank you, and God bless you all.

II. Religion and Prejudice

Dedication of the Mt. Zion African Methodist Episcopal Church[1]

William J. Clinton

President of the United States, 1992– ; born Hope, AR, 1946; B.S., Georgetown University, 1968; Rhodes Scholar, Oxford University, 1968–70; J.D., Yale University, 1973; professor, University of Arkansas Law School, 1973-76; attorney general, Arkansas, 1976-77; governor of Arkansas, 1979–81, 1983-92.

Editors' introduction: Within the past several years there have been numerous church burnings in the United States. More than thirty of those burnings have occurred at predominantly African-American congregations in the South. On June 12, 1996, President Clinton spoke at the dedication of the Mt. Zion African Methodist Episcopal Church in Greeleyville, South Carolina, which had been founded ninety years ago and burned one year prior to Clinton's speech. In this speech, the President remarked that racially motivated church burnings are "everybody's problem." He also pledged to do everything possible "to prosecute those responsible for the rash of church burnings."

President Clinton's speech: Thank you very much, Bishop and Reverend Mackey. Let me begin by thanking you all for being here and making us all feel so welcome. And before I—and thank you for that—[*laughter*]—before I go into my remarks, I want to present the Reverend Mackey a little plaque I brought that is dedicated to the congregation of this church, Mount Zion A.M.E. It says, "We must come together as one America to rebuild our churches, restore hope, and show the forces of hatred they cannot win." I hope you will put this up in your church, Reverend Mackey, and remember this day always. I'm honored to be here with you.

You know, first of all, let me say I'm honored to be here with so many distinguished Americans. I thank Senator Hollings, and Congressman Clyburn for coming down here with me today. I thank Congressman Inglis for being here. And our good friend, John Conyers, from Michigan, is either here or on his way here. Congressman Conyers, I thank him. I want to thank all the dig-

---

[1] Delivered at the dedication of the Mt. Zion African Methodist Episcopal Church, in Greeleyville, South Carolina, on June 12, 1996.

nitaries who have come to join us—Reverend Jesse Jackson for coming back home to South Carolina, and thank you for being here. And I want to thank Reverend Joseph Lowery, the very first person who wrote me to say that our National Government needed to do more about these church burnings. Thank you, Reverend Lowery, for doing that. And I thank my old friend, Bishop James, for coming back here; and Reverend Joan Campbell, Mayor Riley, Mayor Coble, Mayor Kellahan, and others who are here.

And of course, I want to thank the mayor of Greeleyville, who met me at the airport and rode in with me and talked to me about this little community and its challenges and its promise. I thank the Attorney General and the Secretary of the Treasury for coming down with me here today to demonstrate just how important we think it is to get to the bottom of these church burnings, and all of us are going to be working together on that. I thank my good friend, Millard Fuller, from Habitat for Humanity, for being here; and Randall Osborne, the SCLC administrator. Reverend Mack Jones, the NCCC; Reverend Ed Johnson; R.A. Leonard; Reverend Patricia Lohman.

And I'd like to make a special recognition and ask him to raise his hand, the Reverend Larry Hill, of the Matthews Murkland Presbyterian Church in Charlotte, North Carolina, which burned just last week. Reverend Hill, would you raise your hand? Where are you, sir? Here he is. Let's give him a hand. [*Applause*] Good to see you again, sir. Thank you.

First of all, I think it's important to note that we're celebrating a little something today. When the pastor came here, he told me this church had 42 members, and now it has 200 members. This church is like Shadrach, Meshac, and Abednego. They can burn the building down, but they couldn't burn the faith out. And so we celebrate the triumph of the faith of the members of this church. We celebrate those who have walked from the fire unharmed, guarded by God's faith.

We see in the rebuilding of this church that the false idols of hatred and division did not win. The church that burned here, just down the road, was built a long time ago. And when I was driving down that little country road to look at that site, I told Reverend Mackey it was like going down memory lane for me. There's a little road like that off a little highway in southwest Arkansas where my great-grandparents are buried in a country churchyard next to a church that is about exactly the same size that little church was. And I went down there just a few years ago to kind of revisit my past, and I felt like I was doing it all over again today.

Then when we came out here and I saw where this church is, I thought, you know, in just a few weeks this will be one of the few churches in America where everybody can have a fresh ear of corn on the way in or out of church—[*laughter*]—sort of strengthen their bodies as well as their faith as they go alone.

> *"They can burn the building down, but they couldn't burn the faith out."*

You think about what happened 90 years ago when the other church was built, people might have expected things like a church bombing. That was the time of Jim Crow, and there were evening lynchings in the South. It was a time of abject poverty, worse than anything we call poverty today. It was, 90 years ago, an expression of faith and courage for people to get together and build a church.

But it was the church that saved the people until the civil rights revolution came along. And it is, therefore, I think, doubly troubling to people—some of whom are over here on this platform today who spent their entire lives working for equal opportunity among our people, working for an end to the hatred that divided us for too long—to see our native South engulfed in a rash of church burnings over the last year and a half. We have to say to all of you who have been afflicted by this, "We know that we're not going back to those dark days, but we are now reminded that our job is not done." Dr. King once said, "What self-centered men have torn down, other centered men can build up."

The men and women of Mount Zion have shown us the meaning of these words by refusing to be defeated and by building up this new church. Others have come together with you. The pastor told me he got contributions from all over the world to help to rebuild this church. In just a few days we'll have a joyful noise coming out of this church. But today, just as you have come together, I want to ask the people of America to come together. I want to ask every citizen as we stand on this hallowed ground together, to help to rebuild our churches, to restore hope, to show the forces of hatred they cannot win.

I want to ask every citizen in America to say we are not going back, we are not slipping back to those dark days. Every time you hear somebody use race or religion as an instrument of division and hatred, speak up against it—every time you hear somebody do that. If you have the inclination, any evidence of anything you have seen or heard that somebody else might be planning to do something like this, tell the local authorities, and let's stop this before it gets started. If you know anything about any of the unsolved cases, come help us solve them. This is wrong.

The American people are the most religious church-going people of any great democracy. We cannot let someone come into our democratic home, the home of our faith, and start torching our houses of worship. It doesn't matter whether it's this Christian church or the mosque that was burned in South Carolina. People have a right to worship God any way they please. That's what the first amendment of the Constitution is about. We cannot ever let this happen in our country again.

Long before President Lincoln said it, the Lord spoke to us in the Scripture and said, "A house divided against itself cannot stand." It was always true. What a price we paid down here when we forgot it. What a benefit we have gained down here when we let it go. We cannot go back to those days.

"The American people are the most religious church-going people of any great democracy."

But if you look all over the world you see how easy it is for people slowly, step by step, to fall into the patterns of blaming other people who are different from them for the difficulties of the moment. Now we know as we see these fires of racial and ethnic hatred sweeping the world, as we see Africans from different tribes slaughter each other, as we see the ethnic hatred that consumed Bosnia, as we see it place after place all over the globe, we know how easy it is for the heart of human beings to be hardened against one another just because of superficial differences.

I pledge to you I will do everything I can to prosecute those responsible for the rash of church burnings, to prevent future incidents, to help communities to rebuild. But Americans must lead the way, for this is first and foremost an affair of the heart. And our heart must be purged of any temptation to go back to the kinds of divisions that cost us so dearly, especially here in the southern part of our country.

For months, more than 200 Federal agents have been working on these church burnings. There are now 33 active cases. We've closed 10 cases already through investigations, arrests, and prosecutions. Let me say, again, how profoundly grateful I am for the work done by the Attorney General and the Secretary of the Treasury and all those people who work with them. We will continue to probe these crimes. We will continue to use our top law enforcement officers. We will continue to see that these investigations meet a strict code of professional and personal conduct. I expect to get a report on this every week until the job is done. And I want you to help us finish the job.

I also want to say that we must keep this out of politics. This is about America. This is about what it means to be American. I want to say a special word of thanks to a Republican Congressman from Illinois, Henry Hyde, and a Democratic Congressman from Michigan John Conyers, who have together sponsored legislation that will make it easier for us to punish those who burn houses of worship. And I hope Congress will pass the legislation very, very quickly.

We also must work together to rebuild all these churches. We will work with Congress to give HUD the resources they need to guarantee loans by private lending institutions. And I want to applaud the business and community leaders who provide money and folks to assist in rebuilding these churches all across our country.

Already these burnings have sparked an outpouring of concern. The Alabama association of Habitat for Humanity is recruiting volunteers to rebuild several of the churches in Alabama. Today, Habitat for Humanity International has made a commitment to help all the communities that have lost churches in these arson attacks to rebuild. And I want to thank the founder of Habitat, Millard Fuller, who's here, for what his commitment is today. Thank you sir. Thank you.

I applaud the National Council of Churches—and I thank

Reverend Campbell for being here—for their financial commitment to rebuilding. I thank NationsBank for stepping up to the challenge and issuing a $500,000 reward for the arrest of those responsible for church burnings.

But in the end, let me say again, we must recognize that this is everybody's problem. Every citizen, every minister, and religious leader in this country should be speaking out against this violence. Every house of worship in America must be a sacred place, not just Christian churches for those of us who are Christian but our synagogues and our mosques. Any place where people gather to worship according to the dictates of their conscience should be protected from violence.

Reverend Billy Graham wanted to be here today and sent me these words for all of us to reflect on. He said, the problem between various ethnic groups is worldwide; it is a problem of the heart. It seems that much of the world is affected by this terrible disease, which should be called by its right name: sin.

So I ask you today, my fellow Americans, to celebrate the triumph of the rebuilding of this church, to express gratitude for the fact that the huge vast majority of our people of all races deplore what has been done and revere the right of every American to worship God in his or her own way. But I ask you to reaffirm our responsibility to keep working, working together, not to ever let America fall back into those patterns of hatred and division, which can so easily consume any civilized people.

We have to sing a song full of the faith that the dark past has brought us, full of the hope that the present has brought us. Let's face the rising sun of this new day begun. But let us remember we have to march on until victory is won.

Thank you, and God bless you all. Thank you.

"Any place where people gather to worship according to the dictates of their conscience should be protected from violence."

Church Burnings[2]

Carol Moseley-Braun

*Senator (D) from Illinois, 1993– ; born Chicago, IL, 1947; B.A.,
University of Illinois, 1969; J.D., University of Chicago Law
School, 1972; assistant to the U.S. attorney, U.S. District Court of
Illinois, 1973-77; recorder of deeds, Cook County, IL, 1988-92.*

Editors' introduction: On June 13, 1996, Senator Carol Moseley-
Braun supported a Senate resolution that "condemn[ed] arson
against churches as being totally inconsistent with American values." She further denounced church burnings as "domestic terrorism." President Clinton has since ordered the Federal
Emergency Management Agency to help communities form
church-watch programs to deter arson.

Carol Moseley-Braun's speech: Yesterday, Mr. President, I came
to the floor and spoke about what I called the domestic terrorism
that we are suffering in this country with the burning of churches and other hate crimes in our Nation. I spoke at some length
about it and mentioned a time that I will submit a resolution pertaining to the church burnings. I am submitting that legislation
now, Mr. President. I would like it held at the desk until the time
of adoption.

Mr. President, I know there will be other legislative activity
associated with this issue in the days to come. But as the Chair
is no doubt aware, since yesterday, when I first took to the floor,
there has been yet another church burning in this country.

As I said yesterday, the people who are perpetrators of this rash
of hate crimes and church burnings are no more than cowardly
domestic terrorists. These are people who work under cover of
darkness and anonymity to intimidate some and encourage others, and it is out of cowardice.

However, in spite of the objective of these actions, which it has
been suggested are intended to start a race war, there is every
indication that these arsonists are confused about the country in
which their crimes are taking place.

Most Americans—I reiterate, most Americans—are appalled
and outraged. The fact of the matter is, there is in this darkness
some light coming through. The light relates, Mr. President, to
the efforts of Americans, from the President of the United States
down to ordinary people, to stand up, to speak out, to be heard
and to demonstrate that this kind of crime, this kind of heinous

---

[2] Delivered to the United States Senate, in Washington, D.C. on June 13, 1996.

crime and this kind of domestic terrorism is not to be tolerated in this America.

I have been encouraged, Mr. President, by some of the reports from my home State. In Glenn Carbon, IL, there had been a cross burning. In one of the newspapers in Illinois, the headline there was "Neighbors Comfort Black Family Who Found Cross in Yard." The story goes on to say that the people, white and black alike, who live in the community came to the aid of the individuals who suffered the cross burning to indicate their support, to indicate their reassurance that the racial hatred that was symbolized by the cross burning did not reflect the feelings of the neighborhood or of that community. I think that is a very positive and powerful thing.

Another article, Mr. President, from the Alton Telegraph, "Neighbors show good will to victims of cross burning," makes the same point. This article goes on to say that neighbors delivered flowers and food, cards, plants and other gifts to the family on Monday, people reaching outside of themselves to stand up against hatred, to stand up against racism, to stand up against the evil that this church burning represents.

"This America, in this time, is putting the ugly legacy of racism and racial hatred behind."

I think therein lies the key. We can take action here in this U.S. Congress, the Senate and the House, and the President can take action. We can all come together as a collective community through our Government to take leadership in showing that in this America this kind of criminality will not be tolerated, but we can only do that, and it only takes real meaning when we are joined in our official capacity by individual, unofficial action, when the churches, themselves, come together to participate in ceremonies and services and marches and demonstrations in favor of unity and in favor of love.

When we really focus in on the fact that this rash of hate crimes is just that, a rash of evil afoot in the land, and that good people of all races will make it a point to be heard, not to sit back in silence and to allow this evil to take seed among us, but, rather, that we will all stand up as individual citizens to say, "This America, in this time, is putting the ugly legacy of racism and racial hatred behind. We will not go back to the days when these kinds of things can happen with impunity."

We will engage every asset, every resource at our disposal to see to it that these criminals are brought to justice, that the truth is uncovered, that no stone will be left unturned in our efforts to prosecute the perpetrators of these crimes, because they are criminals. We will make it very clear as a national community, all of us, that we will not tolerate this kind of conduct, and that the people who have tried to foist this horror on our community, on our country, will be prosecuted to the fullest extent of the law.

Mr. President, I also say after the speech that I gave yesterday, which is already in the *Record*, I was just really taken personally by the expressions of support, expressions of concurrence and the expressions from my colleagues on both sides of the aisle, people coming up to say, "We think it is just terrible what is going on. We want to do something about it. We want to be heard. We want to make certain that everybody understands that this kind of activity has no place in America." I am encouraged and heartened by that, because I think, if anything, that change of heart, that change of collective consciousness, that change in the climate of opinion is precisely the victory that reflects the moral victory that the civil rights movement achieved.

We have a mindset in this country that does not tolerate this kind of horror, that not only does not tolerate it, but is ashamed by it. Out of our repudiation, out of our rejection of these expressions of evil, I believe we will find a new birth as an American community. We will find a new level, frankly, of coming together and of working together, and of unity in this country, and will, I think, set the stage so the young people that are here today will begin to ask the question, in their time: "I remember the days when race was a debate in the United States, but we got past that. We got smarter, we matured, we moved beyond that." That is my hope for these young people.

If anything, I think with the expressions of support, the expressions of love, the expressions of unity, the good will that is being shown all over this country in reaction and in response to the hatred we have seen, the cross burnings and the church burnings, the moral victory will be ours as a Nation, and we will move forward as a Nation together, a stronger country because of it.

Mr. President, I understand the resolution will be adopted or can be adopted later this evening. I wanted to bring to my colleagues' attention the fact that this resolution is pending. I understand there will be other legislative initiatives in this regard. I am delighted to join with those, as well, because I think it is very important as a body we speak with one voice, that these people who are doing this are not Americans. Their activities fly in the face of the America that we believe in, fly in the face of the values that this America represents to the world, and that we will not allow their evil to shame all of us, and we will not allow them to get away with it. From that, Mr. President, I believe we will be a greater Nation, and we will have found, out of this horror, some light, and from that light we will be able to build a stronger Nation.

I commend my colleagues who have already joined me. Again, thanks to everyone who has stepped up and said something. One other word: There is a tradition that the only thing that allows evil to prevail is for good people to say nothing. Now is the time for good people to be heard. Now is the time for good people to stand up and say, "The America that we know and the America we believe in is an America that cherishes the value of brotherhood and love and unity."

The Issue of Prejudice[3]

Edward M. Kennedy

*Senator (D) from Massachusetts, 1962– ; born Boston, MA, 1932;
B.A., Harvard University, 1956; LL.B., University of Virginia Law
School, 1959; U.S. Army, 1951-1953; assistant district attorney,
Suffolk County, MA, 1961–62; author,* Congregation of the
Condemned *(1991),* Dear Ted *(1994),* Words Jack Loved *(1997).*

Editors' introduction: In response to recent church burnings,
Senators Lauch Faircloth from North Carolina, and Edward M.
Kennedy from Massachusetts, introduced Senate bill 1890, the
Church Arson Protection Act of 1996. In supporting this legislation, Faircloth maintained that, "Senator Kennedy and I stand
here today united in our belief that the rash of church arson must
end and now." In the speech printed below, Senator Kennedy
called upon all Americans to speak with "a united voice in condemning and combating these outrageous acts."

Edward M. Kennedy's speech: Mr. President, recently, the entire
Nation has watched In horror and disbelief as an epidemic of terror has gripped the South. Events we all hoped were a relic of the
past are now almost a daily occurrence. The wave of arsons primarily directed at African American churches is a reminder of
some of the darkest moments in our history—when African-
Americans were mired in a quicksand of racial injustice. We have
come a long way from the era of Jim Crow, the Klan, and night-
ly lynchings. But these arsons are a chilling reminder of how far
we have to go as a nation in rooting out racism.

In the 1960's, at a time when acts of violence against African-
Americans were commonplace, when white freedom workers
were being murdered by cowardly racists, Congress first began to
speak vigorously and in a bipartisan fashion to condemn this
violence and address the many faces of bigotry. Today, we again
speak with a united voice in introducing bipartisan legislation to
address this alarming recent epidemic of church burnings.

I commend my colleague from North Carolina, Senator
Faircloth, for his leadership on the legislation we are introducing
today. It is vitally important for the American people to recognize
that all Americans—Democrats and Republicans, whites and
nonwhites, Catholics, Protestants, Jews, and Muslims—must
speak with a united voice in condemning and combating these
outrageous acts. We must send the strongest possible signal that

---

[3] Delivered to the United States Senate, in Washington, D.C., on June 19, 1996.
Reprinted with permission of Edward M. Kennedy.

Congress intends to act swiftly and effectively to address this festering crisis.

President Clinton has also spoken eloquently on this issue, and has provided strong leadership. I applaud his efforts to commit substantial additional Federal resources to the investigations. Just as it was appropriate in the 1960's for the Federal Government to play an important role in reducing racial unrest, it is vitally important today for the Federal Government to take an active role in combating these racist arsons.

I also commend Congressmen Henry Hyde and John Conyers, who developed the bipartisan House bill that was passed swiftly and unanimously yesterday, and I urge the Senate to act with similar swiftness.

There are four basic components to the Faircloth-Kennedy bill. First, it provides needed additional tools for Federal prosecutors to address violence against places of worship. The bill amends the primary Federal statute dealing with destruction of places of worship to make it easier to prosecute these cases. Current law contains onerous and unnecessary jurisdictional obstacles that have made this provision largely ineffective. In fact, despite the large number of incidents of destruction or desecration of places of religious worship in recent years, only one prosecution has been brought under this statute since its passage in 1988. Our bill will breathe life into this statute by removing these unnecessary obstacles.

In addition, our bill strengthens the penalty for church arson by conforming it with the penalties under the general Federal arson statute. By conforming the penalty provisions of these two statutes, the maximum potential penalty for church arson will double, from 10 years to 20 years. Our bill also extends the statute of limitations from 5 to 7 years, giving investigators needed additional time to solve these difficult crimes.

Giving prosecutors additional tools will enable them to address the current crisis more effectively. However, we must also deal with the aftermath of the arsons that have left so many needy communities without a place of worship. The bill contains an important provision granting the Department of Housing and Urban Development the authority to make loan guarantees to lenders who provide loans to places of worship that have been victimized by arson.

This provision does not require an additional appropriation of funds to HUD. It simply gives HUD authority to use funds it already has. These loan guarantees will serve an indispensable function to help expedite the rebuilding process and the healing process.

These arsons have placed an enormous burden on State and local law enforcement, who also must investigate the crimes and address the tense aftermath within their communities. Our bill contains two measures to assist State and local law enforcement and local communities in responding to these vicious crimes.

The Department of the Treasury is authorized to hire additional ATF agents to assist in these investigations, and to train State and local law enforcement officers in arson investigations. ATF already trains 85 to 90 percent of local law enforcement in how to investigate arson. This authorization will facilitate needed additional training.

The bill also authorizes the Department of Justice to provide additional funds to the Community Relations Service, a small but vital mediation arm established by the Civil Rights Act of 1964. The mission of the Community Relations Service is to go into a community and reduce racial unrest through mediation and conciliation. The Community Relations Service has worked effectively to calm communities during some of the Nation's most difficult moments in the battle for racial justice, and it has earned the respect of law enforcement officials and community leaders nationwide.

In 1996, its budget was cut in half—from $10 million to $5 million. As a result, at a time when its services are in enormous demand, the Community Relations Service is about to be forced to lay off half of its already slim staff. This bill authorizes the restoration of funds to the Community Relations. We must act now, because its services are urgently needed.

"ATF already trains 85 to 90 percent of local law enforcement in how to investigate arson."

Finally, the bill reauthorizes the Hate Crimes Statistics Act. This rash of arsons demonstrates the need to document all hate crimes nationwide. Reauthorizing the Hate Crimes Statistics Act is essential, and law enforcement groups, religious leaders, and civil rights leaders throughout the Nation strongly support it.

Taken together, this bill represents a sensible and practical response to the church arson crisis. We have a constitutional obligation to preserve the separation of church and state, but we also have a Federal obligation to protect the right of all Americans to worship freely without fear of violence. We believe this legislation is a timely and constructive step to stem the tide of violence in the South. If more can be done, we will do it.

In a larger sense, this tragic violence provides an opportunity for all Americans to examine our consciences on the to issue of prejudice. We must work to root out racism and bigotry in every form. If we create a climate of intolerance, we encourage racist acts of destruction. While I respect and indeed cherish the first amendment right of free expression, we must be mindful that words have consequences. It is distressing that hate crimes are on the rise—whether arson of a church or assaults and murders because of bigotry. At other times in our history, we have been able to act together to heal a sudden or lingering sickness in our society, and we will do so now. The fundamental challenge is to re-commit ourselves as a Nation to the basic values of tolerance and mutual respect that are the Nation's greatest strengths.

The courage and faith demonstrated by the parishioners and clergy of the burned churches is an inspiration to the entire country. Their churches may have burned, but their spirit endures, and it is stronger than ever.

I also welcome the outpouring of generosity from numerous sources in the private sector. I commend the many individuals, businesses, congregations, and charitable organizations that have pledged financial support to rebuild the churches. These generous acts, as Martin Luther King once said, "will enable us as a Nation to hew out of the mountain of despair a stone of hope."

I urge my colleagues to join in expediting action on this urgent legislation. America is being tested, and the people are waiting for our answer.

Mr. President, this Faircloth-Kennedy bill addresses the recent spate of arsons that have gripped the South. The bill contains a number of measures designed to assist prosecutors and investigators in pursuit of the cowardly perpetrators of these crimes, and to assist victims and communities in the rebuilding process. This statement pertains to Congress' constitutional authority to amend the criminal provision pertaining to destruction of religious property and violent interference with right of free exercise of religious worship.

The bill amends title 18, United States Code, section 247 to make it easier for prosecutors to establish Federal violations in instances of destruction or desecration of places of religious worship. Although section 247 was passed in 1988, there has been only one Federal prosecution due to the onerous jurisdiction requirements contained in section 247(b).

The interstate commerce requirement of section 247(b)(1) is much greater than in other similar Federal statutes. For example, title 18, United States Code, section 844(i) is the general Federal arson statute and contains a much lower interstate commerce threshold than is found in section 247(b)(1).

The $10,000 requirement of section 247(b)(2) is arbitrary and unnecessary, and does not reflect the serious nature of many bias motivated acts of violence against places of religious worship. For example, there have been a number of incidents of bias-motivated violence committed by skinheads against synagogues which involved firing gunshots into these sacred places of worship, or the desecration of solemn symbols or objects, such as a Torah.

The Justice Department is providing specific examples of the limitations of section 247 which it will present at a hearing scheduled for June 25, 1996 in the Judiciary Committee. The monetary damage amount in these incidents described above is minimal. Yet, the devastation caused by these crimes is enormous, and the Federal Government can and should play a role in prosecuting these heinous acts of desecration.

The Faircloth-Kennedy bill amends section 247 in a number of ways. Most importantly, the onerous jurisdictional requirements of section 247(b) are discarded in favor of a more sensible structure that will better enable prosecutors to pursue the cowardly perpetrators of these crimes.

Section 2 of the bill contains congressional findings that set out in explicit detail the constitutional authority of Congress to amend section 247. A hearing was conducted in the House of Representatives on May 21, 1996, and a hearing will be conducted in the Senate on June 25, 1996, in which substantial evidence has or will be presented to support these congressional findings.

Congress has three separate bases of constitutional authority for amending section 247. First, Congress has authority under section 2 of the 13th amendment to enact legislation that remedies conditions which amount to a badge or incident of slavery. The Supreme Court, in *Jones* v. *Alfred H. Mager Co.*, 392 U.S. 409 (1968), and *Griffin* v. *Breckenridge*, 403 U.S. 88 (1971), held that Congress has broad power under the 13th amendment to enact legislation that addresses societal problems of discrimination. In Griffin, the Supreme Court held that "there has never been any doubt of the power of Congress to impose liability on private persons under section 2 of the [Thirteenth] Amendment.

The arsons that have occurred have been directed primarily at African-American churches. Although a number of the perpetrators have not been apprehended, it is clear from the statement of the Justice Department that a substantial number of the arsons were motivated by animus against African-Americans. Indeed, these events are a tragic reminder of a sad era in our Nation's history, when African-Americans were mired in a quicksand of racial injustice. As such, Congress has the authority under the 13th amendment to amend section 247, and to eliminate the interstate commerce requirement altogether.

Congress also has authority under the commerce clause to enact this legislation. As the record makes clear, the churches, synagogues, and mosques that have been the targets of arson and vandalism, serve many purposes. On Saturdays or Sundays, they are places of worship. During the rest of the week, they are centers of activity. A wide array of social services, such as inoculations, day care, aid to the homeless, are performed at these places of worship. People often register to vote, and vote at the neighborhood church or synagogue. Activities that attract people from a regional, interstate area often take place at these places of worship. There is ample evidence to establish that Congress is regulating an activity that has a "substantial effect" upon interstate commerce.

The Whole World Is Watching[4]

Sam Nunn

Partner, King & Spalding, 1997– ; born Perry, GA, 1938; A.B., Emory University, 1959; LL.B., Emory Law School, 1962; member, Georgia State House of Representatives, 1963; lawyer, Nunn, Geiger, Rampey & Perry, 1972-96; senator (D) from Georgia, 1972-1996.

Editors' introduction: Before retiring from the Senate in 1996, former senator Sam Nunn spoke at the National Prayer Breakfast in Washington, D.C. Begun in 1953, the prayer breakfast is attended by the most powerful politicians in Washington. At this meeting, Nunn discussed the end of the Cold War, and the subsequent lack of a common purpose he believes has been left behind. According to Nunn, this lack of common purpose has resulted in the decay of the family structure and a watering down of moral standards. In response, Nunn feels we must recall those values expressed in religious teachings, in particular those lessons offered by Jesus Christ.

Sam Nunn's speech: Thank you Bob Bennett, President and Mrs. Clinton, Vice President and Mrs. Gore, fellow sinners. Have I left anyone out? I say to my good friend, Alan Simpson, Billy Graham called me also, Alan. He said, as he did in his message, that he was praying for us all. But, he felt particularly compelled to pray for Alan Simpson and for me. Alan, I don't know what he meant by that, but you and I appreciate it.

A few years ago during the Bresznev era, Dr. Billy Graham returned from a highly publicized trip to Moscow and was confronted when he returned by one of his critics with these words, "Dr. Graham, you have set the church back 50 years." Billy Graham lowered his head and replied, "I am deeply ashamed. I have been trying very hard to set the church back 2,000 years."

Today we represent different political parties, different religions and different nations, but as your invitation states, we gather as brothers and sisters in the spirit of Jesus who lived 2,000 years ago, and who lives in our hearts and minds today.

The first prayer breakfast was held in 1953 in a world of great danger. President Eisenhower was newly inaugurated and had just returned from Korea where our young soldiers were fighting desperately. World Communism was on the move. Eastern Europe and the Baltics were locked behind the Iron Curtain. All

---

4 Delivered at the National Prayer Breakfast, in Washington, D.C., on February 1, 1996. Reprinted with permission of Sam Nunn.

across the globe, the lights of religious freedom and individual rights were going out, and the specter of nuclear destruction loomed over our planet.

I wonder this morning how those who attended that first national prayer breakfast 43 years ago would have reacted if God had given them a window to see the world of the 1980's and 1990's.

They would have seen truly amazing things: Catholic nuns kneeling to pray in the path of 50-ton tanks—the power of their faith bringing down the Philippine dictatorship; the Iron Curtain being smashed, not by tanks of war, but by the hands of those who built it and those who were oppressed by it; the Cold War ending, not in a nuclear inferno, but in a blaze of candles in the churches of Eastern Europe, in the singing of hymns and the opening of long-closed synagogues. I believe that God gave Joseph Stalin the answer to his question, "How many divisions does the Pope have?"

They also would have seen a black man in South Africa emerge from prison after 26 years and become the President of his nation, personifying forgiveness and reconciliation; the first hesitant but hopeful steps toward peace between Jews and Arabs in the Middle East, and between Protestants and Catholics in Northern Ireland. They would see that in 1996 we are blessed to live in a world where more people enjoy religious freedom than at any other time in history. Can we doubt this morning that a loving God has watched over us and guided us through this dangerous and challenging period?

During the early days of the Russian parliament, the Duma, I joined several other Senators in attending a meeting with a number of newly elected members of that body. The second day, a few of us were invited to a very small "prayer breakfast" with a group of Duma members who were just forming a fellowship, no doubt stimulated by Doug Coe. As in the larger meeting the day before, the breakfast discussion started with a degree of coldness and tension. One of the Russians, in obvious sadness and a little embarrassment, remarked that Russia was in great economic distress and that the United States was the only remaining superpower. It was clear that this was a very sensitive point for them. It had been abundantly clear the day before.

Senator Dirk Kempthorne and I then pointed out that in the real sense there is only one superpower in the world, our heavenly Father who watches over us all. The tension immediately eased and the spirit of fellowship was built, and we prayed together to that superpower, the God who loves us all.

Our world is a strange and ironic place. The Cold War is now over, but in a tragic sense, the world has now been made safer for ethnic, tribal, and religious vengeance and savagery. Such tragedy has come to the people of Somalia, Bosnia, Rwanda, Burundi, Sudan, Haiti and others.

At home, the pillar of our national strength, the American family, is crumbling. Television and movies saturate our children with sex and violence. We have watered down our moral standards to the point where many of our youth are confused, discouraged and in deep trouble. We are reaping the harvest of parental neglect, divorce, child abuse, teen pregnancy, school dropouts, illegal drugs, and streets full of violence.

It's as if our house, having survived the great earthquake we call the Cold War, is now being eaten away by termites. Where should we turn this morning and in the days ahead?

Our problems in America today are primarily problems of the heart. The soul of our nation is the sum of our individual characters. Yes, we must balance the federal budget and there are a lot of other things we need to do at the Federal level, but unless we change our hearts we will still have a deficit of the soul.

"Two thousand years ago, another society found itself in deeper trouble than our own."

The human inclination to seek political solutions for problems of the heart is nothing new. It is natural. Two thousand years ago, another society found itself in deeper trouble than our own. An oppressive empire strangled liberties. Violence and corruption were pervasive.

Many of the people of the day hoped for the triumphant coming of a political savior, a long-expected king to establish a new, righteous government. Instead, God sent his son, a baby, born in a stable. Jesus grew up to become a peasant carpenter in a backwater town called Nazareth. He condemned sin but made it clear that he loved the sinner. He befriended beggars and prostitutes and even tax collectors while condemning the hypocrisy of those in power. He treated every individual with love and dignity and taught that we should do the same. He died like a common criminal, on a cross, and gave us the opportunity for redemption and the hope of eternal life.

He also put the role of government in proper perspective when he said, "Render unto Caesar that which is Caesar's and unto God that which is God's."

Shortly after I announced that I would not seek reelection, a reporter asked me, "You've been in the Congress for 24 years; what do you consider to be your greatest accomplishment?" I paused for a moment and replied, "Keeping my family together for 24 years and helping my wife Colleen raise two wonderful children, Michelle and Brian." Upon hearing this, the reporter scoffed, "Don't give me that soft sound-bite stuff. What laws did you get passed?"

When he said that, I had several thoughts—only a couple of them I can share with you this morning. Four years ago, my daughter, Michelle, and a few of her friends started an organization in Atlanta called Hands on Atlanta, making it exciting, efficient and fun for young people to volunteer their time to help those in need. Now, about 5 years later, 10,000 volunteers each month render about 20,000 hours of personal, one-on-one service. What laws have I passed that have had this impact?

I also thought about the difference between being a Senator

and being a father. When we in the Senate make a mistake, we
have checks and balances—99 other Senate colleagues, plus the
House of Representatives, plus the President, plus a final review
by the Supreme Court. But, when we as parents make a mistake
with our children, where are the checks and where are the balances?

Congress can pass laws cracking down on those who refuse to
support their children. But we cannot force husbands to honor
their wives, wives to love their husbands, and both parents to
nurture their children. Congress can pass laws on civil rights and
equal rights, but we cannot force people of different races to love
each other as brothers. Congress can promote fairness and efficiency in our tax code, but we cannot force the rich to show compassion toward the poor. We can join with our NATO allies to
separate the warring factions in Bosnia, as we are doing, and
give them a breathing space, but we cannot force Muslims,
Croats and Serbs to live together as brothers in peace.

I recently heard a story on the radio. It happened in Bosnia, but
I think it has meaning for all of us. A reporter was covering that
tragic conflict in the middle of Sarajevo, and he saw a little girl
shot by a sniper. The back of her head had been torn away by the
bullet. The reporter threw down his pad and pencil, and stopped
being a reporter for a few minutes. He rushed to the man who
was holding the child, and helped them both into his car.

As the reporter stepped on the accelerator, racing to the hospital, the man holding the bleeding child said, "Hurry, my friend,
my child is still alive."

A moment or two later, "Hurry, my friend, my child is still
breathing."

A moment later, "Hurry, my friend, my child is still warm."

Finally, "Hurry. Oh my God, my child is getting cold."

When they got to the hospital, the little girl had died. As the
two men were in the lavatory, washing the blood off their hands
and their clothes, the man turned to the reporter and said, "This
is a terrible task for me. I must go tell her father that his child is
dead. He will be heartbroken."

The reporter was amazed. He looked at the grieving man and
said, "I thought she was your child."

The man looked back and said, "No, but aren't they all our
children?"

Aren't they all our children?

Yes, they are all our children. They are also God's children as
well, and he has entrusted us with their care in Sarajevo, in
Somalia, in New York City, in Los Angeles, in my hometown of
Perry, Georgia and here in Washington, D.C.

In the book of Micah, the prophet asks, "Shall I give my first-
born for my transgressions, the fruit of my body for the sin of my
soul?"

The cruelest aspect of our wars and our sins is what they do to
our children. Jesus said, "Suffer the little children to come unto

*"Congress can
promote fairness
and efficiency in
our tax code, but
we cannot force
the rich to show
compassion toward
the poor."*

me... For of such is the Kingdom of God." Too often today we shorten this commandment to—suffer—little children.

Mrs. Clinton, thank you for the emphasis you have put on children and the spotlight you have shined on our challenges. You are great.

The world is watching America today. People around the world are watching not just our President or our Congress or our economy or even our military deployments. They are watching our cities, our towns, and our families to see how much we value our children, and whether we care enough to stop America's moral and cultural erosion. Do we in America in 1996 love our neighbors as our ourselves as explained by Bob Bennett as our theme for the morning and by Tom Lantos and his personal example?

I do not have the answer to these questions this morning, and I don't pretend to. These problems can be solved only in the hearts and minds of our people and one child at a time. I do, however, have a few observations.

The Cold War provided us with a clarity of purpose and a sense of unity as a people. Our survival as a nation was at stake. We came together often in fear. The challenges that confront us today are far different, but the stakes are the same. I pray that our children, all of our children, will be the bridge that brings us together, not in fear, but in love.

Each year millions of our children are abused, abandoned and aborted. Millions more receive little care, discipline and almost no love. While we continue to debate our deeply-held beliefs as to which of these sins should also be violations of our criminal code, I pray that we as parents, as extended families, and as communities, will come together to provide love and spiritual care to every mother and to every child, born or unborn.

Government at every level must play a role in these challenges, but I do not believe that it will be the decisive role. What, then, are our duties as leaders, not just in the world of politics and government, but in every field represented here this morning and throughout our land? Like basketball stars Charles Barkley and Dennis Rodman, we are role models whether we like it or not.

I believe that the example we set, particularly for our young people, may be the most important responsibility of public service. We must demonstrate with our daily lives that it is possible to be involved in politics and still retain intellectual honesty and moral and ethical behavior.

We are all sinners, so we will slip and we will fall. But I have felt God's sustaining hand through every phase of my life—growing up in Perry, Georgia, raising a family, my relationship with my wife Colleen, in Senate floor debates, in committee meetings, visiting our troops in war, or being part of a mission for peace.

In the years ahead, when I think back on my public service, I am certain that my most cherished memories will be those moments spent with my colleagues in the Senate prayer breakfasts and in my meetings with leaders from around the world,

"The challenges that confront us today are far different, but the stakes are the same."

usually arranged by Doug Coe, in the spirit of Jesus.

I have also been blessed by many friends in the Senate and also a small fellowship with a group of Senate brothers like the late Dewey Bartlett, Republican of Oklahoma; Lawton Chiles, Democrat of Florida; Pete Domenici, Republican of New Mexico; Harold Hughes, Democrat of Iowa; and Mark Hatfield, Republican of Oregon. No one can accuse that group of being of like minds politically.

Yet, these brothers have listened to my problems, shared in my joys, held me accountable and upheld me in their prayers. Fellowship in the spirit of Jesus does amazing things. It puts political and philosophical differences, even profound differences, in a totally different perspective.

I believe that 2,000 years ago Jesus was speaking to each of us when he delivered his Sermon on the Mount. And, my prayer this morning for our leaders and our nation is in the spirit of his words then.

May we who would be leaders always be aware that we must first be servants. May we who compete in the arena of government and politics remember that we are commanded to love our enemies and pray for those who persecute us. I can't find any exception for the news media or our opponents. May we who seek to be admired by others remember that when we practice our piety before men in order to be seen by them, we will have no reward in heaven. May we who have large egos and great ambitions recall that the Kingdom of Heaven is promised to those who are humble and poor in spirit. May we who depend on publicity as our daily bread recall that when we do a secret kindness to others, our Father, who knows all secrets, will reward us. May the citizens whom we serve as stewards of government be sensitive to the fact that we are human beings subject to error and that while we need their critiques, we also desperately need their prayers. May we never forget that the final judgment of our tenure here on earth will not be decided by a majority vote, and that an election is not required to bring us home.

May God bless each of you.

Choosing Good Government[5]

M. Craig Barnes

Senior pastor, National Presbyterian Church, 1993– ; B.A., King's College, 1978; Master of Divinity, Princeton Theological Seminary, 1981; Ph.D., University of Chicago, 1986; minister, First Presbyterian Church of Colorado Springs, 1982-87; senior minister, Christ Presbyterian Church, 1988-92; author, Yearning: Living Between How It Ought to Be *(1992);* When God Interrupts: Finding New Life Through Unwanted Change *(1996).*

Editors' introduction: In this sermon Pastor M. Craig Barnes advised his congregation to choose good government by allowing a religious perspective to influence their leader selection process. To illustrate the value of religion to our decision making processes, Barnes drew upon the teachings of the apostle Paul. This sermon was one in a series by Barnes on allowing God to enter our decision-making processes. Other sermons in his series were "Choosing Good Work" and "Choosing Good Sex."

M. Craig Barnes's sermon: Americans have always been ambivalent about authority. We know we need it. We honor and respect it. But we are still suspicious of it.

This is not surprising for a nation whose founding documents include a Declaration of Independence, which we cherish. But that independence has also been written on our hearts. It was what propelled us to explore the frontier and tame it with our hands. It was what almost split the nation in two over a Civil War. Our spirit of independence has led us to honor innovation and creativity, and a competitive economy where we are free to improve ourselves. It has even sent us overseas to fight tyranny and aggression, because we cannot stand the thought of people not being free. Every healthy American teenager knows about the longing to be free, and that longing never goes away.

So we are very careful about giving even some of this freedom away. But we know we have to. We give it to parents and teachers, to employers and to the elders of the church, and we give it to the government who can tell us what to do. They can restrict our activities with laws and regulations and they can direct us toward a particular future. We give these leaders power over our lives because we know we cannot live together without some authority. But we don't really like it.

One of our favorite American beliefs is that the real authority

---

[5] Delivered at the National Presbyterian Church, in Washington, D.C., on September 29, 1996. Reprinted with permission of M. Craig Barnes.

still lies with the individual who at least chooses the people to lead us. Very conscious of this, leadership today has tried to move beyond the hierarchical models of the past where the person at the top ran the show. Now, the last thing anyone wants to be accused of is being authoritarian. So we have developed a new emphasis on "participative management" and "building consensus." But we are discovering this can digress into little more than servicing complaints. In essence, many leaders today are saying, "I'm just here to give you what you want." ("So I can stay here.") This has led many social and political commentators to ask who really has authority in a free society? The leader or those who are led?

According to Romans chapter 13, the answer is neither one. *Let every person be subject to the governing authorities; for there is no authority except from God.* Now that is a rather strong statement. And just in case we want to gloss over it, Paul says the same thing three times in this passage. "There is no authority except from God.... Those authorities that exist have been instituted by God.... Whoever resists authority resists what God has appointed."

At first we want to object by asking what about tyrants like Hitler or Stalin? What about the boss or teacher who abuses their power? Is there authority from God? But then we remember that the Apostle Paul, who was inspired to write these words, lived under incredible tyrants like Claudius and Nero. Paul knew about leaders whose abuse authority, but he also knew about the sovereign power of God.

As a Jew, Paul was steeped in the Old Testament understanding of God's Kingdom—God's reign on earth which is greater than the kingdoms of earth and uses the kingdoms of earth for his own purposes. Which means all governments are under God. To the degree that human leaders obey God they are being faithful to their calling. To the degree that human leaders break God's commandments they are stepping outside of their authority, which can only come from God.

Actually the Bible is filled with illustrations of people who because they obeyed God could not obey their leaders. When Pharaoh ordered the midwives to kill all the Hebrew babies, they began to hide them and Moses' life was preserved. When Nebuchadnezzar ordered everyone to bow before his image, Meshach, Shadrach, and Abednego refused to obey. When Darius outlawed praying, Daniel continued to pray. When Herod ordered the death of the children in Bethlehem, Jesus' parents fled to Egypt with their son. When Peter was told by the Sanhedrin to stop preaching, he told his religious leaders, "We have to obey God rather than man." In everyone of those cases, people of faith were making heroic choices about who would govern them. And in every case, the choices were guided by a prior commitment to serve God the only real authority we have.

The Bible says nothing about either covenants or contracts

between people and their leaders. That makes for good social and political theory, but it is not how the Bible orders our life together. The Bible claims both the people and the leader are under a common obligation to live under God, and the leader is but an instrument of divine purposes. Thus, we must help our government succeed in its calling to serve God. We cannot disregard the laws and direction of our leaders just because we had other preferences. We must still honor good leaders even when they make bad mistakes. In the words of B.B. King, "Only a mediocre man is always at his best." The only time we can refuse to obey our government is when in a great crises in conscience we become convinced it has determined to lead us away from life under God's authority.

Rev. Michael Cassidy, a leader of the South African church's resistance to apartheid tells about the time he was summoned to appear before President P.W. Botha in Pretoria. When he entered his office, the president stood and began reading Romans 13. Botha claimed the passage called for unequivocal support of the Nationalist Government apartheid policy. Rev. Cassidy responded by reminding the president he too had read the Bible and began quoting from Revelation 13, which describes governments that become dragons when they devour God's people. The authority doesn't lie in the leader. The authority lies in God, whom the leader also serves.

Here in the Land of the Free, we are given a wonderful opportunity to make choices about who will lead us. We can elect leaders. We can choose an employer, or a church, or a politician. Behind each of those choices, for people who believe in God, is a decision about which leader will bring us closer to the reign of God. Let me offer two guidelines to help us in our choices about who will lead us closer to God's kingdom.

1. To choose God's leader is always to choose Godly character. We live in an era when the issues of character and integrity have somehow been taken off the table for consideration. Try bringing up the issues of personal morality of a leader at work and you are likely to be told, "That is a private issue. The question is can he or she do the job." But as King David discovered people who do not make good personal choices are compromised in their ability to make good public choices. Biblical leadership is never seen as a job. It is a calling. It is a way of life for which the leader is a symbol.

People who choose to live by the Bible are given rather clear standards of ethical behavior. Some things are right. Some things are wrong. Not wrong because its ineffective or unpopular. But wrong because it isn't the right thing to do. To choose God as your authority is to resist the current privatization of morality and to choose a leader who is clearly trying to be led by God in his or her own life. The evidence of that is not only in things like sex and money, but also in the morals we *don't* talk about as

"To choose God as your authority is to resist the current privatization of morality…"

much in Washington—like humility, and graciousness, and the refusal to become mean just because it helps you survive.

2. Choosing a leader is always a choice about a particular vision of our life together. In a recent article in the journal *First Things*, Thomas Reeves asks why does our country seem to be so spiritually empty when according to the Gallup poll 90% of us claim to believe in God and to pray? One of his suggestions is that our religious leaders no longer have a vision of another way of life. Thus, we are no longer able to call for the sacrifice or discipline necessary to live by the Spirit. So the prayers of the people have become self-indulgent expressions of consumerism, where we keep asking God to give us something we can't get for ourselves.

John Updike's novel, *In the Beauty of the Lilies,* begins with a Presbyterian preacher named Clarence Wilmot who loses his faith at the turn of the century. For Rev. Wilmot it seems Christ is still hiding in the beauty of the lilies across the sea from us. He cannot find the Savior. He's overwhelmed by urban poverty and the injustice of his own parishioners. He finds no answers in the new liberal theology that adores scientific and cultural potential, but has little to say about God. Eventually he drops out of the ministry and becomes an unsuccessful encyclopedia salesman. No longer able to proclaim truth, he now peddles information.

"Without a vision of life, without something more than our current preoccupation with information and success, we are destroying not only ourselves, but our children."

The novel then traces how this loss of faith and vision is visited upon his children and grandchildren. Clarence's son becomes frightened of life. The author writes, "Nothing made Teddy indignant. He was curious about the world but never with any hope of changing it. He had no faith to offer. Only the facts of daily existence." Clarence's granddaughter became what the author calls an ego-theist who is preoccupied with herself. She doesn't seem to be troubled by morals, but finds it useful to pray to God for success. His great grandson became so lost and disillusioned that he fell easy prey to a cult leader who destroyed his followers in a fire.

Throughout the novel, the reader watches these characters make one bad choice after another. The book ends without any redemption or hope, but simply with two words, "The children." I was so upset, I slammed the book shut and threw it across the room. It is an awful book. But it's true. Without a vision of life, without something more than our current preoccupation with information and success, we are destroying not only ourselves, but our children.

To be American means to cherish not only our freedom, but also our vision of life under God. That was what brought Pilgrims and Puritans here. That was what Native Americans and Hispanics had before we came—Life under God. Slaves that were dragged here, found the vision to build a new life in the Biblical stories of God's deliverance. Immigrants that piled into the land came with the vision that there was a life here for them too—as Americans under God.

So those who will now lead us have to offer some vision of our life together. This has to be something more than just helping you get your piece of the pie. It has to be something that will again inspire sacrifice and commitment to the common good, something that will make us refuse to accept the way it is and commit ourselves to the way it can be.

Where will our leaders find a vision with that kind of authority? From their own faith in God. The only authority we have.

III. Race

Social Dynamite[1]

Paul Simon

Professor, Southern Illinois University, 1996– ; born Eugene, OR, 1928; U.S. Army, 1951-53; LL.D., Dana College, 1965; D. Litt., McKendree College, 1965; member, Illinois House of Representatives, 1955-63; member, Illinois Senate, 1963-69; lieutenant governor of Illinois, 1969-73; professor, Sangamon State University, 1972-73; representative (D) from Illinois, 1975-85; senator (D) from Illinois 1985-96; author, Lovejoy: Martyr to Freedom *(1964),* Lincoln's Preparation for Greatness *(1965),* Advice & Consent *(1992),* Freedom's Champion: Elijah Lovejoy *(1994),* We Can Do Better *(1994).*

Editors' introduction: In June of 1995 the Supreme Court ruled that federal affirmative action programs must be "held to an exactly constitutional standard." With that decision, debate over the legality, and worth of affirmative action initiatives accelerated. Many argue that affirmative action practices have run their course; while others believe such programs are necessary to insure equal opportunity. In this speech former senator Paul Simon reviewed recent court decisions, and made the case for continuing affirmative action measures.
\
Paul Simon's speech: Affirmative action, like any good thing, can be abused. Religion can be abused. Education can be abused. But education and religion are beneficial to the nation, and affirmative action is beneficial to the nation.

We all repeat the pledge of allegiance to the nation, incanting the words "One nation, under God, indivisible." The reality is that we are now moving away from becoming that one, indivisible nation, and both the courts and the Congress should weigh actions in this emotion-laden area with great care, lest we further divide the nation. The lessons of Bosnia, Rwanda, and Burundi should be seared into our conscience.

One of the worst court decisions in recent decades came recently from the appellate court of the Fifth Judicial Circuit, the *Hopwood* case, involving the University of Texas law school. This is the state that in 1945 was ordered to provide a legal education for a minority student for the first time, and in order to "comply"

---

[1] Delivered to the United States Senate, in Washington, D.C., on April 30, 1996. Reprinted with permission of Paul Simon.

with that court decision, Texas created a three-room, separate law school in the basement of a building.

Fortunately, that period is history in Texas and this nation, but there remain forces, sincere but insensitive, who want to turn the clock back.

If the *Hopwood* decision, denying the University of Texas the right to have diversity, is upheld on appeal by the United States Supreme Court, it will be the worst decision since the *Korematsu* decision of the Supreme Court denied civil liberties to 120,000 Japanese Americans taken abruptly from their homes and sent to camps in February 1942, when not one had committed a crime. If the Supreme Court upholds the *Hopwood* decision, it will have far-reaching consequences similar to the *Plessy* v. *Ferguson* decision of a century ago, a decision overturned by the Court in 1954, but one that caused decades of disadvantage to all Americans, particularly African Americans, leaving scars in our society to this day.

"...the United States Senate should be sensitive on the issue of racism, not pander to those who would divide our society."

When men in white hoods do the wrong thing, however sincere they may be and no matter how popular their cause may be in certain circles, responsible Americans should stand up. And when men in black robes do the wrong thing, however sincere they may be and no matter how popular their cause in certain circles, responsible Americans should stand up. And the United States Senate should be sensitive on the issue of racism, not pander to those who would divide our society.

I have heard many speeches in the Senate Judiciary Committee about judicial activism, that the lower courts of this nation should not try to write new law. Yet the Fifth Circuit did exactly that, attempting to reverse the *Bakke* decision.

Justice Jerry Smith, writing for the majority, states that race should not be any more a consideration "than would be choices based on physical size or blood type of applicants."

Is he serious? There is no problem in our society of short people and tall people not getting along, or blood type-Os not getting along with type-As. But there are other real problems that the Fifth Circuit ignores. Would the University of Texas law school be justified in admitting all of its students from only Dallas? We recognize that it is important educationally for the students from Dallas to mix with students from Houston and El Paso and other places. Is it any less important for students of differing racial and religious and ethnic backgrounds to study together?

Judge Smith ignores the cultural history of our nation and the history of our laws. Since diminishing percentages of elementary and high school students experience racial diversity in the nation's elementary and secondary classrooms, somewhere students should learn the simple lesson that all human beings share the same hopes and dreams and fears, and universities, to some extent, have been able to fill that void and teach that lesson. Neither the courts nor the Congress should impede universities from that important role.

Let no Senator and no American fool himself or herself. We are dealing with social dynamite. Let us not pander to the forces of reaction but continue to strive to make ours "one nation, under God, indivisible."

A Different Melody[2]

Vernon E. Jordan, Jr.

Senior partner, Akin, Gump, Strauss, Hauer, and Feld, 1981– ; born Atlanta, GA, 1935; B.A., Depauw University, 1957; J.D., Howard University, 1960; executive director, United Negro College Fund, 1970–72; field secretary, president, National Urban League, 1972–81.

Editors' introduction: In response to the passing of California's Proposition 209, which bans affirmative action policies, protesters marched across the Golden Gate Bridge in San Francisco. The law, which was passed by a 54 precent margin by California voters in 1996, went into effect recently. The march was organized by the Reverend Jesse Jackson, who urged those who opposed the law to continue fighting against it. With several state governments and federal courts curtailing affirmative action initiatives, and a more conservative Congress handling federal directives, Vernon E. Jordan, Jr. advised graduates that effective public policy requires that affirmative action programs continue.

Vernon E. Jordan, Jr.'s speech: It has been said that commencement speakers have a lot in common with grandfather clocks. Both are over six feet tall, ponderous in construction, more traditional than functional, and noisily communicate commonplace information.

I shared that view until I started giving commencement addresses. It's amazing how different things seem from this side of the podium.

The address at my own commencement—39 years ago—was one of the longest, most boring speeches I have ever endured, full of sound and fury, signifying absolutely nothing.

So as I rise to address you, I have great empathy and sympathy for your circumstances. However, believing as I do in equal opportunity—I plan to do to you the same thing my commencement speaker did to me!

As you graduate today you are not confronted with the same issues that concerned my generation when we graduated from college. At that time, the issues seemed clear-cut. A cold war was raging, putting the free world against communist dictatorships. Here at home, state-supported segregation denied constitutional rights to black Americans.

Much has changed for the better since then. The cold war is

---

[2] Delivered at the Claremont McKenna College commencement exercises, in Claremont, California, on May 12, 1996. Reprinted with permission of Vernon E. Jordan, Jr.

over. Segregation is illegal. Jim Crow was destroyed.

But alongside such positive global changes, we also see negative ones—ethnic strife, terrorism and economic insecurity are
serious problems throughout the world.

At the same time, rapid technological change has transformed
the world economy into an integrated global economy. The pace
and nature of change have shaken our confidence in old truths
and in a certain future.

The resulting anxiety is leading to major shifts in our political
life. Voters turned to Bill Clinton in 1992 and to Newt Gingrich
and company in 1994.

The Republican majorities in congress thanked the voters by
aggressively pushing a Contract with America that, in my judgment, punishes the poor, heaps even greater rewards on the
wealthy, and increases middle class insecurity.

That's not what the voters wanted or expected. The polls now
show that they might express this dissatisfaction by swinging
back to the Democrats in 1996. The prospects for the President's
reelection and for the return of a Democratic House of
Representatives look better than they did a year ago.

However, we can expect the election campaign to be hard-
fought and close. Voters are still confused, insecure and angry
about layoffs and sluggish income growth.

In that volatile context, we can expect some candidates to
exploit wedge issues—issues that divide people, issues that split
voters from their political allegiances, issues that carry powerful
emotional baggage.

It doesn't take much imagination to predict that affirmative
action and other measures developed to bring blacks, Hispanics,
Asians and women into the mainstream, will be wedge issues in
1996.

For some politicians, serving as the source of this wedge is the
sole function of black and minority citizens. For them, we exist
to be demonized...presented as threats to society and the economic stability of the majority of Americans.

The days of the appeal of blatant racial division are thankfully
no longer with us. Racist attitudes are no longer publicly acceptable, yet some politicians cannot resist the temptation to exploit
racial animosity, wrapping their message in easily understood
code words.

In 1996, you can expect some candidates to play the race card
by focusing on affirmative action programs and policies. They
will say affirmative action is reverse discrimination against
whites, and a quota system favoring blacks and minorities.

They will say that under affirmative action blacks are held to
lower standards than whites. Because they know that affirmative
action is nothing of the sort, raising the issue becomes a trans-
parently cynical election ploy.

I raise these examples for three reasons.

First, to urge you to understand the cynicism that drives so much of today's political discourse, especially about divisive issues such as affirmative action.

Second, to urge you not to become cynical yourselves. You may become disillusioned with the political process because candidates subvert the truth and make appeals to negative emotion they think will win them votes.

However, voters who want to protect the integrity of the political process must see through such ploys and punish those who practice them.

If you turn away from the process in disgust, you leave the field to those who abuse it and those who are influenced by their cynical appeals.

Third, I raise the issue of affirmative action today to urge you to support affirmative action programs because sound, effective public policy requires their continuation.

Whatever your race or ethnic background, I hope you will understand the whys and wherefores of affirmative action, and that you will raise your voices and cast your votes to express your understanding.

Because affirmative action is needed, it works and it benefits all Americans.

Let me just elaborate on those points briefly.

Affirmative action is still needed because—despite impressive gains—blacks and other minorities still do not enjoy equal opportunities socially, economically or politically.

Last fall a bi-partisan national commission concluded that the glass ceiling is firmly in place. It found that 97 percent of the senior managers of fortune 500 companies are white, and almost all of them are male.

It found that black men with professional degrees earn 21 percent less than whites holding the same degrees in the same job categories.

It found that less than half of one percent of managers are Hispanic and that Asian Americans earn less than whites in comparable positions and get fewer promotions, even though they have more formal education than other groups.

Contrary to the impression all the noise about minority preferences gives, the student population of the University of California at Berkeley is only 6 percent black and 14 percent Hispanic.

The prospects for many black Americans are still bleak. The poverty rate is triple that of whites; unemployment is double the white rate; and earnings are about two-thirds of white earnings.

Too many black and minority children today grow up in poverty. In crime- and drug-infested neighborhoods and single-parent homes. They attend inferior and underfunded schools.

Years ago, President Lyndon Johnson said:

> You do not take a person who for years has been hobbled by chains and liberate him, bring him up to the

starting line of the race, and then say you're free to compete with all the others, and justly believe you have been fair.

Those words remain as true today as they were then. Those who believe we are now a colorblind society in which everyone enjoys equal opportunities have lost their vision.

We are far from it. That is why affirmative action is still needed.

My second point is that affirmative action works.

Despite continued disadvantage, America's minorities and women have made extraordinary gains. At least part of that progress can be attributed to affirmative action.

Before affirmative action, minorities were routinely excluded from prestigious schools, from corporate jobs, from skilled trades, and from municipal fire and police departments.

Today, despite their continued under-representation in aspects of American life, all minorities and women have moved into the mainstream—thanks to affirmative action and federal anti-discrimination mandates.

The number of black police officers has gone from 24,000 to 64,000; black electricians increased from 14,000 to 43,000. The number of black students in predominantly white colleges and universities grew from 134,000 in 1961 to 1.2 million today.

Companies that hired minorities only for janitorial jobs now have black managers; colleges that wouldn't admit black students now have black professors; cities that wouldn't hire black cops now have black police chiefs.

As a result, the black middle class has expanded from one in seventeen families a generation ago, to one in seven today.

Such progress would not have been made absent affirmative action programs. And if affirmative action is abolished, such progress would surely be reversed.

That brings me to my third point—affirmative action benefits all Americans.

Let me illustrate. During the Carter Administration, the Secretary of the army—a black man—was presented with a list of candidates for promotion to general. He sent the list back, insisting that more black candidates be added.

When the revised list came back it included a gifted young colonel named Colin Powell, who was duly promoted to general.

The U.S. Army and the nation benefitted from that exercise of affirmative action. Left to themselves, the army brass came up with a limited promotion list. Forced to cast a wider net, they found, not miraculously so, a man whose contributions might otherwise have been lost to the nation and the world.

We can't afford to waste our human talent any more. The world has changed, and America cannot flourish unless it recognizes this change and uses the full potential of all its people.

Demographic changes mean that America must ensure that all groups have access to the mainstream. By the middle of the next

"The number of black students in predominantly white colleges and universities grew from 134,000 in 1961 to 1.2 million today."

century, minorities are expected to make up about half of the Nation's population. About half of all Californians are now black, Hispanic or Asian.

Affirmative action is necessary to ensure that they compete on a level playing field. Without it many will be excluded and discrimination will rob America of talent it desperately needs.

Racial and ethnic feelings have always pervaded American life. If they are manipulated in a way that threatens the very core of this country, everyone suffers.

White Americans and minorities alike must learn to understand and interact with people of other races and cultures. By doing so, they equip themselves with the skills needed to negotiate a diverse, multicolored and multicultural world.

Those who prey on racial antagonisms do not understand the fundamental wisdom and decency of most Americans. Even after all the inflammatory rhetoric and the continuous talk of reverse discrimination, the polls show that the majority of Americans support some form of affirmative action.

Today, affirmative action is under assault from conservative courts, from some running for office, and from people who are no longer concerned about hiding their prejudices.

They would have you believe that affirmative action is wrong, and that the federal measures to help reduce inequality and bring minorities into the mainstream are evil. They say the answer to all our problems is less federal interference and more local control.

But I know from personal experience that the federal government's necessary role must be as guarantor of rights denied by local laws and customs.

When I was growing up in Atlanta, Georgia, local control meant that I had to live in a segregated housing project and that I could not use the downtown public library.

Local control meant that in 1951 I used a plain geometry book used by a white student in 1935. It meant the state of Georgia paid $250 per year to educate black children while it spent $600 a year to educate white children. It meant that black teachers were paid far less than their white peers of equal educational achievement and experience.

Local control meant that my hard-working, god-fearing parents were denied their constitutional right to vote in the democratic presidential primary.

Local control in 1996 means returning to the status quo ante. It means that blacks and Native Americans will be once again targeted as a group denied equal access. It means that prejudice against Hispanics and immigrants will have free rein.

It means that opportunities for women will be questioned. It means that the envy and resentment of the accomplishments of Asian Americans will be unchecked.

Our democracy was warped by bias and injustice, and it was not made straight until the power of the federal government was brought to bear.

Now, voices are raised to tell us not to fear, that the wrongs of the past will not return.

I hope, graduates, that when you hear their siren song of division and devolution you recognize the melody as being the same one used to justify old ways.

I have faith that you will sing a different melody, a song of diversity and inclusion, a harmonious chorus of equal opportunity and respect for the healthy differences and strengths each of us brings to our great nation.

And I fervently hope that as you go forth from this place, you will participate in the great debate...that you will champion America's traditional ideals of justice and fairness and equal opportunity in an open, pluralistic, integrated society.

This commencement marks the beginning of what has been called "the terrific responsibility toward human life." You now share the responsibility fully.

As you share it, hear the timeless words of Herman Melville, who wrote:

> We cannot live for ourselves alone. Our lives
> are connected by a thousand invisible threads,
> and along these sympathetic fibers our actions
> run as causes and return to us as results.

Now as you leave these hallowed grounds of Claremont Mckenna, as you say farewell to classmates and professors, as you accept the responsibilities and duties of citizenship—be steadfast, be strong, be of good cheer, and may your own dreams be your only boundaries, now, henceforth and forever. Amen.

The Moral Decay of America: Racism—Putting the American Dream Out of Reach[3]

Myron H. Wahls

Michigan Court of Appeals Judge, 1982– ; born Rushville, IL, 1931; B.A., University of Michigan, 1952; J.D., Northwestern University School of Law, 1955; LL.M., University of Virginia School of Law, 1957; lawyer, Keith, Conyers, Anderson, Brown, Wahls, Baltimore & Stephens, 1961-74; Wayne County Circuit Court Judge, 1975-82.

Editors' introduction: In 1995 Father John McDonnell of St. Agnes Catholic Church in Kanawha City, West Virginia remarked: "Look around and you'll see a society taut with racial tension." In the commencement address reprinted below, Judge Myron H. Wahls recommended a "rebirth of morality" in America. "Racism," he insisted, "is no longer a problem of civil rights. The issue is now one of social justice." For Wahls, racism is a social divider which places great distance between those seen as "haves" and those seen as "have-nots."

Myron H. Wahls's speech: Thank you, President Vandament. Good morning and congratulations to all of you. I am, of course, delighted to be here.

I was at a breakfast just a few hours ago at which the honors students were recognized—summa cum laude, magna cum laude, cum laude. I was reminded of when I graduated. There weren't any of those three, we were just graduated "Oh Lordy," and glad to be there!

President Vandament's generous introduction of me reminded me of a circumstance where a newspaper was looking for the most highly principled, sober, well-behaved, local citizen, and they got an entry from one fellow who said:

> I don't smoke, I don't touch intoxicants, or gamble. I've been faithful to my wife, never look at another woman. I'm hard working, quiet, and obedient, never go to the movies or the theatre, go to bed early every night and rise with the dawn, and attend chapel regularly every Sunday without fail. I've been like this for the last three years, but you just wait until next spring when they let me out of here.

---

[3] Delivered at the Northern Michigan University commencement exercises, in Marquette, Michigan, on April 27, 1996. Reprinted with permission of Myron H. Wahls.

I don't want to talk too long this morning and be like the preacher in the midst of a long sermon. He said, "I don't mind if you look at your watch to see what time it is, but it really annoys me when you put them up to your ear to see if they're still running."

You've really blessed me with the invitation to be here. I'm deeply grateful for the privilege of being here on this occasion, and it is all the more significant when I think of the distinguished men and women you might have invited here this morning—people I know whose capabilities for articulate creation are firmly established, enabling them to select words to provoke an inspiring celebration providing food of faith for the hungry, spiritual shelter for the homeless, medicine for the sin sick, and compassion and comfort for the weary.

My first contact with Northern Michigan University was in January, 1995 when I had been invited to participate in the birthday celebration of Martin Luther King, Jr. I next visited here in October of last year, with much of the same format—speaking with students, performing with jazz musicians, and enjoying the warm and growing friendship of President Vandament, Vice President Matt Surrell, faculty members, students, and judges and attorneys.

I returned to Detroit humbled and enriched. I have been profoundly impressed with the graciousness and cordiality that I have received from everyone whom I have met during my visits. And it is a deep honor and privilege to be in your midst once again on this, one of the most important days of your lives.

I applaud the University for its courage, dedication, and exciting sense of mission. And I congratulate the University for providing a forum where values are symbolized, choices are clarified, priorities sifted, and where, above all, hope for a brighter future is kept alive.

To the graduates today, you have demonstrated that you have unique abilities in the academic arena, but you must continue to expand the frontiers of your minds. The faculty here have exposed you to their knowledge, experience, and skills with the objective of providing you with the intellectual equipment that leaves you better fortified to meet the responsibilities of your chosen professions, better equipped to more efficiently discharge the duties imposed upon you, and more enlightened as to the important places that you will occupy in your respective communities.

But no matter how well you absorb the learning gleaned from your studies, no matter how determined your resolve to perform in your life work, no matter how successfully you apply the knowledge to your world experience—in the final analysis, the ultimate challenge is not only to make a living, but to make a *life*. This is the continuing saga of everyone's sojourn.

The great jazz trumpeter, Harry "Sweets" Edison, and I were traveling en route to an airport a few years ago. We had just concluded five days at the Lionel Hampton Jazz Festival at the University of Idaho. Harry had performed for several of the concerts and I had served as one of the judges for some of the high school competitions. I observed that many of the young artists displayed a high degree of enthusiasm for the music. However, they were still struggling with the basic understanding of how the music should be interpreted. They lacked the skill to improvise.

"Sweets" shared similar observations and, after a few moments, he concluded his remarks by saying to me, "Judge, if you don't know the tune, you can't improvise.

When I thought about what he had said, I was struck by the simple and powerful truth it conveyed. The more I thought about it, the more I realized that the concept could be applied to everyday life. For, if you don't know the tune, you can't create, compose, conceive, invent, envision, devise or produce. Throughout your years of studies here at the University you have been learning the tune. *You must now begin to improvise.*

"...there is no hope in heroin, no power in a pill, no reason in a reefer, no wisdom in whiskey, no courage in cocaine, and no life in a lottery ticket."

The great thing in this world is not so much where we stand, as in what direction we are moving. To live well, you must have a faith fit to live *by,* a self fit to live *with,* and a work fit to live for. Like everybody else, you will make mistakes, but the cause should be want of information and not unsoundness of judgment or lack of devotion to principle.

It is not only aptitude but attitude that will determine your altitude. If you can conceive it and believe it, you can achieve it. And remember that failure is not falling down, but rather failure is not trying to get up!

One cause of failure could be, for instance, drug addiction. All literature proclaims that nearly a fifth of you will become substance abusers. Let me tell you that there is no hope in heroin, no power in a pill, no reason in a reefer, no wisdom in whiskey, no courage in cocaine, and no life in a lottery ticket. Dope will set you on a high for a moment, but it will hang you up, take you where you don't want to go, and keep you longer than you want to stay.

During the course of your careers, you will no doubt cross paths with people who will try to get you to compromise your integrity. The one thing that you cannot avoid getting in life is a reputation—good or bad.

In the legal profession, the canons of ethics both for lawyers and judges make clear that an admonishment can be forthcoming even for the appearance of impropriety in our conduct. While this standard, you may believe, is harsh, its objective is to make sure that those of us who are called upon to pass judgment on others and to defend those who have been accused of breaking the law have conducted ourselves in a manner that in no way, not even in appearance, calls into question our integrity.

Adopt the same standard for yourselves to ensure that in no way your integrity, even in appearance, is compromised. It will require an integrity that is intact, as well as intelligence, to face the challenges of our society and the world.

If you don't know the tune, you can't improvise.

The challenges of the twenty-first century are burdened with the history of the challenges we have experienced in the twentieth century. Wars, world poverty, human oppression, and economic uncertainty have caught us in the parenthesis of time, spending most of it living somewhere between, 'Thank you, Jesus," and "Lord, have mercy!" as we watch the unjust hand of oppression waved like a wand across the face of the Earth.

Homicide, fratricide, suicide, apartheid—the words affecting us like the acts of a chemist tossing a tiny pinch of some powerful ingredient into a seething, shaking cauldron where, below the fresh confusion, there is heaving some deep and irrevocable change.

Any examination of crime clearly indicates that society fears criminals but is indifferent about what is to be done with them; seeks easy answers to complex problems, and becomes overly dependent upon the criminal justice system while neglecting auxiliary social and economic support systems.

There is still a grudging effort or interest to focus attention on the circumstances that lead to crime, but I see no real concern developing on the horizon. Instead, the cry is for mandatory sentencing, longer sentences, abolishing parole, emphasizing law and order, and capital punishment.

Alternatives to prisons, community-based corrections, pretrial release and diversion, probation and parole are decried in every forum, and the hysteria finds sanctuary in the highest courts of the land—bent on rewriting sacred rites to accommodate an attitude of repression.

One finds himself saying, "Interpret for me the libretto, lest I dilate with the wrong emotion."

The real American Dream is to live in a society experienced by all of its citizens as equitable, just and compassionate. But the widening distance between society's "haves" and "have-nots" is a reflection of the gap between our commitment to meeting human needs and our support for specified strategies by which those needs can be met.

The "haves" have not and the "havenots" have not at all. Repeated studies have shown a direct correlation between the lack of basic human needs being met and the escalation of crime.

If you don't know the tune, you can't improvise.

Of the ideals that characterized the American nation at its beginning, none was more radiant or honored than the inherent equality of mankind. There was dignity in all human flesh. Americans proclaimed that all must have the chance to strive and to excel.

All men and women were to be protected alike from the threat of menacing neighbors and from the prying and coercive tactics of government.

If it is a sin to aspire to conduct of a higher order than one may at the moment be capable of, then Americans surely sinned in professing that all men are created equal, and then acting otherwise. Nor did time close the gap between the profession and the widespread practice of racism in this land.

The nation prospered mightily nonetheless, and few were willing to raise their voices and suggest that what might once have been forgiven as the excesses of a buoyant national youth had widened into systematic and undiminishing cruelty—the cruelty of racism and discrimination.

On the eve of this century, W. E. B. DeBois wrote in his classic work, The Souls of Black Folk, that the problem of the twentieth century was the problem of the "color line." His words were prophetic and he uttered them better than he knew.

No individual, black or white, concerned about justice, liberty and fraternity can stand aloof and remain silent in the face of events we have witnessed in recent years, and in view of the trends that are now emerging in this nation and in this society.

"In the hearts of Black Americans, hope has always sprung eternal in every generation."

Frederick Douglass had already programmed future generations when in 1849 he spoke about the hardships inherent in reform: "The whole history of the progress of human liberty," he said, "shows that all concessions, yet made to her august claims, have been born of earnest struggle.

"If there is no struggle, there is no progress. Those who profess to favor freedom and yet deprecate agitation, are men who want crops without plowing up the ground; they want rain without thunder and lightning. They want the ocean without the awful roar of its many waters."

The nation needs a rebirth of morality, for clearly we have managed to become a society morally confused, morally ambivalent and morally bankrupt. We have no clear and decisive sense of what is fundamentally wrong and what is fundamentally right. The nation's conscience has become muted, or at best, ambivalent.

In short, time has almost run out to make the American idea the American reality. Three centuries is a long time for a people to exercise patience. For they have not only been patient, they have exhibited tolerance and forbearance. In the hearts of Black Americans, hope has always sprung eternal in every generation.

I frankly do not know what else Black Americans must do to exhibit their faith in the American possibility. Until America fully comes to grips with its most historic, endemic and pervasive characteristic at home, it will be incapable of coming to grips with the major problems abroad. Racism is no longer a problem of civil rights. The issue is now one of social justice.

The changes which need to be made are not problems of civil rights but a struggle for social justice. Civil rights sought changes in law and the gaining of the equal protection thereof. But social justice seeks a total restructuring of the American society and the society's institutions—to achieve not simply the integration of Black and White people but to achieve the liberation of Black people from the control and domination of White people.

Social justice has the goal of achieving equity and parity in the access to and participation in all of the opportunities, all of the benefits, all of the rewards, and all of the powers of the total American society.

I haven't given up on the American ideal and the American possibility. This nation stands before the world as perhaps the last expression of the possibility of man devising a social order where justice is the supreme ruler and law but its instrument; where freedom is the dominant creed and order but its principle; where equity is the common practice and fraternity the common human condition.

Yours may be the last generation of Americans that has the opportunity to help our nation fulfill its promise and realize its possibility. Your generation may be the last to be afforded another chance to balance the scales of justice and make them equal; to confront the doors of opportunity and make them open; to seize the chains of bondage and break them free.

"It is a time to remember that you don't use your past to replay your failures..."

It has been and still remains the case that racism, manifested and exemplified in all areas of our national life—economically, socially, culturally, politically, and educationally—is the cancer which is destroying us and happens to be a moral force in the affairs of mankind.

This, then, is the time and this is the place for men and women of good will to take a telescopic view of the journey they take and a microscopic view of themselves. For it is they who demonstrate in their every action and who express in their every utterance, that they are, in the words of Thomas Jefferson, "...committed to the proposition that all men are created equal, that they are endowed by their Creator with certain inalienable rights, and that among these are life, liberty, and the pursuit of happiness."

If you don't know the tune, you can't improvise.

Whatever role you play in life, make sure that your support is from the vantage point of knowledge rather than chaos. Make sure your support is from the point of integrity and not degradation; from selflessness instead of selfishness.

The important thing is that you must play a role, for while not everything that is faced can be changed, nothing can be changed until it is faced. And it is time, then, for discovering instead of dancing, and it is time to look for enlightenment instead of entertainment. There is no time for first-class loyalty to second-class ideas.

It is a time to remember that you don't use your past to replay your failures, and a time to learn that worry, in most instances, is down payment on trouble that never comes. For yesterday is a canceled check; tomorrow is a promissory note; today is ready cash. How are you going to spend that, young people?

Men and women who had lives of struggle and sacrifice gave substance to the proposition that if one is continually surviving the *worst* that life can bring, one ceases to be controlled by *what* life can bring.

And finally, when they tell you—
That you can't and you won't;
That you're out of the race and
    you can't keep pace;
That you don't have a chance,
    and you'll never advance;

I tell you—

When they say you don't belong,
    that you're always wrong;
You don't know enough and can't
    hang tough,
That you just can't take it, that you will never make it;
Then stand up, graduates of
    Northern Michigan University,
    and tell them,
I've trained my mind, and I got a
    new twist;
Take everything else, but you can't
    take this.

Now you know the tune, now go out and improvise!

A House Divided[4]

Johnnetta B. Cole

Professor, Emory University, 1997– ; born Jacksonville, FL, 1936; B.A., Oberlin College, 1957; M.A., 1959, Ph.D., 1967, Northwestern University; professor, Washington State University, 1967-70; professor, University of Massachusetts, 1970-83; professor, City University of New York, 1983-86; director, Latin American and Caribbean studies program, Hunter College, 1984-87; president, Spelman College, 1987-1997; author, Anthropology for the Eighties *(1982),* Conversations *(1994).*

Editors' introduction: Johnnetta B. Cole, former president of Spelman College, Georgia, gave this commencement address to over 3,000 graduates of Emory University. Now a professor at Emory University, Cole felt that her purpose was "to clearly reach the graduates with a message of their responsibility, not only to understand our world, but to help to fix it—especially on the question of difference in our nation." To reach that goal, she drew upon powerful lessons of anthropology, recalling various authorities which cite empathy among the races as necessary to the survival of a civilization.

Johnnetta B. Cole's speech: Members of the Board of Trustees; Brother President Bill Chace; my colleagues of the faculty and staff; alumni and friends of Emory University:

I greet you ever so warmly on this marvelous celebratory morning.

But I save my warmest and most enthusiastic greetings for those for whom we have gathered today: you, my young sisters and brothers of the mighty class of 1996 and your families and friends. As you graduate from this great university, only 67 days before Atlanta hosts the Centennial Olympic Games, may you receive the blessing that is asked for in an old African American song: Guide my feet while I run this race, for I don't want to run this race in vain.

Because I am a college president, I know better than most folks what it has taken for you to get here today. An extraordinary amount of hard work, discipline, determination, and no doubt some good luck too. But you are here, you made it. You certainly would not have done so without the love, the sacrifice and the material support of your families. Surely you have thanked your Moms and Dads and all of your kin folks; but why don't you do

---

[4] Delivered at the Emory University commencement exercises, in Atlanta, Georgia, on May 13, 1996. Reprinted with permission of Johnnetta B. Cole.

it again by standing and applauding all of your loved ones.

I wish that I could give each of you graduates a congratulatory embrace, but since I cannot, please do it for me. Wrap your arms around yourself with a big hug and feel good about what you have accomplished.

A part of the ritual of receiving whatever alphabets you have earned the right to put behind your name: B.A., Ph.D., JD., M.D., MBA—a part of the ritual is that you must also receive a little advice, a little last minute advice before you go.

In a commencement speech at Georgetown University, Bob Hope once said: "To those of you who are about to go into the world and want my advice, here it is: Don't go!"

But you don't have a choice and there is no safer thing to do. The world's problems are your problems, even if you turn your back on them, they are still yours. That is why you and the graduates of Spelman College and all of America's colleges and universities must participate in defining and enacting a common agenda for our nation for the coming century.

So, my young sisters and brothers: "What kind of world are you about to commence to?"

In too many quarters and in too many ways, it is not a pretty place. And our own place? What of our America? It is clearly such an extraordinary country. And for each of us here, there is surely a sense of mighty good fortune that we live in this nation of ours.

And yet, there is so much work that remains to be done to bring into reality the dream that was so eloquently and powerfully articulated in 1963 by Dr. Martin Luther King, Jr.

Today, in some ways even more than when Dr. King shared his dream, ours is a divided house. AND A HOUSE DIVIDED AGAINST ITSELF CANNOT STAND!

Abraham Lincoln uttered those words in the context of slavery in June of 1858, as he spoke before the Republican State Convention in Springfield, Illinois. Many of you will recall that these words are also found in the Bible in the Gospel According to St. Mark, chapter 3 verse 25: "And if a house be divided against itself, that house cannot stand."

All around us there are spokespersons for a divided society, some more frightening than others. Rather than celebrating the magnificence and the strength of so many different kinds of folks all living under one American roof—there are those who call for "keeping certain people in their places." But the uniqueness and the long-term viability of our nation rests on the powerful idea that there is a place of respect in the American house for each and every one of us.

And just look at us, what a people we Americans are! What a people we are in our full array of human diversity; for we Americans are folks of different races and ethnicities; we are women folks and men folks; we are of different ages, religions, and sexual orientations; and we are differently able.

"...the uniqueness and the long-term viability of our nation rests on the powerful idea that there is a place of respect in the American house for each and every one of us."

The problem is that in this house of ours, we have not yet found the way to teach people how to decently, not to mention lovingly, interact with those who are different. We have not yet proven to the satisfaction of all the power of people engaging across communities to solve problems. We have not yet found the way to demonstrate that groups can preserve their distinctiveness and still work together for the common good. And, we have not sufficiently illustrated the benefits of multiple ways of seeing and doing and being. There is a wonderful Chinese saying that captures this point: One flower never makes a spring.

These days, my sisters and brothers all, we feel the bitter return of racism, anti-Semitism and ethnic chauvinism, forms of bigotry that we thought we had dismissed; and we are reeling from assaults on affirmative action, as they come one after another in every sector of our society.

Today, in certain quarters, there are renewed attacks on the rights of women. We see and hear and feel repetitive challenges to an important vision that is captured in an American Indian saying: Women hold up half the sky.

And today, there is a swelling of the ranks of the poor that spells a crisis for us all.

Such a climate of intolerance and mean-spiritedness demands that we in the academic world rededicate ourselves to analyzing and understanding such violent reactions to difference. Inside and outside of the walls of our colleges and universities, we must recommit ourselves to the fundamental principles of a pluralistic democracy.

In calling for a renewed commitment to inclusiveness, to diversity in our schools, colleges, workplaces, and neighborhoods, on one level we are talking about what is fair and just. But there is an additional impetus for respecting diversity and assuring equity for all. It is the demands of the American economy.

We simply cannot afford the social and economic costs of color coding our citizenry so that large numbers of African Americans, Native Americans and people of various Hispanic communities are deprived of the academic skills that are necessary to function in a rapidly changing, technologically complex society. And as the workforce of the coming century is increasingly one of people of color and women, we certainly cannot afford glass ceilings.

On the agenda of those who are successfully involved in the global marketplace, there is no room for old myths and stereotypes about how all Asians are inscrutable, all Mexicans are lazy, and all Africans are insufficiently civilized.

Today, more and more American businesses are coming to grips with a diverse workforce and developing specific marketing for diverse communities at home and abroad. They are doing so not simply as the right thing to do, but because such actions are the economically smart thing to do.

Dear graduates, my message to you must not only identify the problem of a divided house, it must at least suggest how we can

"...more American businesses are coming to grips with a diverse workforce and developing specific marketing for diverse communities..."

begin to rebuild the kind of understanding and unity among diverse peoples that will set our nation for success in the coming century and beyond.

As I search for ideas and materials that might be of use as we try to fortify our house, I turn to the very field in which I was trained. I turn to anthropology, the discipline in which I received my degrees many years ago. Let me share with you now some lessons that we can all learn from anthropology, the study of the human condition.

Lesson number one. While the pitting of one group against another is found in culture after culture and nation after nation, we have yet to find a gene that is the cause of it all. No matter how widespread and tenacious we find racism, sexism and other forms of bigotry, I am here to tell you that this stuff ain't genetic!

We humans learn how to discriminate and we are taught ugly names to call each other. Since we learn how to pit one group against another, then it is possible to unlearn it. And best of all, we could just stop teaching bigotry!

A second lesson from anthropology is this: While certain groups of people have consistently and over time oppressed other groups, there is no group of people immune to practicing intolerance. Look around our world and you will see that from blatant prejudice to the barbaric victimization of one group by another, such expressions of bigotry are not the sole possession of any particular people. Just look at the Middle East, Bosnia, Ireland, India, Mexico, Haiti, Ruwanda, Liberia...and yes, our own nation.

The power of human empathy is a third lesson that anthropology can teach us. Empathy, not sympathy. Trust me when I tell you that if men really work at it, they can come to understand many of the realities in women's lives. We gringos really can come to understand the history and the realities of various Latino communities. And surely one does not have to be Jewish to sense the pain and suffering of the victims of the Holocaust.

What is required to engage in human empathy is so basic. It is simply to imagine oneself in another's shoes. To imagine oneself without any shoes to wear.

I heard Mayor Bill Campbell say that he would spend part of a day in a wheelchair, going about the city of Atlanta in order to better understand and improve what it will be like for all of the athletes who will be competing here during the Paralympics. Every now and then, each of us needs to place ourselves physically or figuratively in a wheelchair. We need to put ourselves in someone else's skin. As the folks say in the Caribbean, we need to be in somebody else's yard.

The fourth lesson from anthropology is grounded in the notion that no matter how much one reads and studies about the condition of another people, one's understanding will be incomplete without participating in their way of life. That is why an anthropologist does fieldwork, living among the people he or she wishes to understand.

Well, my sisters and brothers, each of us has the possibility to get at least a taste of the insights, the excitement, the joy of another way of life. It is yours for the taking whenever you venture beyond your habitual paths to try other peoples languages, foods, films, literature, music and art. Some of you have spent substantial time in someone else's space by participating in study abroad programs, or perhaps by working in the Atlanta Project of the Carter Center, or by doing sustained community service.

Regardless of how you do it, the most powerful insight from a cross-cultural experience is that you come to better understand your own culture, you come to better understand yourself.

The American anthropologist, Clyde Kluckhohn, captured this when he said: "It is scarcely the fish who discovers water."

"It is the will, the determination, the intelligence of ordinary and sometimes extraordinary women and men who transform the world."

Here is the fifth and final lesson that I want to share with you from anthropology as an aid to putting our American house back together: Change is possible! No matter how stubbornly people hold on to ideas and ways that have lost their usefulness, or that are destructive to the very social fiber of the society— they can change.

Anthropology teaches us that the key ingredient in bringing about change is US. It is the will, the determination, the intelligence of ordinary and sometimes extraordinary women and men who transform the world. Think of how an "ordinary" woman named Rosa Parks did so by her simple but courageous refusal to move to the back of a bus in Montgomery, Alabama. Think of how a man named Ralph McGill used the power of a journalist pen to help Atlanta move toward being a city for all of its citizens.

Listen to the words of one of my sheroes, the American anthropologist, Margaret Mead: "Never doubt the ability of a small and thoughtful group of committed citizens to change the world. Indeed, it is the only thing that ever has."

And so, my young sisters and brothers all, I ask of you today that you take these simple but ever so powerful lessons of anthropology and begin to participate in the great American construction project of unifying our house.

I would be a lot prouder today if we in the academy had learned and then practiced these lessons, if we had shown the way. Maybe some of you will join us in the academic world and help.

But each of you, no matter what career or further study you are about to engage in, please lend a hand in putting our house back in order.

As I bring closure on your commencement speech, I want to tell you a story. I must have told it a hundred times, but I do not know of a better way to emphasize who must do the work of putting our house back together again.

This story was often told by one of my sheroes, Fannie Lou Hamer. The final line of the story will say once again who has the responsibility and indeed the power to rebuild our American house.

It is the story of some young boys who decided one day to fool an old lady by asking her a question that they thought she would be incapable of answering. The ring leader would take a bird that they had caught, and placing it behind his back, he would pose a question to the old lady: Old lady, old lady, this bird that I have behind my back, is it dead or is it alive. If the old lady said that the bird was dead, then he would release his hands and the bird would fly away. But if to the question she said that the bird was alive, he would crush it.

They found the old lady and asked if she would respond to a question. She would try, she said. And so, the ring leader put the bird behind his back and said: Old lady, old lady, this bird that I have behind my back, is it dead or is it alive?

With simple but powerful wisdom she said: "The answer is in your hands!"

That is the answer, dear graduates of the class of 1996, putting our divided house back together is in your hands, and it is in mine.

Congratulations on your graduation, and Godspeed.

IV. Arts and the Humanities

Identity Through Art[1]

Jane Alexander

Chair of the National Endowment for the Arts (NEA), 1993– ; born Boston, MA, 1939; TV, film, and theatre actress, 1962– ; winner of Tony Award, 1969; actress, Charles Playhouse, 1964–65, Arena Stage, 1965–68, 1970– ; actress, American Shakespeare Festival, 1971-72.

Editors' introduction: In more than 150 speeches, Jane Alexander has shared with thousands of citizens her vision for the National Endowment for the Arts (NEA). In this speech, Alexander underscores the importance of the NEA, noting that art "is as complex as the human mind dare imagine." Art is therefore a reflection of what we think, and of who we are. As the NEA is devoted to making "the arts accessible to all people," its fundamental value to our own self-image is, according to Alexander, readily apparent.

Jane Alexander's speech: Chancellor Wrighton, trustees, faculty, alumni, parents, friends, and students. It gives me great pleasure to be with you today at this rite of passage for the Class of 1996. I am always honored to be asked to give a commencement address, but particularly so on this occasion at this most prestigious University. I envy those of you who've spent the past four years on the Hilltop. The historic buildings, the Gothic architecture, Forest Park, the Medical Campus, the Edison Theater—which the NEA proudly supports—all of it has given you a rich and pleasant setting in which to learn, to live in community, and to discover your talents.

I know first-hand how important environment is to creativity. As Chairman of the National Endowment for the Arts, I've been to all 50 states and over 150 cities and towns to talk about the arts and meet the community in settings as varied as state-of-the-art theaters to tiny classrooms. In one such schoolroom, I met a group of pre-schoolers who were learning how to paint. I asked one young girl—a painter of exceptional talent—how long she had been making art. This five-year-old said: "All my life."

That's the perfect answer. I thought of this story this week when I picked up the current issue of the *U.S. News and World Report* which had a cover story called "First Genius." It's all

---

[1] Delivered at the Washington University commencement exercises, in St. Louis, Missouri, on May 17, 1996. Reprinted with permission of Jane Alexander.

about how and why human beings became creative thinkers and artists perhaps 60,000 years ago or earlier. As people began to live in larger groups, supported by cooperative group hunting and gathering, the need for expressing group identity *and* individuality intensified. In other words, there is a link between living in a community and the making of art. And the expression of identity through art becomes a necessity for the group and perhaps the individual.

In the dawn of human community, it took about an hour to make a bead out of a piece of ivory or an animal's tooth. Randall White of New York University suggests that primitive people would never have undertaken such a time-consuming process unless personal adornment was vital to human identity. White says: "We have this image of art being the result of people having lots of free time. But that's totally contrary to what we see. For these people, art was a necessity."

"Four hundred centuries ago, people discovered tools that allowed them to paint images on their cave walls."

In short, the beads make the man. Just as today, what you are wearing under your gowns helps express your individuality and your place in the group. We're not so different from our ancient ancestors: we still need visual cues, spiritual icons and rituals, like this graduation ceremony. Four hundred centuries ago, people discovered tools that allowed them to paint images on their cave walls. Music may have accompanied the viewing of these cave paintings, sort of a multi-media event of the time. Today, you are discovering tools that can send those images out to millions over the thin wire of the Internet. How long have we been making art? All our lives.

I have seen this nexus of community and art every where I go in this country. My term as Chairman of the agency is, like your term at Washington University, a four-year stint. I am now sort of in the middle of my Junior year. There have been extraordinary highs—experiencing the abundance, diversity and vitality of the arts in America, and seeing how people everywhere in our country cherish their arts. And, there have been low times, too. Our recent agency cuts were almost 40 percent. The NEA has had its critics, and I've spent most of my time these two-and-a-half years defending the agency and the worth of artists. Politicians generally have had a tough time lately. There's been a lot of mistrust, and I've had my share, let me tell you.

A couple of months ago, I went into a store to buy a soda, and the fellow behind the counter said, "Did anyone ever tell you, you look like that Jane Alexander?" I replied, "Well, yes they have, actually." And the guy said, "Makes you kinda mad, doesn't it?"

There may be some things wrong with government, but there's a lot right, too. That tends to be obscured in the rhetoric today. The Arts Endowment, for example, was created in 1965 to help make the arts accessible to all people in the USA and to attract more money for the arts from the private sector, and it's been immensely successful in doing so. For every dollar we award today, we leverage, on average, 12 other dollars from private and public sources. In this way, we've helped sustain thousands of artists and arts organizations in every pocket of America, including those, as Judy Garland once said, "you meet here in St. Louis."

Yet out of 110,000 grants these past 30 years, we've funded about 40 that have caused some people some problems. And our critics have been making political hay out of those images. Well, I wanted the country to know about the other side of the story, too. Art, both beautiful and challenging, is part of who we are—individually and a society. The caveman knew it, the five-year-old painter knows it, and, I think, even our harshest critic knows it. Art isn't just pretty pictures; art is as complex as the human mind can dare imagine.

What does this have to do with those of you who are graduating today? Whatever the future may hold for you—career as a banker or a baker, an engineer or a doctor, a politician or a playwright, you have been schooled here at Washington University to be creative thinkers. Carry that creativity and the arts with you wherever you go. They will affect how you think and act and respond to others—children, family, friends and acquaintances. I contend that the arts will make you better people, more compassionate citizens, more tolerant and understanding. For the arts demonstrate most clearly our connectedness, our common human nature. They speak to what unites us all under the skin, to the human spirit in all our pain and joy, our disenchantment and beguilement, our anger and our celebration.

"For the arts demonstrate most clearly our connectedness, our common human nature."

What you've accomplished in your time at Washington University hasn't been easy. Four years ago, you arrived as new citizens to this campus. You were wet behind the ears. The time stretched before you in seeming infinity. In retrospect, the years vanish in a snap. It took a lot of commitment to stick it out, to buckle down, to do things you really didn't want to do: exams, papers, research. It took a lot of growing up to get through the heartache or the homesickness. But you've done it. Be proud of what you've accomplished as all of us here today are of you.

When I was leaving college, it was quite a different place, not so fast. I lived through the Beat Generation, the Flower Child and Feminist eras, the hippies, the Me Generation, the Yuppies, and now Generation X and Grunge. What will you live through? What moniker will be hung on you in the next 10 years or so? I hope it will symbolize the "I care" generation, because I know a lot of people your age, and I know you care.

I have great faith in you. You are alive and young and educated at a remarkable time in world history. You are well informed and can surf the Web while many of us wade in the shallows. You actually know how big a mega-byte is! You've seen the prospect of peace in the Middle East, the cease-fire in Bosnia, and Woodstock 2, which I know had exhippies contemplating their gray hairs.

What my generation asks of yours is that you become involved citizens of your community, your state, and your country, that you take good care of the world you inherit at the beginning of the new millennium. The year 2000 is not a specious symbol. It's a place mark in our Western History. Philosopher Hillel Schwartz notes that there are really three millennia ahead:

The first is the year 1999. Just the thought of it is awesome and somehow fraught with danger. It signals the end; it's apocalyptic; it's an omen. If you feel bad about 1999 already, you'll feel a lot worse when it arrives. I know some people who plan to spend the year under the covers.

The second millennium is the year 2000, a mid-point in people's minds, a time of assessment. Not quite the 21st century, yet not really the 20th. In 2000, we as a nation will look back at what we've done, the messes we made, just as we will try to find ways to move forward. A lot of the political turmoil today comes from this unease, I believe. We want a clean slate: balance the budget, shore up the family, protect our children from harm, leave no tracks on the environment. The class of '96 has much to say about where we go. And the way we get there is through the passage of thoughtful laws. So don't waste your voice in this democracy of ours—start voting now, this year.

The third way of looking at the millennium is as beginning with the year 2001. A brave, new world, fresh-scrubbed—a time for amnesty, too, I think, to forgive our trespassers and move on.

Where do you want to be in five years? Which millennium will you choose? 1999, 2000, 2001? Or a combination? Being an optimist by nature, I always think in terms of beginning the new millennium, the new century, rather than ending the one we're in. No matter how you may look at it, this university's given you the tools and great opportunity to seize firmly the challenge of good stewardship.

So care about the legacy you leave behind. When we think of places we've loved, we remember mostly three things: the natural beauty, the cultural stamp of the place, and the people. This one planet we inhabit together is finite. We must keep our Mother Earth whole and healthy.

Long after wars are won or lost, art and science endure. Our cultural legacy tells the next generation about the people who lived then and there—how expansive they were or how prosaic. Great people leave a great testament: beautifully designed buildings, enduring stories in books or on film, timeless visual art, and the legends of the ephemeral performing arts.

Lastly, care about your fellow human beings. It is not good enough when we step over the ill and destitute in the street; it is not good enough that one child goes to bed hungry or bruised. It is not enough when we exclude anyone because they look differently or talk differently. An indignity suffered by anyone is our indignity as well. You have been privileged to receive one of the best educations in the world here at Washington University. Live up to your intelligence. Others have cared for you. Now, it is your turn.

And so, friends, I congratulate you on this day for all you have achieved and for the promise that is vested in each and every one of you. May life be all you make it. Your mothers and fathers, your friends and family, your teachers and I salute you with love.

Worth Defending[2]

Kenneth Lauren Burns

Documentary filmmaker, 1975– ; born Brooklyn, NY, 1953; B.A., Hampshire College, 1975; president, owner, Florentine Films, 1975– ; producer, director, writer, The Brooklyn Bridge (1981), The Shaker (1985); producer, director, Huey Long (1985), The Statue of Liberty (1985), The Congress (1988), Baseball (1996); co-producer, director, The Civil War (1990), Empire of the Air (1992); executive producer, The West (1996), Thomas Jefferson (1997).

Editors' introduction: Speaking alongside several prominent representatives and senators, documentary filmmaker Ken Burns made this plea to maintain funding for the National Endowment for the Humanities (NEH). In the speech, Burns warned that "the marketplace will not produce the good works that have been supported by the NEA." Without such organizations as the NEH, and their funding, Burns remarked that projects such as educational documentaries will simply not be made. In this sense, funding allows history's "excruciatingly wise messages" to reach the ears and eyes of an interested audience.

Kenneth Lauren Burns's speech: Good morning. It is an honor for me to come down from New Hampshire today to express my whole-hearted support for the National Endowment for the Humanities. Let me say from the outset that I am a passionate supporter of the Endowments and their unique role in helping to stitch our exquisite, diverse, and often fragile culture together.

Few institutions provide such a direct, grassroots way for our citizens to participate in the shared glories of their common past, in the power of the priceless ideals that have animated our remarkable republic and our national life for more than two hundred years, and in the inspirational life of the mind and the heart that an engagement with the arts and humanities always provides. It is my sincere belief that anything which threatens these institutions weakens our country. It is as simple as that.

For nearly 20 years I have been producing historical documentary films, celebrating the excruciatingly wise messages American history continually directs our way. The subjects of these films range from the construction of the Brooklyn Bridge and the Statue of Liberty to the life of the turbulent Southern demagogue Huey Long; from the graceful architecture of the

---

[2] Delivered in Washington, D.C., on May 2, 1996. Reprinted with permission of Kenneth Lauren Burns.

Shakers to the early founders of radio; from the sublime pleasures and unexpected lessons of our national pastime to the sear-
ing transcendent experience of our Civil War. I even made a film
on the history of this magnificent building and the much
maligned institution that is charged with conducting the people's
business.

In nearly every instance, these films have been produced with
the support and encouragement of the National Endowment for
the Humanities, either at the state or national level. In every
instance, I have produced these films for national public television broadcast, not the lucrative commercial networks or cable.
For each film project we have worked on, we have willingly sub-
mitted to the Endowment's unique and rigorous proposal
process, sometimes producing documents running to several
hundred pages of detailed scholarly interpretation, budgetary
analysis, and scrupulous preplanning. The months-long application process includes, among many difficult requirements, the
engagement of nationally recognized scholars who advise at
every juncture of the production, insuring balance, adjudicating
differences in historical interpretation, offering a variety of perspectives and modes of inquiry.

Without a doubt, my series on the Civil War or Baseball could
not have been made without the National Endowment for the
Humanities. The Endowment not only provided some of these
project's largest grants, thereby attracting other funders, but also,
through unrelated grants to other institutions, helped restore the
archival photographs we would use to tell our story.

As I produced my own documentaries over the years, I have
watched the Endowment fund literally thousands of other projects that have touched Americans, that have engaged
Americans, that have made a difference in American lives that
belie the relatively small outlay of public funds necessary to sustain these fundamentally good works. I have watched the
Endowments save critical archival documents from decay and
destruction, bring great art to the high plains of South Dakota,
send professors from Nebraska and Georgia on important
research trips their own universities could not underwrite, and I
have watched a man bring Thomas Jefferson to life in the little
towns of my own conservative State of New Hampshire to the
delight and inspiration of all.

But now, and sadly not for the first time, I hear critics saying
that these remarkably efficient Endowments must be scrapped,
that our government has no business in the arts and humanities,
that we must let the marketplace alone determine everything in
our cultural life, that these huge broad based institutions are
essentially elitist, that a few controversial projects prove the left-
ist political bias of not only the Endowments but the entire artistic and academic communities. I feel strongly that I must
respond to these charges.

Since the beginning of this country, our government has been

*"I have watched
the Endowments
save critical
archival
documents from
decay and
destruction..."*

involved in supporting the arts and the diffusion of knowledge, which was deemed as critical to our future as roads and dams and bridges. Early on, Thomas Jefferson and the other founding fathers knew that the pursuit of happiness did not mean a hedonistic search for pleasure in the marketplace but an active involvement of the mind in the higher aspects of human endeavor—namely education, music, the arts, and history. Congress supported the journey of Lewis and Clark as much to explore the natural, biological, ethnographic, and cultural landscape of our expanding nation as to open up a new trading route to the Pacific. Congress supported numerous geographical, artistic, photographic, and biological expeditions to nearly every corner of the developing West. Congress funded, through the Farm Securities Administration, the work of Walker Evans and Dorthea Lange and other great photographers who captured for posterity the terrible human cost of the Depression. At the same time, Congress funded some of the most enduring writing ever produced about this country's people, its monuments, buildings, and backroads in the still much used and universally admired WPA guides. Some of our greatest symphonic work, our most treasured dramatic plays, and early documentary film classics came from an earlier Congress' support.

With Congress' great insight the Endowments were born and grew to their startlingly effective maturity echoing the same time-honored sense that our Government has an interest in helping to sponsor Art and Education just as it sponsors Commerce. We are not talking about a free ride, but a priming of the pump, a way to get the juices flowing, in the spirit of President Reagan's notion of a partnership between the government and the private sector. The NEH grant I got for the Civil War series attracted even more funds from General Motors and several private foundations; money that would not have been there had not the Endowment blessed this project with their rigorously earned imprimatur.

When I was working more than ten years ago on a film about the Statue of Liberty, its history and powerful symbolism, I had the great good fortune to meet and interview Vartan Gregorian, who was then the president of the New York Public Library, and who is now the president of Brown University. After an extremely interesting and passionate interview on the meaning behind the statue for an immigrant like him—from Tabriz, Iran—Vartan took me on a long and fascinating tour of the miles of stacks of the New York Public Library. Finally, after galloping down one claustrophobic corridor, he stopped and gestured expansively. "This," he said, surveying his library from its guts, "this is the DNA of our civilization." He was saying that that library, indeed, all libraries, archives, and historical societies are the DNA of our society, leaving an imprint of excellence and intention for generations to come. It occurs to me, as we debate the very existence of the Endowments, that they, as well as public television, are also part, a critical part, of the great genetic legacy of our nation. They are, in the best sense, modem educational institutions first and foremost.

But there are those who are sure that without the Endowments, the so-called "marketplace" would take care of everything; that what won't survive in the marketplace, doesn't deserve to survive. Nothing could be further from the truth, because we are not just talking about the commerce of a nation, we are not just economic beings, but spiritual and intellectual beings as well, and so we are talking about the creativity of a nation. Now, some forms of creativity thrive in the marketplace and that is a wonderful thing, reflected in our glorious Hollywood movies and our globally popular music. But let me say that the marketplace could not have made and to this day could not make my Civil War series, indeed any of the films I have worked on.

That marketplace does not produce, by the way, the most respected news program on television; that marketplace does not produce the most respected children's, history, and science programs on television either. These are but a small part of the legacy of the Endowments and PBS, institutions supported by 70% of Republicans, 80% of Independents, and 90% of Democrats across the country.

That marketplace does not save the old papers of a founding father, it doesn't fund research into that which enriches our heritage—not necessarily our pocketbooks or what is fashionable at the moment, and it does not fund the local poetry reading, or dance recital, or symphony group, or lecture on great books that take place daily from Maine to California. The Endowments are like posterity's spies—moles penetrating farther and deeper into our political and social landscape than any agent of the so-called marketplace.

No, the marketplace will not produce the good works of the Endowments. Just as the marketplace does not and will not produce a B-2 Bomber, something we are told that is essential to the defense of our country. It has taken government involvement, government sponsorship, government encouragement, government oversight, government absorption of overuns, and government procurement to build a B-2 Bomber. Interestingly, the total cost of both endowments plus the Corporation for Public Broadcasting does not equal the cost of one B-2 Bomber. It is obvious, too, that the National Endowment for the Arts, the National Endowment for the Humanities, and the Corporation for Public Broadcasting have nothing to do with the actual defense of our country, I know that—they just make our country worth defending.

It is a sad commentary when the richest nation on earth cuts its cultural funding 40% and threatens much worse, forcing institutions which serve as the bedrock of our community life to curtail their activities. Don't these overzealous critics realize that 200 years from now whether the military budget increases or

"...the total cost of both Endowments plus the Corporation for Public Broadcasting does not equal the cost of one B-2 Bomber."

decreases a few percent, whether a tax was imposed or repealed will be less important than the quality of our schools, the symphonies we have written, the new museums we have opened. Only in retrospect will they see clearly what we see clearly now the palpable truth that the aesthetics of living are as important as the standard of living to human life.

Even during the Great Depression when some towns were forced to shoot the animals in their zoos and distribute the meat to the poor, even in the Great Depression, public libraries were not forced to shorten hours, as they must do now, during a period of unparalleled prosperity, growth, and riches.

Do not be persuaded by the feeble argument that this is all elitist, that we are funding the superfluous; "opera for the rich." The meat and potatoes of the Endowment's work reaches out to every corner of the country and touches people in positive ways the Federal Government rarely does. Indeed, it would be elitist itself to abolish the Endowments, to trust to the marketplace and the "natural aristocracy" that many have promised over the last two hundred years would rise up to protect us all—and hasn't.

Many have recently criticized the Endowments for certain controversial or political projects; many believe the Endowments and public television are hot-beds of radical thinking. I wonder, though, have they ever applied for an Endowment grant, worked with their staffs or been to a council meeting? I doubt it. These are essentially conservative institutions, filled with people who share the concerns of most Americans. One need only remember that the Endowments are criticized just as vigorously from the far left, to realize at once what a tough job they have, and what a good job they are doing.

And in a free society, the rare examples of controversial scholarship that may run counter to our accepted cannon, need not be the occasion for a new reactionary Puritanism, but ought to be seen as a healthy sign that we are a nation tolerant of ideas, confident—as the recent tide of geopolitical history has shown—confident that the best ideas will always prevail.

One hundred and fifty eight years ago, in 1838, well before the Civil War, Abraham Lincoln challenged us to consider the real threat to the country, to consider forever the real cost of our inattention: "Whence shall we expect the approach of danger?" he wrote. "Shall some transatlantic giant step on the earth and crush us at a blow? Never. All the armies of Europe and Asia could not by force take a drink from the Ohio River or make a track in the Blue Ridge in the trial of a thousand years. No, if destruction be our lot, we must ourselves be its author and finisher." As usual, Mr. Lincoln's words speak to us today with the same force he spoke to his own times.

Most of us here, whether we know it or not, are in the business of words, and we hope, with some reasonable expectation, that those words will last.

But alas, especially today, those words often evaporate, their precision blunted by neglect, their insight diminished by the sheer volume of their ever-increasing brethren, their force diluted by ancient animosities that seem to set each group against the other.

The historian Arthur Schlesinger, Jr. has said that we suffer today from "too much pluribus and not enough unum." Few things survive in these cynical days to remind us of the Union from which so many of our personal and collective blessings flow. And it is hard not to wonder, in an age when the present moment consumes and overshadows all else—our bright past and our dim unknown future—what finally does endure? What encodes and stores the genetic material of our civilization, passing down to the next generation—the best of us—what we hope will mutate into betterness for our children and our posterity? This Endowment provides one clear answer. Please do not be the author of its destruction, the finisher of its important good works. The NEH is the best thing we have to remind us why we all still agree to cohere as a people. And that is a good.

Learning Styles[3]

Claudia Hopkins

Teacher, King Intermediate School, 1989– ; born Baldwyn, MS, 1947; B.A., David Lipscomb University, 1969; manager of Elvis Presley Birthplace, Tupelo, MS, 1982-83; public relations director, Prairie Girl Scout Council, 1983-89; director of An Arts Explosion for at-risk students, Carver School for Innovation, 1996-97.

Editors' introduction: In this speech, Claudia Hopkins hoped to convey that learning is dependent upon a personal connection between teacher and student. She remarked, "it's this connection that compelled me to become a teacher and return to the profession after seven years in the 'real world'!" In this speech, Hopkins discussed the importance of the teaching profession and presented a list of concerns about today's children. According to Hopkins unless teachers *know* their students, information will not be relayed, and the wonder of our culture will be forever lost.

Claudia Hopkins's speech: Thank you, Billy. It's a pleasure to be here and have lunch with people who are talking in well-modulated voices and eating with utensils, and I do apologize to those two men I sent out in the hall for talking with their mouths full.

I. The Background

When Billy asked me to speak to you, I began to reflect on my teaching career. I never planned to teach. I didn't want to. My mother was a career teacher, my father had been a teacher at different times in my life, my aunts were teachers, and I just wasn't interested. I didn't like teachers! They were always so intrusive! I think I was like Winston Churchill who said, "Personally, I'm always ready to learn, although I do not always like to be taught."

I wanted to be a writer, and that's the employment I was seeking as a new college graduate twenty seven years ago in Nashville. I was scheduled for my second interview for a copywriter's position when I came home for the Labor Day weekend to find that the principal of a little school outside of Nashville had called saying he needed a fourth grade teacher. There was only one drawback, he said. My room would be *on the stage*. Well, those of you who know me can appreciate the irony in that! And, sure enough, without really knowing why, I cancelled

---

[3] Delivered to the Rotary Club, in Tupelo, Mississippi, on August 26, 1996. Reprinted with permission of Claudia Hopkins.

my copywriting interview, took that teaching job and with the exception of seven years, have been "on the stage" ever since!

Often I've felt just like Dolly Levi with a business card and a solution for every problem! A teacher makes so many decisions for so many people in one day—our profession ranks second in the number of immediate decisions that must be made every day. Air traffic controllers are first!

They also have the highest suicide rate, but I don't want to dwell on that!

II. "Getting to Know You"

It didn't take me very long that first year to realize that if I wanted my students to be successful, I couldn't teach them as if they were all round pegs to fit into round holes. Some of them are square pegs, some are diamond-shaped—all are unique. I began to read and study and observe. Somewhere along the way, I read what a student had written, and the words had a profound effect on my teaching:

"A teacher makes so many decisions for so many people in one day—our profession ranks second in the number of immediate decisions that must be made every day."

"Can't nobody teach me who don't know me and won't learn me." Let me repeat that: "Can't nobody teach me who don't know me and won't learn me."

Wow, what a powerful statement! I began to try to get to know each one of my students—to search out the learning style(s) unique to each one—to find just the right way to help each child experience success. It's a hard task—often an exhausting one and one I'm still trying to master.

I guess the most outstanding example of tailoring education to fit the child was Fred. Fred was an older boy who'd been held back several years. By the time he was in 4th grade, he was so mature that he wasn't just noticing the girls but the teachers, too! I found him in the sixth grade hall one day getting a drink of water, and as I passed, I patted him on his back and told him that he needed to return to his classroom. He never raised up—I just heard him utter, "Umm, umm, umm!"

Well, at the end of that fourth grade year, the principal decided to by-pass 5th grade and put Fred in my 6th grade class because he was, quote, "getting too old to stay in elementary school" and "it didn't matter where he was anyway; he couldn't learn." Boy, don't ever give me a challenge like that! I discovered right away that Fred COULD learn—in fact, he could learn fast. I showed him how to annex the zero in multiplication in one day. He called that zero the "naked zero!" I don't know why. But it worked for him. He was like that—you could see the light come on in his eyes, and whatever connection he made that year, I supported. He couldn't read very well, and we weren't really successful in overcoming that, but he'd found his own system of deciphering the printed word enough to keep up in science and social studies. In getting to know him, I discovered that he got up before sunrise every day to help his uncle on their farm and that he drove a tractor sometimes late into the night. Yet, he always had his homework that year. His lower elementary teachers couldn't understand the change. I didn't understand it. But Fred did. He understood a lot of things for the very first time, and it felt good to him.

Years later I was back in that little community for a visit, and I attended the very first graduation ceremony in their new high school. Can you imagine how I felt when the principal called his name and there he was in a cap and gown receiving his diploma?! That's why I teach.

III. Have Children Changed?

I'm often asked, "Don't you think children have changed?" I've even said it myself, but I really don't think it's the *children* who have changed. They haven't been here long enough! The world has changed, values have changed, communication has changed, delivery of instruction has changed, I have changed. But I think that children are basically the same in 1996 as they were in 1969.

1. They love to be read to. (I know that sentence ended with a preposition, but as long as I know it, it's ok! Isn't it?) The beauty of the language is as appealing to children today as it ever was. I try to read to my students every day. I choose all kinds of literature, and for many, it's the only time of the day that they're completely quiet and focused on what's being said. That never changes. One of the perks of my job is hearing them say, "The book is better than the movie!"

2. The approval of their peers is as important today as it was when I first started teaching. Last week, one of my students was having a hard time getting anyone to work with him. He said to me, "Nobody likes me," and then he walked off with slumped shoulders. That's what that feeling does to children—to us all—it defeats us. So, he and I had a silent conversation while everyone else was working. Have you ever had a silent conversation? It's where you and someone else *write* your thoughts and questions and comments instead of speaking them. It's a wonderful way to communicate. You're more focused on what you're feeling, you're using more than one or two of your seven intelligences, and it's really hard to whine on paper! Try it in your business this afternoon. Try it at home with your families! Anyway, I suggested that perhaps he was so busy distracting others and being loud that they weren't able to see the real him—the one that was so smart and capable. He didn't write a response—he just looked up at me, grinned and nodded and said aloud, "This was fun" as he joined a group to finish his work.

3. Children today love to be creative, to perform, to improvise— that hunger hasn't changed. But here's the great paradox in education. Even though studies show that children who are stimu-

lated creatively through the arts perform better in school and on standardized tests, the slimness of arts budgets and the strictness of scheduling often cut out the very experiences that children need. Go figure! We're fortunate at King to have the time, thanks to Dr. Cother, and the materials, thanks to AEE, (Association for Excellence in Education), to be able to set up an art museum simulation this year and perform several musicals that extend our social studies, science and literature curricula and meet the creative needs of each child.

4. Children love to see you in a tense, uncomfortable situation, and then they can go in for the kill! That hasn't changed. I'll never forget the first time my superior came into my classroom to observe me. Of course, it was unexpected, but I felt pretty good about the lesson for the day. I'd spent a lot of time cutting out pictures from magazines to reinforce my lesson on writing descriptions. Each student had taken one, written a description, and then I was to read them and let them see if they could guess what the picture was from the description. Well, my supervisor eased in just as I was reading the description of an elephant. "It has fat legs and big hips." One hand went up. I nervously asked, "Yes, honey, who or what do you think it is?" "Sounds a lot like my sister to me!" Well, I handled the laughter as well as I could and said something inadequate like, "No, sweetie, it's not your sister," and went on reading. "It has a little tail." I see you're ahead of me. And of course that same little voice piped up, "Nope, it sure ain't my sister if it's got a little tail. Hers is as big as the Grand Canyon!" Well, you'd think that was the end of it, wouldn't you? Oh, no! Just as I reclaimed control of the class, another student raised his hand, and like a fool, I called on him. "What's that mark on your top?" You know, tact is not a child's long suit. Well, that morning I'd let the iron stay a bit too long on that spot and had a perfect print of an iron right on the front of my top, but I'd convinced myself that it wasn't noticeable. I explained, my humiliation almost complete. Then as we walked out of the classroom, one of the students said, "You need some new shoes, too." My supervisor never said a word, in fact, she never came back.

5. Brace yourselves, parents. Children tell us what you say about us! I really think that there ought to be a contract signed every year between parents and teachers stating: We won't believe everything they say about you if you won't believe everything they say about us! I taught sex education one year—don't laugh—to 6th grade girls. I had looked through my teachers' edition of my science book and noticed that chapter 10 was about reproduction. The principal and I planned for months. We had filmstrips and videos, guest speakers lined up and our lessons all prepared. We'd sent the science books home with instructions for the parents to read chapter 10, sign the permission notes and

be in partnership with us as we went through the unit. On the first day, I opened with, "Girls, I know you all have read chapter 10 and your parents have read chapter 10. What are your thoughts as we begin this unit?" There was just this long silence, so I tried another approach. "Did your parents discuss this with you?" Mary was the only one to raise her hand. "Yes, Mary?" "Well, my mother said it was just like an old maid to get in a stew over this. She said she didn't know what all the fuss was about." I began to respond with something like "Mary, some parents think this is a very delicate subject," and Mary said, "What's delicate about plants?" See, I had read the ALTERNATE chapter in my teachers' edition. The student textbooks were all about cross pollination of pea pods—not sexual reproduction. If those parents had said TO me what they'd said ABOUT me, we could have saved ourselves a lot of stress!

6. Children today are as hungry for an adult's approval as they ever were. Several years ago my students were asked to write in their journals at the beginning of every class period. It was one of those days when the silence was broken SEVERAL times with the question, "What's today?" I'd answered that question over and over and finally, I jumped up, ran to the middle of the room and sang, "Da, da, da, da, da, da! Today's the 29th! Now, everybody knows what today is." On my way back to my seat, I heard one of the boys say to his neighbor, "Everybody but James—he's too dumb to know what today is." Before I could respond, I heard James say—just as quietly, "Uh-huh. Da, da, da, da, da, da! Today's the 29th!" I laughed and said, "James, I love you!" At the end of the week, I took up their journals and there in James' poor spelling and painfully childish writing were these words: "Miss Hockin love me. She say so." That's why I teach.

IV. What, Then, Has Changed?

Am I saying that children are still attending school in Mayberry with Miss Crump? Goodness, no! There ARE differences in our classrooms today. Because of advances in technology, the world can be brought to our doors. We can access research data almost as soon as new discoveries are made. We can communicate with students in other places from our classrooms. We have more materials, more comfortable classrooms, more up-to-date textbooks, more resources.

But, because of drug abuse, we have students who are severely altered in academic ability and in behavioral skills. Because of changes in the home, we have students who withdraw or threaten. Because of neglect, we have students who seek attention in any way they can. Because they've been given too much too soon, we have students who're hopeless and jaded. The dead eyes alarm me more than anything.

Today's differences create more challenges for teachers. What are the greatest challenges I face today? Probably some of the same ones I faced in the early 70's—how to individualize instruction; how to provide a classroom climate where motivation can take place; how to manage behavior; how to communicate effectively with students, parents and other educators; how to meet the needs of every student whether the need be academic, emotional or physical; how to relinquish (quote) "teaching time" to laugh, to enjoy the spontaneous moment, to really look at a child, to really listen, to discover, to explore, to appreciate, to grow; and the continuing challenge of how to give a flawless performance on this education "stage" I've chosen, because…

...a doctor's mistake is buried
...a lawyer's mistake is imprisoned
...a plumber's mistake is stopped
...an accountant's mistake is written off
...a printer's mistake is reprinted
...BUT, a teacher's mistake is never erased!

Custodians of Our Culture[4]

Ingrid Saunders Jones

Vice president and manager of Corporate External Affairs, chair-person, the Coca-Cola Foundation, 1992– ; born Detroit, MI, 1945; B.A., Michigan State University, 1968; M.A., Eastern Michigan University, 1972; executive director, Child Care Coordinating Council, 1974-77; legislative analyst for the president of the Atlanta City Council, 1978-79; executive assistant to Mayor Maynard Jackson of Atlanta, GA, 1979-81; director of Urban Affairs, Coca-Cola Company, 1987-88; assistant to the vice president, Coca-Cola Company, 1988-92.

Editors' introduction: Morris Brown College, named for the second Bishop of the African Methodist Episcopal Church, was founded in 1885 as the first educational institution in Georgia solely under African-American patronage. Ingrid Saunders Jones, vice president of Corporate External Affairs for the Coca-Cola Company, looked to provide "a conversation with the audience on the significance of Morris Brown's history and on our responsibility as custodians of our culture to develop leaders for the present and future generations." To achieve that goal, Jones recalled quotes from great African-American leaders urging that African Americans preserve their culture.

Ingrid Saunders Jones's speech: Good morning. President Jolley, distinguished guests, faculty, staff, students and friends of Morris Brown.

I am humbled, and honored to have been recognized today by an institution known for educating the best and the brightest.

But it is every bit as much an honor just to be invited to be a part of this Founders Day at Morris Brown College; and I am joined here today with colleagues of mine from The Coca-Cola Company, many of whom are graduates of Morris Brown College.

I am so pleased that I finally have the opportunity to meet and talk with Mrs. Merlissie Middleton, an amazing woman who has meant so much to this school and this community.

Mrs. Middleton's reputation and many contributions to Morris Brown are legendary and awesome...she's been a role model for all of us, especially the women of our community. She is the epitome of what this *Month of the Woman* is all about.

Mrs. Middleton, I congratulate you for nearly five decades of service dedicated to teaching and leading our young people, and

---

[4] Delivered at Morris Brown College, in Atlanta, Georgia, on March 28, 1996. Reprinted with permission of Ingrid Saunders Jones.

on a career here at Morris Brown that has helped to instill values in today's and tomorrow's leaders.

You know, Founders' Day is one of those special moments in a college or university academic year...a time to celebrate and honor the visionary leadership of those who helped to establish an educational institution.

But at our historically black colleges and universities...Founders Day is even more important. It is a time to remember the pride, courage and strength of the founders.

It is a time to recognize and to salute the many individuals who, by sheer will, dedication and commitment, decided they could shape the future and the destiny of a people for generations to come by providing the most basic kind of equity... a quality education.

At Morris Brown, it is particularly poignant...because Morris Brown College is the first African American institution of higher learning to be founded for blacks...by black people.

For 115 years, Morris Brown College has been a beacon of hope...a place where young people who want and deserve a quality education can come...a place where leadership is nurtured and where dreams begin to be realized...a place where possibilities begin and potential is taped.

This school has always articulated and executed a very special mission...that of providing "educational opportunity" ...with as much emphasis on opportunity as is placed on education.

That's what the founders of Morris Brown College envisioned...providing the broadest range of opportunities to the broadest cross-section of students.

And we are here today to celebrate this broad vision...the vision of Wesley John Gaines, William F. Dickerson and Steward Wylie, Mary McCree, Annie Thomas and so many more.

Founder's Day is also a day that causes us to take pause...take pause to look at where we've been in order to see where we are going.

John Henrik Clarke, the distinguished scholar and historian at Cornell, said it best, I think. He said:

> *History is not everything, but it is the starting point. History is a clock that people use to tell their time of day.*
>
> *It is a compass they use to find themselves on the map of human geography. It tells them where they are...but, more importantly, what they must be.*

The most instructive aspect of Morris Brown's history is that, as an institution, Morris Brown has demonstrated what I call "effective custodianship."

It is the responsibility of each and every one of us to be the "custodians of our culture."

Our dictionaries tell us that "Culture" is the development and refinement of intellectual and artistic knowledge and under-

"...Morris Brown College is the first African American institution of higher learning to be founded for blacks...by black people."

standing, especially through education that is transmitted to succeeding generations.

The son of a Morris Brown Graduate spoke at Lincoln University's commencement in 1961; he spoke about the importance of "culture" to our civilization. The speaker was the son of Alberta Williams King.

Dr. Martin Luther King Jr. said, and I quote:

> We have allowed our civilization to outdistance our culture. Civilization refers to what we use...culture refers to what we are. Civilization is that complex of devices, instrumentalities, mechanisms and techniques by means of which we live. Culture is expressed in art, literature, religion and morals. The great problem confronting us today is that we have allowed the means by which we live to outdistance the ends for which we live. We have allowed our civilization to outrun our culture...and so we are in danger now of ending up with guided missiles in the hands of misguided men.

Dr. King's message is clear. We, as individuals and institutions, must take the responsibility of protecting, educating, and providing hope...and we must protect and support *institutions* like Morris Brown College...that educate our young people, that teach our young people, and that transmit the values of our "culture" to our young people.

Thank you, Morris Brown College, and thank you to the Founders and Leaders of Morris Brown.

This *is* an extraordinarily important time for Morris Brown and I want to speak on three important things that have occurred recently.

First and foremost, this college has come out from under a dark cloud that threatened its very existence a few years ago. That did not happen by happenstance...it was the dedication, vision and hard work of the Morris Brown Board of Trustees, Morris Brown Graduates and supporters that turned that around on a dime.

The Coca-Cola Company was proud to be an early supporter of the College during that time of need.

Morris Brown can now once again concentrate on the main mission of providing "educational opportunity" and preparing young people for the future.

The second thing falls under the category of leadership...Morris Brown now has the bold and visionary leadership of President Samuel Jolley, a great educator who clearly relishes the opportunity to lead this institution into the 21st century.

Thank you Dr. Samuel Jolley for hearing the call and answering it...the ancestors are pleased.

And finally, this is an extraordinary time for Morris Brown because the world is coming to Atlanta this summer. Thousands and thousands of people from all over the world...people who may never have heard of Morris Brown, are going to come streaming down M. L. K. Boulevard toward Herndon Stadium, for the Olympics.

This past Sunday, I personally toured the campus to view the construction activities surrounding the Olympics; and I had the opportunity to see and walk on the grounds of Herndon Stadium as they were beginning the field preparation to lay the Astroturf.

I also went back on Tuesday to just gaze at the stadium. Herndon Stadium is incredible! And Dr. Jolley, I look forward to sitting with you next year for at least one football game.

Yes, it is also an extraordinary time for Morris Brown because of the "people commitment" ...people of the past and people of the present, like Gary Holmes, Chief Beverly Harvard and Dr. Johnny Clark and, most of all, people and students of the future.

As I look out and see the faculty, staff, graduates and supporters of Morris Brown College (the institution)...what I know is that each one of us represents a special commitment, a special set of talents and a special power that can make a difference in this institution and this community. And I think this difference can be summed up in one word..."Leadership."

Leadership is about direction and change. It is about being able to grow from each mistake made; and it is about stretching our comfort zone to the limits. We must be willing to use our talents, interests and insights to help shape a society that bridges the gulf between what "is" and what "ought" to be.

It's not easy to lead...you have to be willing to take risks, to move fast, and have the ability to see around corners even when it's dark. That is when you call on faith...and, in your faith, you find a level of comfort that you can feel from within...it tells you that it's going to be okay, that you need not fear taking a risk as you lead. And leadership produces results, many times, that are beyond expectations.

Andy Young, in his book, "A Way Out of No Way," writes very eloquently about the moments of destiny that make up our lives...the times when one simple action can bring a new world of change, potential and possibility. Andy writes:

> *Most of the successful men and women I have known can point to moments of destiny in their lives...times when a simple decision produced complex and meaningful results which were totally beyond anticipation.*

> *It is the interrelationship of multiple coincidences of one's life that makes for success, and that makes many of us believe that there is a divine purpose and power in human life.*

A very powerful observation.

For many young men and women, coming to Morris Brown is their moment of destiny...it is here that their experiences often produce complex and meaningful results that are totally beyond their expectations. It is here that lives are shaped and leaders are molded.

By the same token, I suggest to you that we should never underestimate how our personal leadership effects the lives of young people and how we become a part of the "multiple coincidences" that lead to their success. When we care, nurture and protect, we become a part of the power of human life.

I thank you all for meaning so much to this special institution.

I want to thank all of you here today who have been so generous in helping make the Morris Brown annual campaign a success.

I thank you for letting me share this Founder's Day with you and for the high honor you have bestowed on me this morning.

Thank you.

V. Government

Second Inaugural Address[1]

William J. Clinton

*President of the United States, 1992– ; born Hope, AR, 1946; B.S.,
Georgetown University, 1968; Rhodes Scholar, Oxford University,
1968–70; J.D., Yale University, 1973; professor, University of
Arkansas Law School, 1973-76; attorney general, Arkansas, 1976-
77; governor of Arkansas, 1979–81, 1983-92.*

Editors' introduction: As the first Democrat to win reelection to
the executive office since Franklin Delano Roosevelt, Bill Clinton
secured a relatively easy victory by running on a platform that
pledged an end to big government. In his second Inaugural
Address, President Clinton challenged Congress to be partners
rather than partisans. Clinton also warned of the American racial
divide, and promised that we shall overcome the plague of prejudice that has polarized the population.

President Clinton's speech: My fellow citizens, at this last
Presidential Inauguration of the 20th century, let us lift our eyes
toward the challenges that await us in the next century. It is our
great good fortune that time and chance have put us not only at
the edge of a new century, in a new millennium, but on the edge
of a bright new prospect in human affairs, a moment that will
define our course and our character for decades to come. We
must keep our old democracy forever young. Guided by the
ancient vision of a promised land, let us set our sights upon a
land of new promise.

The promise of America was born in the 18th century out of
the bold conviction that we are all created equal. It was extended and preserved in the 19th century, when our Nation spread
across the continent, saved the Union, and abolished the awful
scourge of slavery.

Then, in turmoil and triumph, that promise exploded onto the
world stage to make this the American century. And what a century it has been. America became the world's mightiest industrial power, saved the world from tyranny in two World Wars and
a long cold war, and time and again reached out across the globe
to millions who, like us, longed for the blessings of liberty.

Along the way, Americans produced a great middle class and

---

[1] Delivered in Washington, D.C., on January 20, 1997.

security in old age, built unrivaled centers of learning and opened public schools to all, split the atom and expired the heavens, invented the computer and the microchip, and deepened the well-spring of justice by making a revolution in civil rights for African-Americans and all minorities and extending the circle of citizenship opportunity, and dignity to women.

Now, for the third time, a new century is upon us and another time to choose. We began the 19th century with a choice: to spread our Nation from coast to coast. We began the 20th century with a choice: to harness the industrial revolution to our values of free enterprise, conservation, and human decency. Those choices made all the difference. At the dawn of the 21st century, a free people must now choose to shape the forces of the information age and the global society, to unleash the limitless potential of all our people, and yes, to form a more perfect Union.

When last we gathered, our march to this new future seemed less certain than it does today. We vowed then to set a clear course to renew our Nation. In these 4 years, we have been touched by tragedy, exhilarated by challenge, strengthened by achievement. America stands alone as the world's indispensable nation. Once again, our economy is the strongest on Earth. Once again, we are building stronger families, thriving communities, better educational opportunities, a cleaner environment. Problems that once seemed destined to deepen, now bend to our efforts. Our streets are safer, and record numbers of our fellow citizens have moved from welfare to work.

And once again, we have resolved for our time a great debate over the role of Government. Today we can declare: Government is not the problem, and Government is not the solution. We—the American people—we are the solution. Our Founders understood that well and gave us a democracy strong enough to endure for centuries, flexible enough to face our common challenges and advance our common dreams in each new day.

As times change, so Government must change. We need a new Government for a new century, humble enough not to try to solve all our problems for us but strong enough to give us the tools to solve our problems for ourselves, a government that is smaller, lives within its means, and does more with less. Yet where it can stand up for our values and interests around the world, and where it can give Americans the power to make a real difference in their everyday lives, Government should do more, not less. The preeminent mission of our new Government is to give all Americans an opportunity, not a guarantee but a real opportunity, to build better lives.

Beyond that, my fellow citizens, the future is up to us. Our Founders taught us that the preservation of our liberty and our Union depends upon responsible citizenship. And we need a new sense of responsibility for a new century. There is work to do, work that Government alone cannot do: teaching children to read, hiring people off welfare rolls, coming out from behind locked doors and shuttered windows to help reclaim our streets from drugs and gangs and crime, taking time out of our own lives to serve others.

Each and every one of us, in our own way, must assume personal responsibility not only for ourselves and our families but for our neighbors and our Nation. Our greatest responsibility is to embrace a new spirit of community for a new century. For any one of us to succeed, we must succeed as one America. The challenge of our past remains the challenge of our future: Will we be one Nation, one people, with one common destiny, or not? Will we all come together, or come apart?

The divide of race has been America's constant curse. And each new wave of immigrants gives new targets to old prejudices. Prejudice and contempt cloaked in the pretense of religious or political conviction are no different. These forces have nearly destroyed our Nation in the past. They plague us still. They fuel the fanaticism of terror. And they torment the lives of millions in fractured nations all around the world.

"Our rich texture of racial, religious, and political diversity will be a godsend in the 21st century."

These obsessions cripple both those who hate and of course those who are hated, robbing both of what they might become. We cannot, we will not, succumb to the dark impulses that lurk in the far regions of the soul everywhere. We shall overcome them. And we shall replace them with the generous spirit of a people who feel at home with one another. Our rich texture of racial, religious, and political diversity will be a godsend in the 21st century. Great rewards will come to those who can live together, learn together, work together, forge new ties that bind together.

As this new era approaches, we can already see its broad outlines. Ten years ago, the Internet was the mystical province of physicists; today, it is a commonplace encyclopedia for millions of schoolchildren. Scientists now are decoding the blueprint of human life. Cures for our most feared illnesses seem close at hand. The world is no longer divided into two hostile camps. Instead, now we are building bonds with nations that once were our adversaries. Growing connections of commerce and culture give us a chance to lift the fortunes and spirits of people the world over. And for the very first time in all of history, more people on this planet live under democracy than dictatorship.

My fellow Americans, as we look back at this remarkable century, we may ask, can we hope not just to follow but even to surpass the achievements of the 20th century in America and to avoid the awful bloodshed that stained its legacy? To that question, every American here and every American in our land today must answer a resounding, "Yes!" This is the heart of our task. With a new vision of Government, a new sense of responsibility, a new spirit of community, we will sustain America's journey.

The promise we sought in a new land, we will find again in a land of new promise. In this new land, education will be every citizen's most prized possession. Our schools will have the highest standards in the world, igniting the spark of possibility in the eyes of every girl and every boy. And the doors of higher education will be open to all. The knowledge and power of the information age will be within reach not just of the few but of every classroom, every library, every child. Parents and children will have time not only to work but to read and play together. And the plans they make at their kitchen table will be those of a better home, a better job, the certain chance to go to college.

Our streets will echo again with the laughter of our children, because no one will try to shoot them or sell them drugs anymore. Everyone who can work, will work, with today's permanent under class part of tomorrow's growing middle class. New miracles of medicine at last will reach not only those who can claim care now but the children and hard-working families too long denied.

"Parents and children will have time not only to work but to read and play together."

We will stand mighty for peace and freedom and maintain a strong defense against terror and destruction. Our children will sleep free from the threat of nuclear, chemical, or biological weapons. Ports and airports, farms and factories will thrive with trade and innovation and ideas. And the world's greatest democracy will lead a whole world of democracies.

Our land of new promise will be a nation that meets its obligations, a nation that balances its budget but never loses the balance of its values, a nation where our grandparents have secure retirement and health care and their grandchildren know we have made the reforms necessary to sustain those benefits for their time, a nation that fortifies the world's most productive economy even as it protects the great natural bounty of our water, air, and majestic land. And in this land of new promise, we will have reformed our politics so that the voice of the people will always speak louder than the din of narrow interests, regaining the participation and deserving the trust of all Americans.

Fellow citizens, let us build that America, a nation ever moving forward toward realizing the full potential of all its citizens. Prosperity and power, yes, they are important, and we must maintain them. But let us never forget, the greatest progress we have made and the greatest progress we have yet to make, is in the human heart. In the end, all the world's wealth and a thousand armies are no match for the strength and decency of the human spirit.

Thirty-four years ago, the man whose life we celebrate today spoke to us down there, at the other end of this Mall, in words that moved the conscience of a nation. Like a prophet of old, he told of his dream that one day America would rise up and treat all its citizens as equals before the law and in the heart. Martin Luther King's dream was the American dream. His quest is our quest: the ceaseless striving to live out our true creed. Our history has been built on such dreams and labors. And by our dreams and labors, we will redeem the promise of America in the

21st century.

To that effort I pledge all my strength and every power of my office. I ask the Members of Congress here to join in that pledge. The American people returned to office a President of one party and a Congress of another. Surely they did not do this to advance the politics of petty bickering and extreme partisanship they plainly deplore. No, they call on us instead to be repairers of the breach and to move on with America's mission. America demands and deserves big things from us, and nothing big ever came from being small. Let us remember the timeless wisdom of Cardinal Bernardin, when facing the end of his own life. He said, "It is wrong to waste the precious gift of time on acrimony and division."

Fellow citizens, we must not waste the precious gift of this time. For all of us are on that same journey of our lives, and our journey, too, will come to an end. But the journey of our America must go on.

And so, my fellow Americans, we must be strong, for there is much to dare. The demands of our time are great, and they are different. Let us meet them with faith and courage, with patience and a grateful, happy heart. Let us shape the hope of this day into the noblest chapter in our history. Yes, let us build our bridge, a bridge wide enough and strong enough for every American to cross over to a blessed land of new promise.

May those generations whose faces we cannot yet see, whose names we may never know, say of us here that we led our beloved land into a new century with the American dream alive for all her children, with the American promise of a more perfect Union a reality for all her people, with America's bright flame of freedom spreading throughout all the world.

From the height of this place and the summit of this century, let us go forth. May God strengthen our hands for the good work ahead, and always, always bless our America.

Four Points of the Compass: Restoring America's Sense of Direction[2]

Balint Vazsonyi

Director of the Center for the American Founding, 1995– ; born Budapest, Hungary, 1936; Artist Diploma, Liszi Academy, Budapest, 1956; M.M., Florida State University, 1960; Ph.D., University of Budapest, 1982; professor of music, Indiana University, 1978-84; dean of music, New World School of the Arts, 1993-95.

Editors' introduction: Balint Vazsonyi interrupted his musical career to launch the Center for the American Founding, a political think-tank sponsored by The Potomac Foundation of McLean, Virginia. A refugee who left his native Hungary after the unsuccessful revolt against Stalin (1956), Vazsonyi explained that the purpose of this speech was to launch a national initiative to return "back to the path of our existing Constitution." To achieve that goal, he emphasized "the unique properties of American society, the ingredients on which it depends, [and] the means by which to ensure its survival."

Balint Vazsonyi's speech: Senator Grams, Dr. Spalding, distinguished guests:

Although the press appeared not to notice, President Clinton, in his Inaugural Address, called for a new Constitution. He borrowed language from the Declaration of Independence where in 1776 Thomas Jefferson presented the argument for new government. On January 20th, 1997, Mr. Clinton proclaimed, 'We need a new government for a new century." He proceeded to set forth all the things this new government would *give* the American people.

Today, I come before you to argue that we need just the opposite. We, at the Center for the American Founding, believe that a tool is necessary to guide us back to the path of our existing Constitution. We offer this tool to the decision makers, legislators and judges of America and ask all of you to help us develop it to its full potential. Because it points the way, we think of it as a compass.

What kind of country will exert its best efforts for the benefit of all mankind? Or engage in war without expectation of gain? What kind of country makes it possible that a person who did

---

[2] Delivered to The Heritage Foundation, in Washington, D.C., on February 13, 1997. Reprinted with permission of Balint Vazsonyi.

not grow up in it feel sufficiently at home to step forward with a major initiatives What kind of country has long-time professionals come together to hear a relative novice with a foreign accent speak on national issues? What kind of country? A country which is one of a kind.

As we contemplate the future, it is essential that we keep in mind that America, indeed, is one of a kind. Some believe with all their heart that people, and their aspirations, are the same everywhere. This may be so. But the *nation* established here more than two hundred years ago has neither precedent nor a parallel in the known history of this planet. Not its capacity for success; not its capacity for strength; not its capacity for goodness. It is one of a kind.

One-of-a kind. A big word. You hear it and think of Shakespeare. Or Beethoven. Or George Washington. We look at their work and try to understand what makes it so. It is a hopeless endeavor. But with America, there are definite ingredients we can identify quite easily: the rule of law, individual rights, guaranteed property and so forth. A funny thing, ingredients. We acknowledge their importance in all sorts of scenarios, yet ignore them when it comes to matters of life and death. If we eat something memorable, we want the recipe. With food, we know without the shadow of a doubt that the ingredients make the thing.

Chocolate ice cream, for example, takes chocolate, cream and sugar. If, instead, you use ground beef, mustard and "A1" sauce, you don't expect chocolate ice cream to come out of the process. Whatever else it will be, chocolate ice cream it will not be. Ice creams come in many varieties. America is one of a kind. Do we honestly expect it to remain America if the ingredients are changed?

Over the past decades, the Rule of Law has been displaced by something called "social justice." Group rights and arbitrary privileges make a mockery of the constitutional rights of the individual. Where not so long ago all Americans could feel secure in their right to acquire and hold property, government today is no longer discussing whether—only how *much* of it to confiscate, and how to redistribute it. As you see, the ingredients have already undergone drastic change. Is it reasonable to hope that America will nevertheless remain America?

And the greatest variety of assaults is launched against something I have come to refer to as "national identity." Now, I realize that some people might have a reaction to that phrase because the term has been used by others as a wedge. I use it as a magnet. As such, it is a necessity. Something needs to bind people together, especially when they have converged, and continue to converge upon a place from every corner of the globe.

Identity is about being similar or being different. Since our differences have been amply provided for by nature, we have to agree about those aspects of our lives which will make us similar. For the shared history which other nations have, Americans have

"Some believe with all their heart that people, and their aspirations, are the same everywhere."

successfully substituted a shared belief in, and adherence to, certain principles. A common language took the place of a shared culture. No state religion was established, but a Bible-based morality taken for granted. Add to this a certain work ethic, an expectation of competence in your field of work (whether you spilt the atom or sweep the floor), a spirit of voluntary cooperation, insistence on choice, a fierce sense of independence—and you have the ingredients of the American identity. And, if you prefer to call it American character or, as George Washington, "national character," it will serve our purpose so long as we remain agreed about the ingredients. *For it is these ingredients that have distinguished us from other societies, and enabled those who sweep the floor today to split the atom tomorrow.*

Today, our nation's leaders are engaged in choosing a path to pursue. Yet, all along, we have had a path to *follow.* It is clearly pointed in the Declaration of Independence and our founders complemented it with a superb road map they called the Constitution of the United States. Add to this the glossary we know as The Federalist Papers and it is hard to see why and how we could have lost our sense of direction. But lost it we have. That is why we need a compass—the compass in the title of these remarks.

Between 1776 and 1791, our compass was calibrated to keep us on the path of betterment—as individuals and as a nation. We even had a kind of "North Star," a magnetic North, in what we call the Rule of Law. But instead, we now have rule by the *lawmaker.* Every member of the Executive, every member of the Judiciary has become a potential lawmaker and in most cases they use the potential to the hilt.

Yet the Rule of Law stands for the exact opposite. As its basic property, it places the fundamental tenets beyond the reach of politics and politicians. Whereas it confers legitimacy upon subsequent laws that spring from its eternal well, it denies legitimacy to all legislative maneuvers that corrupt its purpose. It holds the makers, executants and adjudicators of the law accountable at all times. Above all, it demands equal application to every man, woman and child. Within its own framework, a prescribed majority may amend the law. But as the law stands in any given moment, it must be applied equally. If accomplished, nothing in the history of human societies can match the significance and magnificence of equality before the law.

The aspiration for equality before the law began with the Magna Carta or even earlier, in King Arthur's court, where knights sat at a *round* table. But it took Thomas Jefferson to etch the concept in the minds of freedom-loving people everywhere, more permanently than posterity could have etched the words in the marble of the Jefferson Memorial. And even then, after those immortal words of the Declaration of Independence had been written, it took most of two centuries before America, land of the many miracles, almost made it a reality for the first time ever.

But it was not to be. The rule of law, our only alternative to the law of the jungle, came under attack just as it was about to triumph. The attacker displayed the irresistible charm of the temptress, the armament of the enraged avenger, dressed itself in intoxicating clichés, and wore the insignias of the highest institutions of learning. It called itself "social justice."

Let me make it clear: I do not speak of social conscience. *That* is a frame of mind, a noble sentiment, a measure of civilization. Precisely for that reason, while it has everything to do with our conduct, it has nothing whatever to do with laws. "Social justice," on the other hand, aims at the heart of our legal system by setting an unattainable goal, by fueling discontent, by insinuating a permanent state of hopelessness.

But above all, social justice is unacceptable as the basis for a stable society because, unlike the Law, it is what anyone says it is on any given day. We need only to move back a few years, or travel a few thousand miles, and one is certain to find an entirely different definition of social justice. At the end of the day, it is nothing more than an empty slogan, to be filled by power-hungry political activists so as to enlist the participation of well-intentioned people.

The Rule of Law and a world according to "Social Justice" are mutually exclusive. One cannot have it both ways.

What have the Rule of Law and the pursuit of "social justice" respectively spawned over time? The Rule of Law gave birth to a series of individual rights. In other words, rights vested solely in individuals. Only individuals are capable of having rights, just as only individuals can be free. We say a society is free if the individuals who make up that society are free. For individuals to be free, they must have certain unalienable rights, and others upon which they had agreed with one another.

Social justice has spawned an aberration called group rights. Group rights are the negation if individual rights. Group rights say in effect, "you cannot and do not have rights as an individual—only as the member of a certain group." The Rule of Law knows nothing about groups, therefore it could not provide for, or legitimize rights of groups. Groups have no standing in the eyes of the Law. And, since their so-called rights are invariably created and conferred by persons of temporary authority, they are "subject to change without notice," as the saying goes, just like the definition of social justice itself.

Individual rights recognize and promote similarity. Group rights promote differences and stereotypes. Individual rights and group rights are mutually exclusive. One cannot have it both ways.

Among our individual rights, the right to acquire and hold property has a special place. If ever a concept came to be developed to protect the weak against the strong, to balance inborn gifts with the fruits of sheer diligence and industry, *property inviolate* is its name. But who am I to speak, after John Locke,

> *"Only individuals are capable of having rights, just as only individuals can be free."*

Thomas Jefferson and James Madison have pronounced on this topic. They held that civilized society is predicated upon the sanctity of private property, and that to guarantee it is government's primary function. Without absolute property there is no incentive. Without absolute property there is no security. Without absolute property there is no liberty. The freedom to enter into contract, the freedom to keep what is mine, the freedom to dispose of what is mine underlies all our liberties.

Neither the search for "social justice" nor so-called group rights recognize, or respect, private property. They look upon flesh-and-blood individuals as faceless members of a multitude who, together, create a certain amount of goods. These goods belong to what they call "The Community." Then certain people decide who needs what and, being privy to some higher wisdom, distribute—actually redistribute—the goods. Redistribution is pursuant to group rights expressed in something called *entitlement*. Entitlements are based neither on law nor on accomplishment. Entitlements are based on membership in a certain group, and we have seen that groups are designated by persons of temporary authority, rather than the Law.

The right to property and entitlements through redistribution are mutually exclusive. One cannot have it both ways.

We have been ordered by the prophets of social justice to replace our national identity with something they call "multi-culturalism." I will confess that some time in the past, I might have shared the allergic reaction some of you experience in the face of "national" and "identity." But then I noticed the enormous importance the social-justice crowd attaches to the destruction of the American identity. Just think: bilingual education and multilingual ballots. Removal of the founding documents from our schools. Anti-American history standards. Exiling the Ten Commandments. Replacing American competence with generic "self esteem." Replacing voluntarism with coercion. Encouraging vast numbers of new immigrants to ignore the very reasons which brought them here in the first place. The list goes on, and sooner or later will affect national defense, if it hasn't already.

And for those who would point to Yugoslavia as proof of the tragedy nationalism can cause, let me say that a healthy national identity is utterly distinct from nationalism. Like the United States, Yugoslavia was created. But unlike in the case of the United States, ingredients for a national identity were not provided, and Yugoslavia imploded at the first opportunity precisely for that reason. Had it not done so, it would have succumbed to the first external attack, for no Croat would lay down his life for the good of Serbs or Bosnians. Will Americans lay down their lives if America is nothing but a patchwork of countless group identities?

Will the Armed Forces of the United States fight to uphold, defend, and advance the cause of multiculturalism?

This is not a frivolous question.

The questions before us are serious, and legion. We are virtually drowning in what we call "issues," and they are becoming increasingly difficult to sort out. How do we find our position? And, once we find our position, how do we argue its merit? Above all, how do we avoid the plague of every issue coming at us like an octopus and, just as we figure out how to tackle each arm, turning into a turtle inside its impenetrable shell?

We asked you to hear me today, because the Center for the American Founding has a proposal to submit. We call it "Four Points of the Compass" because these points provide direction, because—in a manner of speaking—they constitute a re-calibration of our compass which the events of the past thirty years have distorted. They are the Rule of Law, Individual Rights, the Sanctity of Property, and the sense of National Identity. As you have seen, they are interconnected, they literally flow from one another, just as the false compass-points which have come to displace them—social justice, group rights, redistribution and multiculturalism—are interconnected and flow from one another. What is multi-culturalism if not a redistribution of cultural "goods?" What is redistribution if not a group right? What is a group right if not the implementation of some political activist's version of "social justice?"

For thirty years, we have acquiesced in a steady erosion of America's founding principles. The time has come to reverse the movement. Rather than contending with countless individual issues, all we need to do is take the debate down a few notches, closer to the core. Let me repeat: we need to take the debate down a few notches, closer to the core. We submit that all future policy and legislative initiatives be tested against the four points of the compass. Does the proposed bill negate the Rule of Law? Does it violate individual rights? Does it interfere with the sanctity of Property? Does it constitute an assault on National Identity? Only if the answer is "No" in each case, would the proposal proceed. In other words: *Only if the answers are NO is the bill a GO.*

A few items need tidying up. How do we know what the Rule of Law can accommodate, and how far do we take individual rights? The answer, in both cases, comes from Article VI of the Constitution. **"This Constitution, and the laws of the United States which shall be made in Pursuance thereof...shall be the supreme Law of the Land; and the Judges in every State shall be bound thereby..."** It is as uncomplicated as that.

In the coming months, we intend to approach the citizens of this great nation and their representatives at all levels with a call to consider adopting this approach. We will hold panel discussions and town meetings so as to invite, engage and incorporate the wisdom and experience of Americans everywhere. There will be retreats and, by year's end, there will be a book with all the details. We do not underrate the magnitude of the step we are proposing, but we honestly believe that it will make life a great deal easier. With a simple stroke, it will become clear that one cannot take an oath upon the Constitution and support group rights. One cannot take an oath upon the Constitution and support the confiscation of property without compensation. One cannot take an oath upon the Constitution and support measures which are clearly at odds with the mandate for national defense.

We cannot have it both ways. We have to choose our compass and remember the four points. They are, as we have seen, inseparable. Therefore: *Only if the answers are NO is the bill a GO.*

I do not believe that last November the people of this country voted for the luke-warm bath of bi-partisanship. I believe the people of this country said: If you don't give us a real choice, we won't give you a real election. Yes, people probably have grown tired of the "issues," but they are, I am certain, eager to partake in an effort to choose either a return to our original path, or a clean and honest break with the past.

Those who feel that the time has come to change the supreme law of the land should come forward, say so, and engage in an open debate. But let us not continue a pattern of self-delusion. We are heirs to a remarkable group of men who, two hundred plus years ago, had every reason to feel similarly overwhelmed by the number of decisions they had to make. Their response was to make very few laws, for they knew that the fewer the laws, the broader the agreement. They knew people find it hard to agree on everything. So they sought agreement on core principles they held to be non-negotiable.

Today, we propose the four that ought to be non-negotiable. They are, as we have seen, inseparable. We call them the four points of the compass. Together, they can and will restore America's sense of direction.

Proud of Liberal Accomplishments[3]

Patricia Schroeder

President, chief executive officer, Association of American Publishers, 1997– ; born Portland OR, 1940; B.A., University of Minnesota, 1961; J.D., Harvard Law School, 1964; field attorney, National Labor Relations Board, 1964-66; private law practice, 1966-72; law instructor, Community College of Denver, 1969-70; faculty, University of Colorado, 1969-72; law instructor, Regis College, 1970-72; hearing officer, Colorado Dept. of Personnel, 1971-72; representative (D) from Colorado, 1973-96; author, Champion of the Great American Family (1989).

Editors' introduction: On September 30, 1996, Patricia Schroeder, former representative from Colorado, gave this farewell speech to the House of Representatives. Here, Schroeder praised "liberal accomplishments," her goal being "to outline the liberal accomplishments of the 20th century and to reaffirm the relevance of progressives in the 21st century." Throughout her tenure as a representative, Schroeder proudly upheld and advocated what can be termed a liberal agenda.

Patricia Schroeder's speech: Mr. Speaker, I am not quite sure what to call this, whether I call it a "Fem-fomercial," or "I am liberal, hear me roar," or "I am a progressive, hear me roar,"—or what. I wanted to take this floor one last time and say, for those who want to demean Progressives or demean liberals in this body, and for those who want to hurl labels at them, I want to say I am proud to be in that category, and I wanted to say why.

If you look back on this last century, think of what it would have been like if there had not been Progressives or there had not been liberals. There clearly would not have been any civil rights enacted. The voting rights would not have transpired. Women would not be voting. We would not be dealing with the environment the way we are now, and much more knowledgeable about it. We would not have Social Security. That, clearly, was a very stark difference. We would not have had Medicare. There was a stark difference.

We would not have had the Marshall Plan, which President Truman introduced when he was at about a 17 percent approval rating. We would not have had the nuclear test ban. We would

---

[3] Delivered in the House of Representatives, in Washington, D.C., on September 30, 1996. Reprinted with permission of Patricia Schroeder.

not have had the food safety laws or the drug safety laws. We would not have had things like air bags.

I remember those fights and how people laughed at those of us who were advocating air bags and the threatening stuff we were hearing from people, and now everybody is delighted that we have them and lives have been saved.

We would not have had the educational opportunities that the Federal Government is putting out there, whether it is for Head Start to going on to college. And I could go on with a lot of things that were introduced in this century that I think made this place a better place to live.

One of my frustrations has been, in my 24 years in politics, watching the people who fought us tooth and nail on these issues, then, after they passed they start trying to get in front of the train and pretend like its theirs and say trust me, I will take care of this if you just put me in power. Well, I do not think so. And at the same time trying to hurl labels at the people who advocated these issues like there was something really terrible about it although now of course they agree with the issues.

So as we go into this election year, I hope Americans are a lot more sophisticated and start thinking about how far this country has moved in 100 years. That is hard for us as Americans because one of our strong suits is we do not really deal in the past and we really do not deal too far in the future. We deal in the here and now and reality. That is good news, but that can be bad news, because we have to at some time think about how deep is our rudder, where is our compass set, and what do we see out there on the horizon.

So I guess what I am saying is the challenge of every one of us as we start to enter this new century is to think about where is our compass set and where do we want to go, and do we want to wipe out all these people we now call liberals, liberals or progressives, that have any of these kind of ideas? Do we want to just stay right where we are, marching in place, or do we want to march backwards and start undoing things?

As you know, they are already in the Presidential campaign talking of let us undo family medical leave, we do not like that. Let us undo all sorts of things that we have made gains on. I always feel after we gain that ground, it is almost like a military campaign, we have to sit there and sleep with one eye open like the lioness at the den because we never know what could be undone.

But I hope all Americans engage in this and think about it because I do not think liberal is a bad word. I think the great progress that this country has made has been because of people who have been courageous enough to come to this floor and say this is a Nation where hope is the bottomline and the Federal Government must find a way that hope becomes reality to every American.

I have said over and over again that I was raised in a family that said we all came from countries where we were what our parents are, but in this country we are what our children become. So we desperately need to think about what our children are going to become in the 21st century and what our Nation is going to become in the 21st century and what kind of opportunities are going to be out there for everyone.

And that, I hope, is the level of debate we have this fall. I hope that that starts to be a little more of a vision thing for every voter. It is not just the vision thing for the candidates. What are the vision things of the voters? This is where the people come in, and this is where I hope they speak.

"Private" Gambling and
Public Morality[4]

George Anastaplo

Professor, Loyola University of Chicago, 1977– ; born St. Louis, MO, 1925; B.A., 1948, J.D., 1951, Ph.D., 1964, University of Chicago; author, The Artist as Thinker (1983), The Constitution of 1787 (1989), The American Moralist (1992), The Amendment to the Constitution (1995), Campus Hate-Speech Codes and Twentieth Century Atrocities (1997).

Editors' introduction: Prohibitionists have increasingly targeted the legalization of gambling. At present 24 states have casinos, including betting houses run by 126 different tribes of American Indians. Last year, Americans spent in excess of $40 billion on gambling, up from $10 billion in 1982. Over the past two years however, the National Coalition Against Legalized Gambling has thwarted plans for casinos and slot-machines in 23 states. Opponents of gambling use metaphors of invasion and addiction that characterize bettors as passive victims. George Anastaplo, professor of law at Loyola University of Chicago, asserted that "organized gambling depends upon the systematic fleecing of the ignorant by the informed." It is Anastaplo's belief that widespread, legalized gambling prevents law and government from effectively sustaining any sort of positive morality. It follows that Anastaplo believes it is government's obligation to recognize the "ugly side" of gambling and assume the moral responsibility of curtailing it.

George Anastaplo's speech: A quarter of a century ago the following report on the status of gambling in this country was issued by the National Institute of Mental Health (Gilbert Geis, *Not the Law's Business?* [1972], p. 224):

Major concern in the United States today centers about four kinds of gambling operations: (1) numbers; (2) casino-style gambling; (3) lotteries; and 4) pari-mutuel betting at race tracks and its extension, offtrack betting. Numbers remain illegal throughout the United States; casino gambling is legal only in the State of Nevada; lotteries have recently been started in New Hampshire, New York, New Jersey, Pennsylvania, and Massachusetts; and offtrack betting was inaugurated in New York City in April 1971, in a move that has been watched with

---

[4] Delivered at a convention sponsored by the American Culture Association, in Las Vegas, Nevada, on March 25, 1996. Reprinted with permission of George Anastaplo.

special care by other jurisdictions, particularly those—and there are but few which do not fit the category—looking desperately for new sources of revenue.

I

Thus, twenty years ago only two states had legalized gambling; now all states but Hawaii and Utah have it. Even more telling is the fact that today the states themselves are often in the gambling business.

Gambling is in evidence all around us. For example, Texas bingo halls took in $63,000,000 in 1994. (*USA Today*, Nov. 13, 1995) The pervasiveness of gambling is evident to anyone who follows sports: the "point spread" helps make each encounter of even mismatched opponents "interesting" and hence the occasion for wagering. Officials of professional leagues used to worry about the influence of gambling. For example, it was once argued, "The values of football are hard work, disappointment, and honest competition, which must exist in an honest environment." Gambling, it was feared, would "accentuate" the pressures on football players beyond a tolerable point, and change a sporting event into a gambling spectacle. (Geis, pp. 247-48) Now, the officials of professional leagues cooperate with the gambling industry to make sure that games are not "fixed." (Dan Pompei, *Chicago Sun Times*, Oct. 12, 1995.)

"... twenty years ago only two states had legalized gambling; now all states but Hawaii and Utah have it."

But, it can be noticed, the sports contests that are gambled upon may often be intrinsically interesting—and can attract attention without any organized wagering. But lotteries, slot machines, and the like are far less interesting in themselves. Even so, they can be quite entertaining, even thrilling, for participants. Thus, it has been observed, "Unlike narcotics, which creates droves of criminals who prey on the generally poor black community, the numbers game seems to many people to be just a potent, daily titillation for poor people seeking a rainbow's end." The head of an offtrack betting corporation, upon being accused of taking money from the poor, asked rather rhetorically, "Who's to say what's gambling and what's entertainment?" (Fred J. Cook, in Geis, pp. 229, 235-37) But then, nicotine, too, can be engaging for the addict, however deadly cigarette-smoking may be.

II

We tend to be much more relaxed, as a community, about the damage done by gambling than were some of the earlier generations in this country. Tolerance for lotteries, in the first quarter of the Nineteenth Century, gave way because of growing abuses to efforts by state governments to put lotteries out of business. In 1895 Congress provided support for these states with its own legislation, "An Act for the Suppression of Lottery Traffic through National and Interstate Commerce and Postal Service, Subject to the Jurisdiction and Laws of the United States." (28 Statutes at

Large 963)

A constitutional inquiry into what was indeed "subject to the jurisdiction and laws of the United States" elicited this question in 1903 from the United States Supreme Court in *Champion* v. *Ames*:

> If a state, when considering legislation for the suppression of lotteries within its own limits, may properly take into view the evils that inhere in the raising of money, in that mode, why may not Congress, invested with the power to regulate commerce among the several states, provide that such commerce shall not be polluted by the carrying of lottery tickets from one state to another?

Further on the Court argued:

> [B]ut surely it will not be said to be a part of anyone's liberty, as recognized by the supreme law of the land, that he shall be allowed to introduce into commerce among the states an element that will be confessedly injurious to the public morals.... We should hesitate long before adjudging that an evil of such appalling character, carried on through interstate commerce, cannot be met and crushed by the only power competent to that end.

It is thus evident how people in authority in the first decade of this century were expected to speak about such gambling as the lottery. The dissenting opinion in *Champion* v. *Ames* made no defense of lotteries, arguing instead that the power to suppress such "a harmful business" belonged to the states, not to the national government.

The majority of the Supreme Court in *Champion* v. *Ames* insisted that Congress should be able to act:

> to protect the country at large against a species of interstate commerce which, although in general use and somewhat favored in both national and state legislation in the early history of the country, has grown into disrepute, and has become offensive to the entire people of the nation. It is a kind of traffic that no one can be entitled to pursue as a right.

I mention in passing the likelihood that the current indulgences in lotteries and the like will, because of emerging abuses and harmful consequences, eventually be subjected once again to severe restrictions. In fact, it is already likely that lotteries (if put to a popular vote by referendum) would not be approved in most of the states where they now operate.

No one on the 1903 Court doubted that state governments could try to suppress lotteries if they wished. *Phelan* v. *Virginia* was cited to this effect. The opinion in that 1850 case, upholding an 1834 act of Virginia forbidding the sale of lottery tickets, includes this reminder of how lotteries were once regarded in this country:

The suppression of nuisances injurious to public health or morality is among the most important duties of government. Experience has shown that the common forms of gambling are comparatively innocuous when placed in contrast with the widespread pestilence of lotteries. The former are confined to a few persons and places, but the latter infests the whole community: it enters every dwelling; it reaches every class; it preys upon the hard earnings of the poor; it plunders the ignorant and simple.

III

This, then, is the sort of public opinion, running back to 1850 and earlier, that the Supreme Court could invoke in the opening years of this century. Now, at the end of the same century, not only are lotteries no longer spoken of in this fashion by officials, but the states of this Union are themselves in the business of running and vigorously promoting lotteries with ever-growing prizes. In Illinois, for example, the gambling industry contributed more than a million dollars to political candidates in 1995. Furthermore, it has even been able to hire a former governor of the state and other former Illinois officials as paid lobbyists.

"In Illinois...the gambling industry contributed more than a million dollars to political candidates in 1995."

This is not just an American phenomenon, of course. State lotteries are very much in evidence in Europe and elsewhere. The "pools" have long been a feature of British life. And something *is* to be said for legalizing (or at least decriminalizing) what is likely to be done anyway, thereby permitting both regulation and taxation. But is not the state's doing it, and promoting it, something significantly different from toleration, taxation and regulation? Is it as if the state had gotten into the business of producing and selling firearms, prostitutes, alcoholic beverages, cigarettes, and other narcotics?

The newest gambling rage in this country, however, is not lotteries but rather casinos. These are licensed by states which, as virtual partners in such enterprises, count on a hefty cut of the revenues. Respectable newspapers prod their legislatures to take measures to counter the competition from the casinos in neighboring states. Consider, for example, the opening and closing sentences of a recent *Chicago Sun Times* editorial (Dec. 7, 1995):

> Two Illinois riverboat casinos got no satisfaction from the Legislature last month when they asked for help in competing with Iowa boats across the Mississippi River.... While the Legislature fiddles, Illinois gaming revenue floats across the Mississippi to lucky Iowa.

It is the practice of the gambling industry, by the way, to refer to the "entertainment" it offers as "gaming," not as "gambling."

A recent *Chicago Tribune* editorial, supporting an effort to exact more revenues from riverboat casinos, begins with these observations (March 8, 1996):

Who says gambling doesn't pay?

Last year the Empress Casino in Joliet hauled in $200 million, after paying off bettors. For Harrah's, also in Joliet, the figure was more than $190 million.

Gov. Jim Edgar's proposed 1997 state budget would impose on those and other high-rolling casinos a graduated tax to tap some of the windfall for the state's schools—and rightly so.

Under current law, all casinos are taxed a flat 20 percent of their adjusted gross receipts (that's what they have left after they've paid out winnings), regardless of how much money they're making.

For a struggling operation (and there are some), 20 percent is too much; for the wildly successful ones, it's a bargain, and for the state it's an inefficient approach to taxation of this protected industry.

Immediately following this *Tribune* editorial about how the state should take further advantage of "this protected industry" is an editorial, "No more cosying up to gangsters," commenting upon the conviction of eight members of a gang for distributing narcotics in Chicago and the suburbs. There is much to be said, of course, for the decriminalization of drug sales in this country, just as there has been for the decriminalization of gambling. But "cosying up" to, and relying upon, such activities and even promoting them for their revenues pose questions that we seem to have lost sight of about the role of law in sustaining morality. (See Anastaplo, "Governmental Drug Testing and the Sense of Community," 11 *Nova Law Review* 295 [1987]. "If Illinois were not surrounded by legalized gambling, its leaders surely would have to think twice before bringing it to their communities." *Chicago Tribune*, Editorial, June 13, 1996.)

IV

An overriding issue here is whether there is an appropriate public morality that the community should promote. Perhaps even more critical is the issue of whether there are any enduring standards of good and bad, or of right and wrong, aside from what the law may do to help establish or to protect what is taken to be public morality. It can be sobering to notice how reluctant even law professors, who are in the service of ministering to law-abidingness, are to endorse an objective morality.

In anticipation of the gambling industry that we have become accustomed to in this country, I had occasion to observe in 1975 (*Human Being and Citizen*, p. 281):

What do we believe to be the source of the desires we happen to have? And what is the legitimate role of the community in shaping those desires?... Consider the implications of the deliberate appeal to and even the intensification of the lowest desires seen in the blatant promotion in Illinois the past year of a State Lottery. See Editorial, "Why Isn't the Church Fighting Lotteries?" 91 *Christian Century* 1163 (Dec. 11, 1974; Adam Smith, *The Wealth of Nations* (index: "Lotteries"). Our desires, we are inclined to say these days, are no legitimate concern of the public, however troubled we may be by what happens when a deterioration in private desires has serious public consequences. Certainly, we have come a long way from that Colonial America in which a Cotton Mather could argue (Geis, p. 223):

> [L]ots, being mentioned in the sacred oracles of Scripture, are used only in weighty cases, and as an acknowledgment of God sitting in judgement.... [They] cannot be made the tools and parts of our common sports without, at least, such an appearance of evil, as is forbidden in the word of God.

But we need not go back that far for a healthier approach to these matters. We have noticed how the Supreme Court could speak of lotteries in 1903 as "an evil of...appalling character" which was "injurious to public morals." This kind of talk, which we today would tend to find embarrassing from any politician with intellectual pretensions, came from the pen of one of the great Justices of that period, John Marshall Harlan, the champion of a color-blind Constitution. It is symptomatic of what we have become since then that Justice Harlan's grandson, of the same name, should have been the author of the Supreme Court's opinion in *Cohen* v. *California*. The privatization, or rather the depolitization, of our morality may be seen in a passage in that 1971 opinion which the original Justice Harlan would probably have considered outrageous once he was persuaded that it was not a series of misprints (emphasis added):

> [P]ersons confronted with Cohen's jacket [with its "distasteful" four-letter word]were in a quite different position than, say, those subjected to the raucous emissions of sound trucks blaring outside their residences. Those in the Los Angeles courthouse could effectively avoid further bombardment of their sensibilities *simply by averting their eyes*. And, while it may be that one has a more substantial claim to a recognizable privacy interest when walking through a courthouse corridor than, for example, strolling through Central Park, surely it is nothing like the interest in being free from unwanted expression in the confines of one's own home.

There is no issue here of public morality (including the level of public discourse), but rather that of the extent of the right to privacy. Further on we were told, in this 1971 Harlan opinion,

> For, while the particular four-letter word being litigated

here is perhaps more distasteful than most others of its genre, it is nevertheless often true that one man's vulgarity is another's lyric. Indeed, we think it is largely because governmental officials cannot make principled distinctions in this area that the Constitution leaves matters of taste and style so largely to the individual.

The advice, "Avert your eyes," reinforced by the "discovery" that "one man's vulgarity is another's lyric," can serve as the epitaph for civic-minded morality in our time.

The distortion seen here of the First Amendment has been carried even further by the Supreme Court with its ever-widening protection of advertising. The primary purpose of the First Amendment, with a view to unfettered discussion of public issues, has long been neglected by the court. (See Anastaplo, *The Amendments to the Constitution*, p. 47f.)

V

"To some extent... gambling is a form of entertainment less harmful in many ways than some other forms of entertainment one might choose."

Far from encouraging morality, we find ourselves catering to vices and trying to exploit them. To some extent, as we have noticed, gambling is a form of entertainment less harmful in many ways than some other forms of entertainment one might choose. It tends to be for most of the "players" more self-correcting than several other forms of self-abuse, such as indulgence in alcohol, cigarettes, and drugs.

But this sort of entertainment is not likely to be intrinsically satisfying, requiring as it does constant intensification in order to maintain its interest for participants. Thus, it has been noticed by a Haverhill, Massachusetts newspaper (*USA Today*, Nov. 13, 1995):

> We've gone from the Sweepstakes era, with a once-a-week, 50-cents-per-ticket drawing, to a state-run and fostered gambling industry which is worth millions. The state government is addicted to gambling, as government finds ways to avoid dealing with the issues of how much money it should spend and what tax it ought to levy. But something is drastically wrong when government becomes increasingly dependent on the misfortunes of its people to finance its operations.

There is something "realistic" in recognizing that people *will* gamble, however much government attempts to suppress it. The considerable lure of gambling, sometimes with catastrophic consequences, has long been known. (See, for example, the Hindu epic, *The Mahabharata*.) But what seems to be forgotten from time to time is the price paid, even in economic terms, for widespread gambling. The next decade should see the publication of more and more studies which expose to public view the hidden costs of the revenues that are derived from the gambling industry.

These include the effects upon small businesses as large sums of money are siphoned out of communities by casinos. These hidden costs include, as well, the social services that have to be provided the families that are victims of gambling addictions.

Even more important than the economic and social costs of intensified addiction is what has been happening (but not only because of the gambling industry) to the authoritative opinions of the community. Hedonism is encouraged along with the notion of getting "something for nothing." Self-centeredness is thereby legitimated, as may be seen in the growing scandal of the level of compensation these days for the chief executive officers of our major corporations (especially when their compensation is compared to that of their equally successful European and Japanese counterparts). It sometimes seems that shamelessness has become the order of the day. Underlying these developments may be the corruption of the sacred. A billboard recently on display in Chicago (at LaSalle and Kinzie) invited us to a Wisconsin Dells casino with the slogan, "Come to the Land of Milk and Money." (This advertisement was illustrated by the drawing of a slot-machine showing three cows lined up: a real winner!) *That*, we are thus told, is the new Promised Land. (What then, if anything, is still sacred? That one should pay one's gambling debts?)

VI

The public should be encouraged in these matters to face up to two sets of delusions. This can help us face up in turn to what we are doing and how best to accommodate ourselves to the vices that human beings are bound to have.

The first set of delusions has to do with what organized gambling depends upon: the systematic fleecing of the ignorant by the informed. Professional gamblers do not believe in gambling any more than professional panderers believe in love: gambling magnates are no more gamblers than casino riverboats are boats. The huge outlays that casino operators are willing to devote to securing licenses reveal what a treasure-trove the well-placed casino must be. The sooner that casino customers recognize that they are suckers, the sooner most of them are likely to try to entertain themselves some other way.

The second set of delusions has to do with the notion that revenues derived from the gambling industry are a painless substitute for the taxation required for schools and other essential community services. Thus, it can be said that "money raised through legalized gambling is one of the few forms of taxation that people voluntarily and cheerfully pay." (Geis, p. 237) But for an action to be truly voluntary a minimum of understanding is required. Consider, for example, these observations (*Chicago Sun-Times,* Sept. 28, 1955):

> Some $330 billion was wagered legally in 1992, up 1,800
> percent from 1976. In Mississippi last year, gamblers

wagered $29.7 billion, while total retail sales were only $27.6 billion. Since casinos opened in Atlantic City in 1978, 100 of the 250 restaurants have closed, as have all the movie theaters.

Despite evidence that gambling may not be the panacea once thought, legislators continue to legalize gambling as a way to bring money into state coffers. But what are its costs long-term?

The need for reliable information here, to which I have already referred, may well be served by the current efforts in Congress, by Senator Paul Simon and others, to investigate gambling in this country. The thesis to be tested is that offered last year by a syndicated columnist (William Safire, "New Evil Empire," *New York Times*, Sept. 28, 1995):

Gambling is a [massive] industry that is inherently immoral, corrupting public officials, enriching criminals, addicting and impoverishing the young and vulnerable.

But the gambling racket—whether in state-licensed casinos, state-sponsored lotteries or on glitzy reservations of phony Indian tribes—has been promoted by public officials as a great way of painlessly raising revenues, with state voters acting as suckers. As a result officially endorsed and govenment-advertised gambling now has America by the throat.

A report from Deadwood, South Dakota sums up the suicidal course we have followed in our delusions. A woman who had supported the effort to legalize casinos in 1989 is now appalled upon seeing that the casinos "have all but wiped out [her] town's retailers" (*New York Times*, Nov. 24, 1995; emphasis added):

Strolling past storefront casinos that have replaced everything from the state social services office to the insurance broker and department store, [she] commented,

"I'm homesick all the time and I never left home. We were completely unrealistic."

Perhaps the most troublesome feature of all this may be that we have drifted into a much-changed way of life without much serious study or deliberate choice.

VII

I return to another anticipation, this one in 1979, of these developments (Anastaplo, *The American Moralist*, pp. 194-95):

One effect of our distortion of the promptings of nature and of the fashionable insistence that the community has little if any legitimate power to regulate our "private lives" is what is said and done these days about "victimless crimes." It has led to such scandals as the recourse we have had to government-promoted gambling in this State [Illinois]. Our lottery is a blatant effort to exploit the weaknesses of some among us in order to save the rest of us the taxes that would otherwise have to be raised to pay for what we believe ourselves to need. Or consider the increasing tolerance being shown to the doing of things that supposedly hurt only oneself, whether they be indulgence in drugs, corrupting film and print, or dangerous stunts. All this culminates in the supposed right to commit suicide, about which one hears more and more these days.... [N]ature prefers that the strong should rule the weak, that the wise should rule the ignorant, that the good should rule the bad. In any event, it should be evident upon examination not only that there are few private actions which do not affect others (a suicide, for example, can have devastating effects on a wide circle of survivors), but also that the supposedly private person very much depends on his community as well as on his family to become what he is. For both sets of reasons, and for other reasons as well, his duty to the community is considerable.... Related to the enthronement of the principle of private choice, of "doing one's own thing," is a corresponding depreciation of political life and of politicians....

"At the very least we should insist that those who profit from organized gambling should pay the full costs of their industry."

It should at once be added, however, that direct suppression of various of our vices is not likely, in our circumstances, to do much good. We should be reminded again and again of the harm that the moralistic can do to the cause of morality. Guidance here is provided by Abraham Lincoln's Temperance Speech of 1842 which is brilliantly discussed by Harry V. Jaffa in his book, *The Crisis of the House Divided* (1959). Sensible remedies, including a steady retreat from public reliance upon gambling revenues, should suggest themselves as we come to recognize what we have let ourselves in for by countenancing and even promoting gambling the way we do. (We have come a long way, most of it downhill, from private poker gatherings and church bingo games, social occasions which once afforded more or less harmless pleasures to many.) At the very least we should insist that those who profit from organized gambling should pay the full costs of their industry.

The recognition needed here includes an awareness of the ugliness of much of the organized gambling that we have. The least offensive, in a way, is horse-racing: the horses can be majestic creatures when thus put on display, however abused they may sometimes be. Much is made of the glitter of Las Vegas. (Even the cover of the Program for this American Culture Association annual convention can feature a sign welcoming us to "Fabulous

Las Vegas.") But my one visit to Las Vegas, like my single visits to deadly-serious Monte Carlo and to the grim Ho Chunk Indian Casino in Wisconsin (our billboard casino), has left me with the feeling that once is more than enough in each case. And in the United States, I presume to add, one Nevada is more than enough, a place where tightly-regulated casinos can minister to the "needs" of those who "must" have that sort of "excitement." Homesickness may be contagious wherever casinos infest a community. Certainly, the sense of community is readily sacrificed to the compulsion of private gratification. It is perhaps symptomatic of the disintegration to be expected in civic mindedness that Las Vegas should have the highest proportion of unlisted telephone numbers of any city in this country.

VI. Foreign Policy

Completing Marshall's Plan in Europe[1]

William J. Perry

Professor, Stanford University, 1997– ; born Vandergrift, PA, 1927; B.S., 1949, M.S., 1950, Stanford University; Ph.D., Pennsylvania State University, 1957; director of electronic defense laboratories, GTE Sylvania Co., 1954-64; co-founder, president, ESL Inc., 1964-77; U.S. under secretary of defense, 1977-81; managing director, Harnbrecht & Quist, 1981-85; founder, president, Technology Strategies and Alliances, 1985-93; U.S. deputy secretary of defense, 1993-94; U.S. secretary of defense, 1994-97.

Editors' introduction: Former U.S. secretary of defense William Perry's experience working in both the private and public sectors has proved invaluable during his tenure at the Pentagon. In a period of stringent budget restraints, he maintained research and development funding with a clear understanding of the value of new technology. In this speech, Perry discussed the expansion of NATO into Eastern Europe.

Andrei Kokoshin, the Deputy Defense Minister of Russia, warned conference delegates that "enlargement of NATO could topple Russia's reform process." Kokoshin insisted that the "prospect of NATO membership for countries in eastern and central Europe aggravates in Russia the feeling of vulnerability with unpredictable political implications." Perry admitted that, when he contended that an expanded NATO would fortify the "security of Russia...most of the Russians I talked to fell off the cliff."

William J. Perry's speech: Behind my desk at the Pentagon hangs a portrait of the great statesman George C. Marshall. Marshall, who was the third secretary of defense in the United States, is a role model of mine. He had a great vision for Europe—a Europe which from the Atlantic to the Urals was united in peace, freedom and democracy—and a strong trans-Atlantic partnership sustained by bipartisan political support in the United States.

Marshall not only had this vision, he also had a plan to make this vision a reality in postwar Europe. And in a famous speech

---

[1] Delivered at the Wehrkunde Conference on Security, in Munich, Germany, on February 4, 1996.

at Harvard University in 1947, he outlined what came to be called the Marshall Plan.

A little known fact is that joining Marshall on the dais that day was the famous poet T.S. Eliot, who 10 years earlier had written:

Footfalls echo in the memory
Down the passage we did not take
Towards the door we never opened.

These words by T.S. Eliot foreshadowed the fate of Marshall's plan in Eastern and Central Europe, because on that day 50 years ago, as the footfalls of World War II still echoed across a shattered continent, the Marshall Plan offered Europe a new passage toward reconstruction and renewal. Half of Europe took this passage and opened the door to prosperity and freedom. Half of Europe was denied this passage when Joseph Stalin slammed the door on Marshall's offer. And for 50 years, the footfalls of what might have been echoed in our memories.

"NATO's challenge is to provide these Europeans a path for achieving their security goal."

Today, as the Cold War becomes an echo in our memory, we have a second chance to make Marshall's vision a reality: To go down the passage we did not take 50 years ago, towards the door we never opened. Behind that door lies George Marshall's Europe. To open this door, we do not need a second Marshall Plan, but we do need to draw on Marshall's vision.

Marshall recognized that peace, democracy and prosperity were ultimately inseparable. And Marshall understood that if you identify what people desire most and provide them with a path to reach it, then they will do the hard work necessary to achieve their goals.

In the late 1940s, what Western European countries desired most was to rebuild their societies and economies. And the Marshall Plan provided a path for achieving this goal. By taking this passage, the nations of Western Europe built an economic powerhouse. And along the way, they built strong democracies and a strong security institution called NATO.

Today, countries in the other half of Europe are struggling to rebuild their societies and economies, and the one thing they all desire is greater security. NATO's challenge is to provide these Europeans a path for achieving their security goal. And along the way, we want them very much to develop strong democracies and strong economies.

This other half of Europe includes the nations of Central and Eastern Europe and the newly independent states. It includes Russia, and it includes the nations of the former Yugoslavia. Today, NATO is reaching out to all three areas and providing a path to Marshall's Europe.

The primary path NATO has provided is the Partnership for Peace. Just as the Marshall Plan worked because it was rooted firmly in the self-interest of both the United States and Europe, so too does the Partnership for Peace work because it is rooted firmly in the self-interest of both NATO and the partner nations.

PFP is bringing the newly free nations of Europe and the former Soviet Union into the security architecture of Europe as a whole. Our nations are working and training together in military joint exercises. But make no mistake, the Partnership for Peace is more than just joint exercises. Just as the Marshall Plan had an impact well beyond the economies of Western Europe, PFP is echoing beyond the security realm in Central and Eastern Europe, and into the political and economic realms as well.

Just as the Marshall Plan used economic revival as the catalyst for political stabilization—and ultimately the development of the modern Europe—the PFP uses security cooperation as a catalyst for political and economic reform.

PFP members are working to uphold democracy, tolerate diversity, respect the rights of minorities and respect freedom of expression. They are working to build market economies. They are working hard to develop democratic control of their military forces, to be good neighbors and respect the sovereign rights outside their borders. And they are working hard to make their military forces compatible with NATO.

For those partner countries that are embracing PFP as a passage to NATO membership, these actions are a key to opening that door. For many of these nations, aspiration to NATO membership has become the rock on which all major political parties base their platforms. It is providing the same overlapping consensus that NATO membership engenders in NATO countries, making compromise and reconciliation possible.

In Hungary, all six major political parties in the Parliament united to pass a resolution in support of IFOR [implementation force], the Bosnia peace implementation force, by a vote of 300 to 1. In Poland, the new president—a former member of the former communist party—reaffirmed Poland's NATO aspirations. In Slovakia, Hungary and Rumania, governments are quietly resolving border disputes and putting into place protection for ethnic minorities. For these countries, the Partnership for Peace is becoming a passage to democracy and market reform, as well as a passage to security cooperation with the West.

But even those countries that do not aspire to NATO membership are realizing many of the same political and social gains from active participation in the PFP. Moreover, PFP is providing them the tools and the opportunities to develop closer ties to NATO, and learn from NATO—even as they choose to remain outside the alliance. And PFP is building bonds among the partner nations—even outside the framework of cooperation with NATO.

That is why defense ministers from many partner nations have said to me that even if, or when, they eventually join NATO, they want to sustain their active participation in PFP. In short, by creating the Partnership For Peace, NATO is doing more than just building the basis for enlargement. It is, in fact, creating a new zone of security and stability throughout Europe.

That is why I believe that the creation of the Partnership for Peace has been one of the most significant events of the post-Cold War era. By forging networks of people and institutions working together to preserve freedom, promote democracy and build free markets, the PFP today is a catalyst for transforming Central and Eastern Europe, much as the Marshall Plan transformed Western Europe in the '40s and '50s. It is the passage this half of Europe did not take in 1947; it is the door that we never opened.

To lock in the gains of reform, NATO must ensure that the ties we are creating in PFP continue to deepen and that we actually proceed with the gradual and deliberate, but steady, process of outreach and enlargement to the East. NATO enlargement is inevitable. And if NATO enlargement is a carrot encouraging reforms, then we cannot keep that carrot continually out of reach. So it is critical that we implement the second phase of NATO enlargement agreed upon at the NAC (North Atlantic Council) Ministerial Meeting in December.

"Unlike with the Marshall Plan 50 years ago, Russia today has chosen to participate in the Partnership for Peace."

And even as some countries join NATO, it will be important to keep the door open for others down the road. We must make sure that PFP continues to provide a place in the security architecture of Europe so that we keep the door open to Marshall's Europe even for those nations that do not aspire to become NATO members.

For Marshall's vision to be truly fulfilled, one of the nations that must walk through this door is Russia. Russia has been a key player in Europe's security for over 300 years. It will remain a key player in the coming decades, for better or for worse. Our job is to make it for the better.

Unlike with the Marshall Plan 50 years ago, Russia today has chosen to participate in the Partnership for Peace. And in the spirit of Marshall, we welcome Russia's participation and hope that over time it will take on a leading role in PFP commensurate with its importance as a great power.

But for Russia to join us as a full and active partner in completing Marshall's vision, NATO and Russia need to build on our common ground, even when we don't agree with each other's conclusions. It is fair to say that most members of Russia's political establishment do not welcome or even accept NATO's plans for enlargement. Anybody that doubted that yesterday, if you heard Mr. [Andrey] Kokoshin's [first deputy minister of defense] speech, realized the extent of the opposition to NATO enlargement in Russia.

When I was in Russia last June, I had a number of conversations with Russian government leaders and Duma members about the future of European security. I offered them a series of postulates about that future. I told them if I were in Russia's shoes, I would want the future security picture in Europe to have the following characteristics:

First, I said, if I were a Russian leader, I would want the United

States to be involved in the security of Europe. They agreed with that postulate.

Then, I said, if I were a Russian leader, I would want to see Germany an integrated part of the European security structure. And they agreed with that postulate.

And third, I said, if I were a Russian leader, I would want Russia to be in the security architecture of Europe, not isolated outside of it. They agreed with this postulate also.

Finally, I asked them how could a Russian leader best achieve these goals?

I concluded they could only be achieved through a healthy and vibrant NATO. That is, NATO, far from being a threat to Russia, actually contributes to the security of Russia as well as to the security of its own members.

When I reached that conclusion, most of the Russians I talked to fell off the cliff. They agreed with each of my premises, but they did not agree with my conclusion. But in the absence of NATO and its partnership arrangements, I do not see any way of achieving those goals—our shared goals—of a safe and peaceful Europe.

I have to tell you that I did not persuade my Russian colleagues with my argument. But I do believe that as Russia deepens its involvement with NATO, it will come to believe in the truth of my conclusion as well as my premises. And I believe that Russia will want to have a cooperative relation with NATO and a leading role in the Partnership for Peace and that Russia will come to understand that NATO enlargement means enlarging a zone of security and stability that is very much in Russia's interest, not a threat to Russia.

But the way for this new understanding to occur is for NATO to continue to reach out to Russia not only from the top down but from the bottom up. Last year at Wehrkunde, I proposed that NATO and Russia begin a separate plan of activities, outside the Partnership for Peace. Since then, we have all discussed and even agreed upon this proposal in principle, but we have not yet put it on paper. We must do so. We cannot let disagreements over the "theology" of building NATO-Russia relations get in the way of "here and now" opportunities to work together where our interests clearly overlap. Instead of letting theology dictate our practice, we should let our practice shape our theology.

One example of where the United States is already doing this is with our program of bilateral training exercises with Russia. We have held four such exercises in the last year, each a great success, and each conducted in a spirit of trust and good will. This summer, the United States and Russia will move beyond the bilateral and jointly participate in a major regional Partnership For Peace exercise with forces from Ukraine, Russia, United States and other regional powers.

Our bilateral contact program with Russia is not confined to joint exercises or even to just the security field. Through the Gore-Chernomyrdin Commission, it extends to the fields of science and technology, space, defense conversion, business development, the environment, health care and agriculture.

Just this past week the commission met in Washington, and Mr. Kokoshin and I both participated in the defense conversion program of this commission. I urge all NATO nations to build on this model. These contacts provide important exchanges of information. They help break down years of distrust and suspicion. They weave the Russians into the kind of personal and professional networks that have long characterized relations among all of the allies. These are the kind of activities that will build trust between Russia and NATO. And these are the kind of activities that will keep Russia on the passage toward integration with Europe, to pass through that open door.

Mr. [Russian Defense Minister Army Gen. Pavel] Grachev and I attended the joint U.S.-Russia exercise in Kansas last October. And we met after the exercise with the American and the Russian soldiers conducting that exercise, and talked to them. He told the Russian soldiers what they were doing was very important, that they should extend their friendship and cooperation with the American soldiers and that this was the basis for creating a peaceful world for their children. The American soldiers were as much interested in what he was saying as the Russians were, I can assure you.

Ironically, the place where a distinct NATO-Russia relationship is occurring in practice is in Bosnia. Today, as we speak, a Russian brigade is serving in the American Multinational Division of IFOR. It took an enormous amount of work to make this happen. Minister Grachev and I met four times over a two-month period to iron out the details. Gens. [Army Gen. George] Joulwan and [Army Maj. Gen. William] Nash work closely every day with their counterparts, Gen. [Col. Gen. Leontiy] Shevtsov and Col. [Alexandr] Lentsov. NATO and Russia do have a special relationship today in Bosnia, and Russia is demonstrating its commitment to participating in the future security architecture of Europe.

The reason we are all working so hard to make this relationship successful is not just because of the additional troops Russia brings to Bosnia, but because Russia's participation in Bosnia casts a very long shadow that will have an impact on the security of Europe for years to come. When we deal with the most important security problem which Europe has faced since the Cold War was over, we want to have Russia inside the circle working with us, not outside the circle throwing rocks at us.

Indeed, the more you think about what NATO and Russia are doing together in Bosnia, the more amazing it becomes. I can only imagine what Gen. [Dwight D.] Eisenhower, the first SACEUR [supreme allied commander Europe], would think if he saw a general from Russia sitting with Gen. Joulwan, today's SACEUR, at the SHAPE [Supreme Headquarters Allied Powers Europe] compound reviewing a secret NATO OPLAN [operational plan]. We need to build on this model, to institutionalize it and expand it to cover the entire range of NATO and Russia's overlapping security interests. By so doing, NATO and Russia can move forward as full partners in completing Marshall's vision.

Just as the NATO-Russia relationship is being forged in Bosnia, so too is the future of NATO itself. I was in Bosnia several weeks ago. I was struck by the dedication and professionalism of every unit from every country that is participating. I was also struck by the stark contrast between the devastation and suffering I saw in Sarajevo, and the rebirth and renewal I have seen in the other capitals of Central and Eastern Europe.

Bosnia is what happens when newly independent nations focus on old hatreds instead of new challenges. Four years ago, some people in the former Yugoslavia chose not to join Marshall's Europe. And the death and bloodshed that resulted will long echo in our memory. But today, the door to Marshall's Europe is open again for them—and holding that door open are NATO, Russia and the newly free peoples of Central and Eastern Europe.

The success or failure of IFOR is crucial to whether or not we will complete Marshall's vision. It is in Bosnia where we are sending the message that NATO is the bedrock on which the future security and stability of Europe will be built. It is in Bosnia where NATO is first reaping the benefits of joint peacekeeping training with our new peace partners. It is in Bosnia where future NATO members are showing themselves ready and able to shoulder the burdens of membership. And it is in Bosnia where we are showing that we can work as partners with Russian forces. Bosnia is not a peacekeeping exercise. It is the real thing.

Bosnia is also teaching us important lessons about the kind of NATO that Marshall's Europe will require. Ever since the end of the Cold War, NATO has struggled to develop a mechanism for executing the new missions using NATO assets with the voluntary participation of NATO members.

In the conference room, we have so far failed to come up with an agreement on a combined joint task force, CJTF. But in the field, we have cut through these theological arguments and put together IFOR, which is a CJTF. As with the NATO-Russia relationship, we need to take the practical lessons learned in putting IFOR together and extrapolate back until we have a CJTF that works.

Bosnia also casts in sharp relief something we have suspected for some time: that it is time for NATO to adapt itself internally to deal with the new challenges of this new era. NATO was not well structured for the Bosnia mission. At a time when our political and geostrategic thinking has been completely reoriented, symbolized by our partnership in peacekeeping with former adversaries, and at a time when our individual military forces have streamlined and modernized for the battlefield of the future, NATO's command and decision-making structure is still geared for the challenges and the battlefields of the past. The time has come to streamline and modernize NATO, recognizing that our challenge is no longer simply to execute a known plan with already designated forces, as it was during the Cold War.

We must make NATO's command structure more responsive and more flexible, and streamline the planning and force preparation process, and simplify and speed up the entire decision-making process. And we must complete the task of giving NATO's European members a stronger identity within the alliance. These kinds of internal changes will ready NATO for enlargement and will allow us to better respond to the future challenges to European security and stability.

"NATO's command and decision-making structure is still geared for the challenges and the battlefields of the past."

It is in this context that we welcome the French decision to participate more fully in NATO's military bodies. And we look forward to working with France as we transform the alliance and realize Marshall's vision of a Europe united in peace, freedom and democracy.

In 1947, Marshall told America that it must "face up to the responsibility which history has placed upon our country." Today, it is not only America, but also Russia; is not only NATO nations, but all of Europe—all of us must face up to the responsibility which history has placed upon us. This means reaching out to each other not only in the spirit of friendship, but also in the spirit of self-interest. This means working towards our goals not only from the top down, but also the ground up. And it means recognizing that when the outside world changes, we must look inside our institutions and see what changes are needed there.

If we do these things, then next year, when we commemorate the 50th anniversary of the Marshall Plan, we will be able to say that we made Marshall's vision our own; that Partnership for Peace is a strong, permanent pillar of Europe's security architecture; that NATO and Russia have a relationship where trust, understanding and cooperation are givens, not goals; that all the nations of the former Yugoslavia are adding, not detracting, from Europe's security; and that we have taken the passage to a new Europe and opened the door to a new era of peace, freedom and democracy.

Thank you very much.

U.S. Policy Toward Latin America and the Caribbean: Building Upon a Solid Foundation[2]

Jeffrey Davidow

*Assistant secretary of state for inter-American affairs, 1996– ;
born Boston, MA, 1944; B.A., University of Massachusetts, 1965;
M.A., University of Minnesota, 1967; political officer, Santiago,
Chile, 1974-76, Republic of South Africa, 1976-78; desk officer,
South African Affairs, 1978-79; head, U.S. Liaison Office,
American Embassy, Zimbabwe, 1982-83; fellow, Center for
International Affairs, Harvard University, 1983-85; director,
Office of Regional Affairs and Office of South African Affairs,
1985-86; deputy chief of mission, American Embassy, Venezuela,
1986-88; U.S. ambassador to Republic of Lusaka, 1988-90;
deputy assistant secretary for African affairs, 1990-93; author,*
Dealing with International Crises *(1983),* A Peace in Southern
Africa *(1984).*

Editors' introduction: In these remarks at the Miami
Conference on the Caribbean and Latin America, the assistant
secretary of state for inter-American affairs, Jeffrey Davidow,
examined U.S. policy toward Latin America and the Caribbean.
According to Davidow, America shares with Latin America and
the Caribbean a clear vision of the future, as well as a belief in
the strategy to achieve that vision. With the policy agenda of
this speech in place under the second Clinton Administration,
the United States pursues four basic objectives: 1) promoting
free trade and economic integration, 2) strengthening democracy and the rule of law, 3) encouraging sustainable development
and poverty alleviation programs, and 4) combating drug trafficking, migrant smuggling, and environmental degradation.

Jeffrey Davidow's speech: Over the past 20 years, this conference has helped define the direction of economic policies in the
hemisphere. It has made a major contribution to the intellectual
revolution which is transforming the region. So it is a particular
pleasure and honor for me to address this forum, and to use this
occasion to outline U.S. policy toward Latin America and the
Caribbean for the second Clinton Administration.

---

[2] Delivered at the Miami Conference on the Caribbean and Latin America, in
Miami, Florida, on December 9, 1996.

A Solid Foundation

As policymakers, we have the uncommon luxury today of building upon an unusually solid foundation. Freely elected and reformist governments are in place throughout the hemisphere. The region is stable and economies are growing. Per capita income has increased this decade by an annual average of about 1%, in contrast to its decline over the 1980's. Inflation continues to recede, with ECLAC projecting an average rate for this year somewhere in the low 20's, the lowest level in a quarter-century. Having been tested and found reliable, the region's commitment to market economics within a democratic framework is continuing to attract foreign and—more importantly over the long run—domestic investment.

Above all, we have a unity and clarity of vision that was both celebrated and made concrete by the 1994 Summit of the Americas in Miami. It's not just that we have an unprecedented hemispheric consensus on the broad goals of democracy, economic integration, protection of the environment, and combating poverty. What is most impressive is the depth of the commitment to those general goals not only by the hemisphere's governments, but also by private sector leaders and the public. The commitments we made in Miami have been a steadying force that has helped the region withstand the shocks and stresses of the past two years without backtracking on essential reforms.

And of course, the Summit vision is much more than a vision. We still have a long way to go in achieving all our goals. But there has been remarkable progress toward implementing the 23 initiatives of the Action Plan established by our leaders in Miami. Specific achievements include the world's first anti-corruption convention, agreements on cooperation to fight terrorism and to combat money laundering, establishment of a hemisphere-wide capital markets committee to liberalize and improve financial markets, as well as major initiatives underway for health and education, and to clean up and conserve the environment. I am happy to report that the Summit on Sustainable Development which just concluded in Santa Cruz, Bolivia, gave a strong additional impulse to work in these areas. Finally, we have made very substantial progress toward the Free Trade Area of the Americas, which I will address in a little more detail later.

A Continuing Commitment to Reform and Cooperation

As in the first Clinton Administration, three principal objectives will guide U.S. policy in the region:

- Strengthening democracy, the rule of law, and respect for human rights;

- Working cooperatively to address transnational problems–particularly combating the menace of the illegal drug trade, crime, migrant smuggling, and terrorism, as well as meeting new challenges such as environmental degradation; and finally

- An objective which is of great interest to you and to us, promoting economic integration through an open and fair trade policy and the building of a Free Trade Area of the Americas—FTAA.

Our action agenda within the second Clinton Administration will closely track these objectives. As to particular initiatives, it is clearly premature to get into specifics. However, I can share with you some of my general thinking about what we will need to accomplish.

If there is to be an overall theme to our efforts during the next four years, I would say it would be institutionalizing the reforms which are now underway. The past two years have shown that the reform process is not as fragile as some feared, but neither can we be confident that it is irreversible. There is a strong momentum for policy changes, but what is still under construction in most countries are the detailed regulations, enforcement practices, and efficient administration which make policies effective and responsive to people's needs.

I want to emphasize also that the Summit will continue to provide the framework on which we will build our action agenda. As you know, Chile will be hosting the next Summit of the Americas in early 1998. Building on the accomplishments achieved since the Miami Action Plan in December 1994, and on our experience in the intervening four years, we believe the Santiago Summit can focus on a limited number of new initiatives—perhaps a half-dozen or so—which will address three priority areas: democracy and human rights, poverty, and economic integration.

"The past two years have shown that the reform process is not as fragile as some feared, but neither can we be confident that it is irreversible."

An Action Agenda

Let me say just a few words about each of these areas.

First, the region has made truly remarkable progress in achieving peaceful resolution of disputes, strengthening democracy, and enhancing human rights. We must consolidate and further this progress.

In Guatemala, the support of the U.S., other international "friends," and the UN is helping the parties reach a final settlement to their 36-year civil war.

Between Peru and Ecuador, the U.S., Argentina, Brazil, and Chile are strongly supporting direct negotiations to find a just and lasting settlement to a border dispute which flared into open conflict less than two years ago.

In Haiti, the U.S.-led Operation Uphold Democracy directly restored a democratic government. We are also working in less dramatic ways to nurture new democratic institutions, to share our experience on the appropriate role of the military in a civil society, and to strengthen the administration of justice and rule of law.

On Cuba, we are committed to challenging peacefully the Cuban Government's 37-year reign of tyranny and denial of basic individual and political rights.

Another challenge, and probably the most difficult single issue which we must address, is the region's persistent poverty. A very large proportion of Latin America's people live in conditions that are highly unhealthy and with extremely limited opportunities—probably more than a third according to several recent estimates, which amounts to well over 150 million people.

Concerns about the sustainability of economic reforms in the face of widespread poverty and wide income disparities make poverty alleviation a key issue at the Santiago Summit. But addressing this issue is critical not only to sustain political support for reform, but also to build a modern economy, with a broad base of consumers and workers for growth.

"The alleviation of poverty requires a well-targeted and comprehensive strategy."

The alleviation of poverty requires a well-targeted and comprehensive strategy. Over the long run, the most powerful single weapon against poverty is education. "Education as investment" has been suggested as a key Summit theme by President Frei. I strongly agree.

This brings me to the third focus for our work over the next few years—making the FTAA a reality. There has already been very considerable movement toward that goal including: two successful ministerial meetings in Denver and Cartagena; the establishment of a private sector trade forum; and the formation of 11 working groups to collect and analyze data and develop recommendations for negotiating procedures in a wide variety of areas.

At the third ministerial this coming May in Belo Horizonte, I anticipate that the ministers will determine when and how to launch formal negotiations. We need a decisive beginning in Brazil; we need to answer the fundamental questions and define practical negotiating goals and procedures for the FTAA. If we don't answer these questions decisively by the time all the presidents reunite in March of 1998 in Santiago, then I think we can be accused of having failed—failed to meet the mandate given us by our leaders, and failed to meet the expectations of our publics.

I can assure you that President Clinton remains deeply committed to the creation of the FTAA by the year 2005. He is personally interested in the Summit process and is determined that the United States will continue to be an active player in building a peaceful, democratic, and prosperous hemisphere.

On the much-discussed issue of fast-track, again I can assure you that the President remains deeply committed to seeking a dialogue with our Congress and working in a bipartisan fashion to obtain this important authority promptly. I personally remain optimistic on this issue. I believe it is increasingly well understood that it is in our interest to negotiate strong and balanced trade agreements, whether through the FTAA, bilateral free trade agreements, or accession to NAFTA by Chile. When we have flexible and comprehensive negotiating authority, we are in a better position to exercise leadership in the international trading system.

Let me add also that this Administration recognizes the concern expressed by many Caribbean and Central American countries that they were put at a disadvantage with the passage of NAFTA. The Administration remains committed to the goal of enhancing trade benefits for the CBI region, and we will be working closely with the 105th Congress to achieve it.

Looking back on what I have just outlined as our action agenda in moving toward the next Summit, I must admit these are large and ambitious goals. They are also goals which are achievable only with the broadest cooperation, not only among governments, but also with the private sector—business, labor, academia, nongovenmental institutions, and concerned citizens everywhere. I am confident that this conference will contribute significantly to those cooperative efforts.

Conclusion

Let me conclude by noting that, in my view, U.S. policy toward Latin America today is unusually strong and resilient.

We share with Latin America and the Caribbean a clear vision of where we want to go. We have a common strategy to achieve that vision which is specific and comprehensive. And we have an ongoing dialogue among governments, and with the other key players of this hemisphere's societies, which ensures that our goals and our strategies reflect changing realities. I view today's meeting as an important part of that dialogue, and I wish this conference every success.

U.S. Policy Toward the Middle East: Steering a Steady Course[3]

Robert H. Pelletreau

Assistant U.S. secretary of state for Near Eastern Affairs, 1994– ; born Patchogue, NY, 1935; U.S. National Reserve, 1957-58; B.A., Yale University, 1957; LL.B., Harvard University, 1961; U.S. foreign service, 1962-78; ambassador to Bahrain, 1979-80, Tunisia, 1987-91, Egypt, 1991-93; deputy assistant secretary of defense, 1980-81, 1985-87; deputy assistant secretary of state, 1983-85.

Editors' introduction: In this address, Robert H. Pelletreau, Jr., the assistant secretary of state for Near Eastern Affairs, examined U.S. policy toward the Middle East as well as American diplomacy there, which, over the years, has worked to bridge the Arab-Israeli divide. Pelletreau also reevaluated America's interests in the Middle East, the challenge posed by extremist groups, and U.S. negotiations with Israel, Syria, and Lebanon.

Robert H. Pelletreau's speech: Ladies and Gentlemen, thank you for that warm welcome. When I arrived at this wonderful place last night, I noticed that my lecture was listed on this week's schedule between presentations by Professor Moshe Maoz of Hebrew University and my friend Abdullah Toukan, who is the personal adviser to King Hussein of Jordan. I think it is wholly appropriate for a lecture on U.S. policy toward the Middle East to be positioned between presentations by an Israeli and a Jordanian. American diplomacy over the years has worked hard to bridge the Arab-Israeli divide, at no time harder and more successfully than during the Clinton Administration. Today, at least part of that divide has been bridged: Israel and Jordan are at peace, as Israel and Egypt before them. The Palestinians and Israel have concluded several agreements on the way to working out the terms of their co-existence, and Syria and Israel have expressed interest in finding a common basis for negotiations. It is fair to say that the core of the Arab-Israeli agenda has moved on from how to make and avoid war to how to make peace and how to make peace bring economic and other benefits for those who have courageously reached agreements across the negotiating table.

Engaging U.S. Interests

Everyone in this audience is aware that we live in a time of rapid and fundamental change in world politics. The end of the Cold

---

[3] Delivered to the Chautauqua Institution, in Chautauqua, New York, on August 21, 1996.

War has challenged analysts, policymakers, and the American public to make sense of a fluid international situation. Halfway between the end of the Cold War and a new century, Americans are debating such basic questions as how to engage internationally to advance national goals, when to use force to protect our national interests, and how we can best support international institutions like the United Nations and the World Bank.

Finding our bearings in a complex world was not always as difficult as it is today. For more than 40 years, our foreign policy was governed by a single, overriding goal—to contain the Soviet Union's expansionist tendencies. It was never an easy task to contain a massive empire armed with nuclear weapons and the capacity to threaten our interests around the world. During the Cold War, flare-ups in tension regularly occurred, but at least our goals were clear to everyone. Building new security alliances and institutions, forging close ties with other nations, and providing foreign assistance all contributed to this clear purpose.

Today, most current and foreseeable threats to our interests from other nations do not jeopardize the actual survival of the United States. Other nations do not even jeopardize our prosperity except through improvements in their own international economic competitiveness. We have even embarked on a cloudy and still incomplete program of cooperation with our erstwhile Russian opponents. Yet, we as a nation are not comfortable with the current state of affairs, and we cannot afford to be complacent. Terrorism disrupts our tranquility both at home and abroad, and the proliferation of weapons of mass destruction has not been adequately checked. Ethnic conflicts rage on several continents. Global problems of daunting dimensions such as population growth, desertification, disappearance of the rain forests, and global warming are all growing.

"...we as a nation are not comfortable with the current state of affairs, and we cannot afford to be complacent."

When Americans look out over the world, they can take pride in the fact that more people live free and at peace than ever before. But is that enough? Can we be certain that positive trends will continue and negative ones will wither without our active leadership, engagement, and financial underpinning?

These are questions which are driving the restless search for a convincing new paradigm for U.S. foreign policy in this decade. At the beginning of the decade, we heard there was a "new world order" and that America had a free hand to lead the international community in turning back such lawless acts as Saddam Hussein's invasion of Kuwait. We were also told that the "end of history" was at hand, with democracy and the free market triumphing over communism and all other possible forms of human organization.

But then the paradigms took a pessimistic turn. There were lurid predictions of "coming anarchy" in a world where nation-states would collapse under the weight of overcrowded, ungovernable cities and roving bands of lawless thugs. Finally, we heard that we were teetering toward a "clash of civilizations," where traditional fault lines between peoples and cultures would widen and tear apart the fragile political and economic ties that bind the world's nations.

Each of these paradigms is by necessity oversimplified, and each contains important insights into the central question: What are our interests and how do we pursue them? But none so far has provided a convincing answer.

In the Middle East, I would argue, our interests are broadly engaged, no matter what paradigms we apply. Standing threats like aggression by rogue states such as Iraq against our allies and oil supplies loom large as ever. New threats represented by the terrorists who bombed U.S. troops in Saudi Arabia underline the need to maintain a strong and vigilant stance in the region.

Let me be more specific at interests in the Middle East. They include, first and foremost, achieving a just, comprehensive, secure, durable Arab-Israeli peace; helping maintain the security and well-being of Israel; preventing regional conflicts and supporting friendly nations; ensuring the free flow of oil from the Gulf upon which we and the other industrial nations depend for our economic security; enhancing business opportunities for our companies and jobs for our citizens; suppressing terrorism and the spread of weapons of mass destruction; containing rogue regimes in Iran, Iraq, and Libya; advancing respect for human rights, the rule of law and open, and participatory societies; and preserving the deep cultural ties we have to the origins of Western civilization and the birthplace of the great monotheistic religions—Judaism, Christianity, and Islam. All of these give our nation a concrete and lasting stake in the Middle East.

Many of these interests and objectives overlap, and sometimes they cross cut. The peace process, for example, profoundly influences the stability of the entire region. The work of every U.S. ambassador in the region is made easier if there is an active peace process with strong U.S. involvement. Progress in the peace process strengthens governments in Egypt, Jordan, and Saudi Arabia and others which are friendly to the U.S.; it helps isolate Iran and Iraq whose leaders are hostile; and it helps secure our access to Persian Gulf oil. The absence of progress in the peace process, on the other hand, increases tensions and spurs rearmament and violence, endangering our access to oil and undercutting Israeli security. These are only a few examples of the interconnectedness of developments in the Middle East. In general, a successful peace process enhances regional stability, removes a rallying point for fanaticism, and enhances prospects for political and economic development. With so many complex interests at stake, the United States cannot step back from this turbulent and difficult sector of the globe, however tempting it might be at times. Let me now sketch what the United States has been doing to promote Arab-Israeli peace and bring a more peaceful and secure life to the people of Israel and the

Palestinians, Syrians, Lebanese, Jordanians, and Egyptians who are their neighbors.

The Long Quest for Peace

The goal of peace between Israel and the Arab world has been a cornerstone of our Middle East policy since the Truman Administration. The Israel-Egypt peace brokered at Camp David by President Carter was a significant breakthrough. But after that, until the 1990s, progress toward this goal was limited. The climate for peacemaking was poor. Israel and the Arabs shared a profound animosity, suspicion, and sense of vulnerability. Both sides saw themselves as victims; neither side could contemplate compromise on the scale necessary for peace.

For decades, the Middle East was a tinderbox, threatening to embroil us in its deadly wars. This volatility was aggravated by Soviet efforts to gain influence through fueling radicalism and conflict. The Arab-Israeli conflict emboldened radicals, intimidated moderates, and left Israel—except for its friendship with the United States—in a lonely state of siege.

Throughout the long struggle, only one Arab state—Egypt, under the extraordinary leadership of Anwar Sadat—bravely bridged the Arab-Israeli divide to make peace with Israel. For 17½ years, that heroic achievement has held strong. Egypt stood nearly alone until 1993, when Israel and the Palestinians signed the Declaration of Principles on the White House lawn and the Arab world began to see that Egypt, its largest and most powerful member, was in reality a pathfinder rather than a pariah.

It was not until the Cold War began to wane that new opportunities arose to promote peace. The Gulf War was a watershed. With the United States and its coalition partners working together, Saddam Hussein's invasion of Kuwait and bid to become the dominant power in the Gulf were decisively turned back. Our overwhelming display of power, principle, and leadership during the Gulf War provided us with enhanced influence in the Middle East. It also tilted the regional balance of power toward moderate forces committed to peace and stability. We moved rigorously to seize the historic opportunity for peace in 1990 and 1991 because we know that, in the Middle East, such opportunities do not last very long.

The current peace process was launched in October 1991 in what we generally refer to as the Madrid Middle East peace conference, co-sponsored by the United States and the Soviet Union. As our ambassador to Egypt, I was a member of our delegation. It was a moving experience to see, for the first time in my professional career, Israel, the Palestinians, Jordan, Syria, Lebanon Egypt, the Europeans, Russia, and the United States together around one table, each saying in his own way, "Let's try to reach a peaceful settlement." The Madrid conference launched a series of bilateral and multilateral talks that proved useful in shattering taboos on political dialogue and helping each side to focus on the practical concerns of the other side. This architecture of mutually reinforcing bilateral and multilateral levels of negotiation has proven both resilient and productive, enabling us to overcome serious obstacles and make some remarkable progress.

Breakthrough in 1993

The first real breakthrough after the Madrid conference was the dramatic moment on the White House lawn in September 1993 when Chairman Arafat and Prime Minister Rabin reached out and shook hands following the signing of the Israel-PLO Declaration of Principles. With mutual recognition and a mechanism for resolving differences through negotiation and compromise, the Declaration marked a true turning point in the history of the Israeli and Palestinian communities.

In the nearly three years since the signing of the Declaration, Israel and the Palestinians have been engaged in almost continuous negotiations. These talks have resulted in three landmark agreements, including the comprehensive Interim Agreement signed in Washington last September. As a result of these agreements, Palestinians now govern themselves throughout Gaza and most cities of the West Bank. Israeli soldiers no longer face the burden of patroling those streets. Where once there was an *intifada*, Israeli and Palestinian security forces now cooperate to root out the terrorist infrastructure of Hamas and the Palestinian Islamic Jihad.

"The Palestinian National Council subsequently voted by an overwhelming margin to cancel the anti-Israeli portions of the PLO charter."

We have emphasized to the Palestinians that the success of this process will depend on the confidence they engender in their Israeli partners. In response to Hamas suicide bombings in Israel last February and March, Chairman Arafat, with strong U.S. encouragement, has taken serious and effective Steps against the Hamas infrastructure and has made important progress toward eliminating its terrorist capabilities. Cooperation between Palestinian and Israeli security services has improved. The United States has stressed to Arafat and other Palestinian leaders the need to keep up a comprehensive, sustained, and systematic approach to combating terrorism within the rule of law.

We have also stressed the importance of continuing to make progress on democracy and human rights. We were pleased to see that the Palestinians defied the Hamas call to boycott elections last January and gave Chairman Arafat and the Palestinian leadership a strong mandate to pursue peace. The Palestinian National Council subsequently voted by an overwhelming margin to cancel the anti-Israeli portions of the PLO charter.

These are no small achievements. They are tangible steps toward Arab-Israeli reconciliation and reflect the fundamental desire of the people of the region to secure what President Clinton has characterized as the "quiet miracle" of normal life.

For Israel, these agreements with the Palestinians have begun to lift the heavy moral and political burden of ruling a hostile foreign population. Israel's elder statesman, Abba Eban, has pointed out other benefits. They include a bustling economy with Pacific Rim potential, a GNP rating that would delight any major industrial power, and a wider breach than Israel has ever known in the Great Wall of Arab and Moslem hostility. There is also a series of commercial commitments that may still carry the area to an unexpected renewal of its vitality.

With the psychological barrier between Israel and the Palestinians breached, there is a new basis for expanding inter-action between Arabs and Israelis. In the past three years, Jordan has joined Egypt in signing a peace treaty with Israel. Over 100,000 Israelis have traveled to Jordan, and a large number of Jordanians have visited Israel. In many ways it has become a model peace, a warm peace with numerous sub-agreements being signed and joint exploration of areas of mutual benefit such as civil aviation and transport, trade and tourism, and development of water resources. Beyond Jordan, as many as eight Arab League members have made official visits to Israel, all but three Arab states have participated in some aspect of the peace process, and Israel has exchanged diplomatic offices with Morocco and Tunisia and opened commercial offices in Qatar and Oman.

The peace process has also acquired an increasingly important economic dimension called the economic summit process. It began in Casablanca in 1994 and moved forward in Amman last year, mobilizing private business to take advantage of new opportunities opened up by the peace process and encouraging business activities to cross newly opened borders and help con-solidate peace agreements. At this year's economic summit in Cairo, we expect to see major new commercial developments. Overall, the economic summit process brings together the public and private sectors of the Arab world and Israel, and representa-tives of large and small businesses from all over the world, in ways you would never have seen three years ago, but which now are beginning to seem almost routine.

The U.S. is working with the newly elected Netanyahu govern-ment to keep up the momentum of Israeli-Arab cooperation across a broad range of issues. Sustaining our momentum requires a viable peace process which offers Arab partners incen-tives for progress. We are, therefore, encouraged that the new Israeli Government has agreed to honor and abide by the agree-ments reached by its predecessors and has expressed its desire to continue the peace process and build on those agreements. It has recognized that important changes have taken place in the Middle East since the Likud was last in power—new agreements, the beginnings of new relationships with the Arab states, and a new prosperity for Israel which has resulted at least in part from these political developments. Prime Minister Netanyahu has shown in his visits to Cairo and Amman, his contacts with other Arab leaders, and the beginnings of renewed high-level and working-level contacts with the Palestinian Authority and first steps to ease the closure on the West Bank and Gaza that he understands this reality and does not want to see the dismantling of what has been accomplished. We have stressed to the new government the key importance of intensifying channels of communication with the Palestinians, and we have cautioned about the harmful effect that major new settlement activity could have on the negotiating process. We have also impressed on Palestinian leaders the need for maximum effort and vigilance to root out and prevent acts of terrorism and respond to Israel's deep-seated security concerns which played such a large role in the recent elections. This would accelerate the current gradual relaxation of the tight closure imposed on Gaza and the West Bank and put renewed focus on promoting Palestinian economic development which the United States strongly supports.

"You can't pursue peace in isolation, just as you can't deal with terrorism in isolation."

The Extremist Challenge

Progress on the peace process has not, of course, been free of controversy or pain. With each step forward, there has been a determined challenge from the enemies of peace. The Princeton historian Bernard Lewis, who has viewed regional developments against a 2,000-year continuum of rivalry and conflict, has remarked that:

> The real threat to peace…comes from those who see any peace as a betrayal and a surrender. They will continue to use every means to prevent a peaceful end to their various holy wars. The test of all the seekers of peace will be their ability to cope with these forces.

One of the messages we received from Prime Minister Netanyahu when he visited Washington last month was that he is going to take a very determined approach to terrorism while Israel pursues peace with its neighbors.

That approach is certainly an approach we can support, and it is consistent with our own long-standing efforts to rally an international consensus against terrorism, turn off foreign sources of funding for terrorists, and track down and punish the perpetrators of terror, including state sponsors. We recognize that peace and security are indivisible. Waging peace and fighting terrorism are opposite sides of the same coin: You can't pursue peace in isolation, just as you can't deal with terrorism in isolation. You have to do both at the same time.

That is how we approached the suicide bombings in Israel in February and March, as well as the crisis involving Israel and Lebanon in April. Both represented not only human tragedies but serious challenges to security and the peace process.

In both cases, the United States took the initiative to deal with the immediate human crisis, safeguard the peace process, and refocus attention on negotiations. Following the suicide bombings in Israel, President Clinton initiated the Sharm el-Sheikh summit, which brought together leaders from around the world to send a clear message that terrorism from any source must be confronted and beaten.

In the Lebanon crisis last spring, the understanding brokered by Secretary Christopher allowed people to return to their homes and will protect civilians on both sides of the Israel-Lebanon border.

The Secretary spent more than a week in the Middle East shuttling seven times between Damascus and Jerusalem to resolve the crisis. It was a grueling exercise. At one point, we had to trade in our Air Force 707 for a C-141 owing to crew rest requirements. At another, we had to enter Lebanon via land convoy across the Bekaa Valley when the air route was judged too dangerous.

Secretary Christopher's work in bringing the parties to closure was one of the finest diplomatic performances I have witnessed. The set of understandings he negotiated to help defuse the conflict between Israel and Hezbollah guerrilla forces improved in several ways upon the U.S.-brokered understandings of 1993. First, the understandings are now written to ensure the clarity and consistency of commitments. Second, the understandings called for a five-party monitoring group to review complaints about implementation of the understandings. The modalities governing the monitoring group were completed in a five-sided negotiation during Prime Minister Netanyahu's visit in July, and just last week, the group successfully dealt with its first complaint. The April understandings will help protect both Israeli and Lebanese civilians but are not meant to be a substitute for lasting peace agreements between Israel and Lebanon and Israel and Syria.

Israel, Syria, and Lebanon

When Prime Minister Netanyahu was here, he stated that he had been elected to pursue peace with security and not to promote a stalemate. And he emphasized to us he was prepared to work with the U.S. to try to achieve those goals. He and his Foreign Minister have since stated repeatedly that they are prepared to negotiate peace with Syria. The Syrian Government has told us privately and publicly that it, too, is interested in negotiations. The Lebanese Government has been somewhat more reserved in public, but we are convinced that Lebanon also seeks peace. Just how these two tracks, which are separate but, clearly linked, can be engaged productively is still being worked out.

We are encouraged by the recent public statements from Jerusalem and Damascus, but we are not under any illusion that achieving peace between Israel and Syria and Israel and Lebanon will be quick or easy. Their conflict has evolved over many years, and the resolution must evolve over time as well. We have long felt that peace between Israel and Syria is essential for closing the circle of peace and producing a comprehensive settlement. We are committed to working toward this goal. The effort must not be put on the shelf just because it is difficult.

Neither Israel nor the United States sees the current Israeli posture in southern Lebanon as a desirable or even acceptable long-term alternative to peace. Israel claims no land from Lebanon. Again, it is a question of security. We, for our part, support Lebanon's sovereignty, independence, and territorial integrity and look forward, as the Lebanese people do, to the day when Lebanon is free of all foreign forces and in charge of its own destiny. The United States stands ready, yes even determined, to facilitate dialogue and act as an honest broker whenever an opportunity for further peace negotiations arises. Let me close by saying that neither U.S. policy nor the U.S. posture has changed. We are actively working with the parties in the region to achieve our long-sought goal of a truly comprehensive and durable Middle East peace.

Ukraine at Five:
A Progress Report on U.S. Policy[4]

Strobe Talbott

Deputy secretary of state, 1994– ; born Dayton, OH, 1946; B.A., Yale University, 1968; M.Litt., Oxford University, 1971; U.S. department of correspondents, 1973-75; White House correspondent, 1975-77; diplomatic correspondent, 1977-84; chief, Washington bureau, 1984-89; author, Endgame *(1979),* The Russians and Reagan *(1984),* Deadly Gambits *(1985),* The Master of the Game *(1989).*

Editors' introduction: In the five years since the Ukraine achieved independence from the former Soviet Union, the country has been transformed, but there is much hard work still to be done. In this speech, Deputy Secretary of State Strobe Talbott discussed taxes and bureaucracy that must be cut in order for the Ukraine to fulfill its tremendous economic potential. He also promoted land reform and the legal foundation for a future market economy. The country does not face this challenge alone however, as President Clinton has urged the international community to secure $1.9 billion in cash commitments for Ukraine, and has gone beyond the mandates of Congress to provide the Ukraine with $330 million in trade and investment credits.

Strobe Talbot's speech: Thank you Jaroslav [Voiko], and thanks to The Washington Group for including me in your celebration.

To those of you who arrived today from other parts of the country for this weekend's conference, welcome to Washington. During the Cold War, this city used to be called the "capitol of the free world." Well, Washington still qualifies as exactly that. In fact, with the collapse of Soviet communism, with the disappearance of the U.S.S.R., and with the dissolution of the Warsaw Pact, the free world is a much bigger place than it was just a few years ago—and today the free world includes an independent, democratic Ukraine.

Over the past 3½ years, I've had six opportunities to visit that brave young democracy. It's good to be back on sovereign Ukrainian territory this evening. I'm grateful to the embassy for opening its doors to me and my colleagues from the Administration—John Deutch, the Director of Central Intelligence; Carlos Pasqual of the National Security Council; Melanne Verveer of the Office of the First Lady; Teras Bazyluk of

---

4 Delivered at the Washington Group 1996 Leadership Conference, in Washington, D.C., on October 11, 1996.

the Arms Control and Disarmament Agency; and Bill Taylor and Bruce Connuck of the State Department.

The President and the Secretary of State have asked me to convey two messages to all of you: First, they have asked me to extend their greetings and their thanks for all that everyone here has done both for Ukraine and for U.S.-Ukrainian relations; and second, they have asked me to review briefly, from the vantage point of the Clinton Administration, the past five years.

Everyone here tonight knows very well how far Ukraine has come in that short time. This room is filled with witnesses of Ukraine's transformation. Some of you were a part of the "Chain of Unity" that stretched from Kiev to Lviv on January 22, 1990. Some of you were in the Verkhovna Rada on August 24, 1991, the day when an honor guard brought in a giant blue and yellow flag and Ukraine declared its independence. Others here were in Kiev or Lviv or Kharkiv during the landmark presidential election in 1994, when Ukraine became the first New Independent State of the former Soviet Union to transfer power from one democratically elected government to another. Or you've been back for subsequent regional elections that have produced victories around the country for a new generation of leaders who have made the cities and towns they lead into hubs of reform and sources of new ideas. Or maybe you were there this past June, when Ukraine adopted a new constitution that has codified the country's commitment to democracy and equal rights for all its citizens.

"For more than seven decades of Soviet domination, the Ukrainian-American community kept alive the dream of an independent and democratic homeland."

Many of you—I'd guess most of you—have seen with your own eyes the industry and entrepreneurship of the Ukrainian people, which have spawned thousands of small businesses throughout the country. They now account for more than half of Ukraine's national income. You've seen the hospitals where there are now MRIs and other modern diagnostic equipment, and you've seen the maternity wards where there are now incubators for premature babies. You've seen the churches and synagogues that are once again filled with worshippers.

In fact, many of you have been more than just witnesses of all this—you've been benefactors and participants, and your contribution goes back a lot longer than five years. For more than seven decades of Soviet domination, the Ukrainian-American community kept alive the dream of an independent and democratic homeland. Your faith nurtured the spirit and the substance of independence until the dream finally came true in 1991. Since then, you have labored on behalf of Ukrainian democracy, Ukrainian rule of law, Ukrainian freedom of the press, Ukrainian medicine and science, the Ukrainian environment, and Ukrainian prosperity.

Many of you have worked hard to put the Ukrainian economy on the right track. It has been a monumental effort, and there were some scary moments along the way. Not too long ago, Ukraine was looking over the abyss of hyperinflation. Last month, inflation was running at only 2%—a huge and hopeful improvement. Also in September, Ukraine successfully launched its new currency, the hryvnia, which is already stronger than the kharbovanets, the provisional currency it replaced.

If Ukraine is to continue this progress—if it is to fulfill its tremendous economic potential—there is much hard work still to be done. That means cutting taxes and bureaucracy, promoting land reform, and building the legal foundation for a market economy.

But Ukraine does not face the challenge alone. The American people as a whole have followed the example of the Ukrainian-American community. We've all joined together in the great task of supporting a free Ukraine. President Clinton has led the way by calling on the international community to secure $1.9 billion in cash commitments for Ukraine in 1996. He has gone beyond the mandates of Congress to provide Ukraine with $330 million in bilateral grants and $860 million in trade and investment credits.

We're in Ukraine not just with our dollars, but with our know-how, our expertise, our own can-do bent for licking the toughest problems. We're on the ground making a difference for the better, working with real people. Americans are in Ukraine today training the next generation of entrepreneurs. And by the way, our exchange programs work both ways. Through the U.S. Information Agency and the Agency for International Development, nearly 8,000 Ukrainians have come to our country to share our ideas, to learn first-hand about our way of life and work.

By early next year, we will have helped Ukraine privatize virtually its entire small business sector and a significant share of its larger enterprises. We have already helped Ukraine build democracy by sponsoring town hall meetings, sending legal advisors and constitutional experts, and assisting Ukraine's growing independent media.

Let me also make special mention of America's effort—both public and private—to help Ukraine deal with one of the defining disasters of our time. Ten years ago, an obscure town on the Prypiat River became world-famous overnight. When Reactor Number Four at the Chernobyl nuclear power plant blew its top, it was more than an isolated accident; it marked the beginning of the meltdown of the Soviet Union. But Chernobyl also left Ukraine with a health crisis that will last a generation—and it left the world with an obligation to ensure that such a tragedy never happens again. Through the work of numerous volunteer groups—many of whom are represented in this audience—there has been an outpouring of support for the victims, especially the children of Chernobyl.

A number of you were present at the White House when Vice President Gore and the First Lady commemorated the anniversary of the disaster—not just by looking backward at the horror, but by looking forward with hope and resolve. In this spirit, the United States has delivered over 100 tons of medical supplies to hospitals in Ukraine and Belarus. We have also used our leadership position in the Group of Seven major industrialized democracies to make available $3 billion to support Ukraine's decision to close Chernobyl by the year 2000.

Let me assert a key point: Everything we've done for Ukraine—and everything we will do in the future—we do not just because we Americans are a generous people, although that is certainly the case. We've done it and we'll keep on doing it also because it is in our own nation's interest to see an independent, secure, democratic Ukraine survive, succeed, and prosper.

Let me explain why that is by echoing our President. I was with him—as was Marta—on a lovely spring day in May 1995, when he spoke to an audience of enthusiastic, welcoming students in front of the main building at Shevchenko University in Kiev. President Clinton told that young audience that support for Ukraine's young democracy reflects our most deeply held American values and advances our most fundamental interests. He said a Ukraine that fulfills the hopes of its 52 million citizens will also, as he put it, "provide an essential anchor of stability and freedom in a part of the world still reeling from rapid change."

"Ukraine was the first New Independent State to join the Partnership for Peace program in February 1994."

We've said over and over—and we mean it every time we say it—that Ukraine is a key European country. It is a bellwether for a vast region that matters deeply and enduringly to the United States. If Ukraine stays on course toward a better future for its own people, that will be good for all of Europe and for the larger transatlantic community of which we are a part. If, however, Ukraine goes off course, that will be bad for all of us. The rationale for a steadfast policy of American support for Ukraine is just that simple.

The fact is, while Ukraine still faces numerous challenges, it has already emerged as a force for stability and integration in Europe. It has done so through its courageous decision in 1994 to join the Non-Proliferation Treaty as a non-nuclear-weapons state. In exchange for assurances worked out with the help of the United States, Ukraine enhanced its own security, and it set a valuable example for the rest of the world. As a result of that landmark of Ukrainian wisdom, the whole world is safer today, and it will be safer still in the next century.

Ukraine has shown similar statesmanship and strategic foresight by forging strong new ties with the west while maintaining constructive relations with its neighbors to the east and to the north. Ukraine was the first New Independent State to join the Partnership for Peace program in February 1994. This past summer, American, Ukrainian, Russian, and Polish troops trained together for peacekeeping operations on Ukrainian soil.

That training is already paying off. Today, American and Ukrainian soldiers are together in Bosnia, working side by side to deal with the first major threat to the peace in Europe since the end of the Cold War. And a Ukrainian-Polish peacekeeping battalion is taking shape.

Ukraine has also managed its complex relationship with Russia with prudence and balance, working hard to defuse problems before they become crises. From time to time, when both parties have asked us to do so, the United States has helped, and it stands ready to do so again in the future.

We in the U.S. Government fully understand the difficulty that often attends the right decisions. Therefore, we will use every occasion, including this one, to reaffirm our determination to ensure that there is a proud and prominent place for Ukraine in the growing community of market democracies—and in the institutions that undergird our common values, our common interests, and our common aspirations.

My boss, Secretary Christopher, recently delivered a major speech on European security in Stuttgart. He laid out the President's strategic vision for a Europe that is increasingly stable, secure, prosperous, and democratic—a Europe that will be undivided for the first time in history. Let me quote just one part of what Secretary Christopher had to say about Ukraine in that speech. "A critical goal of the New Atlantic Community," he said, "is to achieve Ukraine's integration with Europe."

That statement will serve as a guiding principle for the United States in the months and years ahead. It means that we will support Ukraine's active participation in the Council of Europe and in the Organization on Security and Cooperation in Europe, the OSCE. It means that we will continue to assist Ukraine in its effort to join the World Trade Organization, and that we endorse Ukraine's interest in the Central European Free Trade Area, the European Union, and the Organization for Economic Cooperation and Development, which is the international forum for monitoring economic trends in free market democracies.

That same guiding principle—that same commitment to Ukraine's integration into the community of nations—will also dictate our leadership of the North Atlantic Treaty Organization. NATO is, and will remain, essential to the evolution of a new, post-Cold War Europe.

A solid, cooperative relationship between NATO and Ukraine is vital to European security. As you all know, NATO is preparing to take in new members. There will be concrete steps in that direction next year. We are determined that the process of NATO enlargement serve the larger cause of peace, security, prosperity, democratization, and integration on the continent of Europe.

This is more than just a matter of asserting a negative: it is more than being determined that NATO enlargement not create new dividing lines or harm the legitimate security interests of any of the new democracies emerging from the old Soviet empire. It is also a matter of asserting a positive proposition—that NATO must respect and enhance the security of the region as a whole and the security of all European states that deserve and aspire to integration. That emphatically includes Ukraine.

As a vigorous, pathbreaking participant in the Partnership for

Peace, Ukraine is already cooperating closely with NATO. We've laid the basis for a steadily developing relationship of cooperation and consultation. There is nothing to limit how that enhanced relationship might develop over time.

Let me underscore here two simple statements of fact—and of principle: First, Ukraine and only Ukraine will decide what associations or memberships it aspires to in the future; and second, NATO and only NATO will decide whom to admit to its ranks.

The watchwords of NATO enlargement bear repeating here: the process will continue to be deliberate; it will be transparent; it will be open; it will be inclusive; it will be respectful. "Inclusive" means that none of the emerging democracies is to be excluded. None means none. It means there will be no special categories for inclusion into NATO, and none for exclusion from NATO. "Respectful" means that the rights and interests of all those states will be taken fully and properly into account in the way that enlargement occurs. Both those principles apply to Ukraine.

"...our own democracy has been a work in progress for 220 years."

How we apply those principles is one of the most important items on the ever-growing agenda of U.S.-Ukrainian cooperation and consultation. No subject has occupied more attention than European security in the dealings that Secretary Christopher and I have had with our friend Foreign Minister Hennadiy Udovenko, or in the talks that Tony Lake and I recently had with Volodymyr Horbulyn, the very able Secretary of the National Security and Defense Council. By the way, Foreign Minister Udovenko will be here again in just over a week for meetings with Secretary Christopher, Secretary Perry, and National Security Advisor Tony Lake.

The subject of Ukraine's important role in the building of a new Europe will also figure, along with a wide array of other topics, in a new channel that is opening between Washington and Kiev: the U.S.-Ukraine Binational Commission, to be headed by President Kuchma and Vice President Gore.

I do not want to impose on your kind attention much longer. Nor do I want to delay the next stage of the embassy's hospitality. I just want to make one final point.

All of us in the Clinton Administration—starting with the President and Vice President themselves—are optimistic about Ukraine's future, and I sense you are too. One reason for our optimism is that Ukraine has come so far in such a short period of time.

The United States' own historical experience should make us Americans patient, persistent, and admiring when we look at Ukraine. After all, our own democracy has been a work in progress for 220 years. We must remember how long it has taken us to get it right. In fact, we're still working at it. The United States became a "new independent state" in 1776. When we celebrated the fifth anniversary of our own independence in 1781, we still had a very long way to go. It would take us another six years to draft a constitution. Independent, democratic Ukraine accomplished that task before it turned five. In our own evolution as a civil society and a multiethnic democracy, it took us 89 years to abolish slavery, 144 to give women the vote, and 188 to extend full constitutional protections to all citizens.

All of which is to say that, even by the accelerated, fast-forward standards of the modern world, Ukraine at the tender age of five has much of which to be proud, much to make it confident about the future, and much that we Americans can be proud to support, to applaud, and to join in celebrating—for Ukraine's sake, and for our own. So happy birthday, Ukraine. *Mnohaya Lita, Ukraino.*

The U.S. and China: Building a New Era of Cooperation for a New Century[5]

Warren Christopher

Partner, 1958-93, 1997– , O'Melveny & Myers; born Scranton, ND, 1925; B.S., University of Southern California, 1945; U.S. National Reserves, 1943-46; LL.B., Stanford, 1949; law clerk for Supreme Court Justice William O. Douglas, 1949-50; lawyer, private practice, 1950– ; deputy attorney general, 1967-69; deputy U.S. secretary of state, 1977-81, U.S. secretary of state, 1993-97.

Editors' introduction: Now more than ever, America and China have a shared interest in confronting threats, such as terrorism, drug trafficking, disease, and environmental destruction. In an address at Fudan University, Shanghai, China, former secretary of state Warren Christopher discussed the challenge facing America and China. Both countries have a huge stake in building an open global trading system for the 21st century, as the two countries account for almost one-third of all global trade and output. In this speech, Christopher also examined the ability of China and America to advance other global and regional goals.

Warren Christopher's speech: Good morning. President Yang, thank you very much for that nice introduction. Vice Mayor Zhao, honored guests: I am delighted to be here today. It really gives me great pleasure to be at this center which has played such a valuable role in promoting the study of American history, culture, and foreign policy. I am honored to meet with the scholars and students of Fudan University, one of China's most distinguished institutions of intellectual achievement. Here in this city where East and West have long met and mixed, you are helping to shape a modern China with growing links to the wider world.

On behalf of President Clinton, I have come to this great city to speak to you about the challenges now facing our two nations. My message is clear: Now more than ever before, the American and Chinese peoples can and must work together to advance our interests. Like all great nations, we will no doubt at times have divergent views. But history has given our two countries a remarkable opportunity—the opportunity to build a new era of cooperation for a new century. It is an opportunity which we simply must seize.

---

[5] Delivered at Fudan University, in Shanghai, China, on November 21, 1996.

The shape of the world is changing almost as dramatically as this city's skyline. Today, the Cold War is over, the risk of global nuclear conflict has been greatly reduced, and the free flow of goods and ideas is bringing to life the concept of a global village. But just as all nations can benefit from the promise of this new world, no nation is immune to its perils. We all have a great stake in building peace and prosperity and in confronting threats that respect no borders—threats such as terrorism and drug trafficking, disease, and environmental destruction.

To meet these challenges most effectively, China and the United States must act together—must act in concert. Some have argued that with the Cold War's end, the strategic importance of the United States-China relationship has somehow diminished. I believe they have it exactly backwards. As a new century begins, the importance of strengthening the ties between the United States and China will grow even stronger.

Last May, I proposed that we deepen our cooperation by developing a more regular dialogue, including meetings at the highest level. During the last few months, contact between our government officials has intensified across a broad range of issues—a healthy sign of maturing relations. Yesterday in Beijing, I had the opportunity to meet with President Jiang Zemin; Premier Li Peng; and my counterpart, Vice Premier Qian Qichen. And just three days from now, President Clinton and President Jiang will meet at the APEC Leaders' Meeting in the Philippines.

These meetings have one overriding purpose: to reach new understandings that will bring concrete benefits to the citizens of both countries and the citizens of the world. The United States is convinced that by expanding our cooperation at every level—global, regional, and bilateral—we will advance our shared interests. Let me outline briefly why.

First, I want to talk about the need for the United States and China to work together on the international stage in dealing with global events. Our great nations share a weighty, heavy responsibility: As nuclear powers, as permanent members of the UN Security Council, and as two of the world's biggest economies, we simply must lead. We have a common stake in building and upholding an international system that promotes peace and security and prosperity around the globe.

Nowhere has cooperation been more crucial than in our efforts to halt the spread of weapons of mass destruction. The last few years demonstrate just how much the U.S. and China can accomplish when we work together. Together, we helped ensure the indefinite and unconditional extension of the nuclear Non-Proliferation Treaty and together helped achieve one of the landmarks of this current period, namely the conclusion of the Comprehensive Test Ban Treaty. These two giant steps have made our citizens safer. Americans and Chinese will be even more secure if we can redouble our efforts to end the production of fissile material for nuclear bombs, if we can work together to

"Some have argued that with the Cold War's end, the strategic importance of the United States-China relationship has somehow diminished."

join the global convention to ban chemical weapons and to strengthen the ability of the international community to detect and stop illicit nuclear programs.

While the United States and China have worked side by side to reach important understandings on nonproliferation, much remains to be done. Indeed, in my meetings yesterday in Beijing we advanced our work together toward this goal. The new regular dialogue that we will have between officials from the United States and China on non-proliferation and arms control issues will facilitate further progress. We have a shared interest in preventing the introduction of sensitive technologies into volatile regions such as South Asia and the Persian Gulf. Let me be particularly clear on one point: Countries such as Iran that sponsor terror and work against peace cannot be trusted to respect international norms or safeguards. Their attempts to acquire nuclear and chemical weapons and missile technology threaten the interests of both of our countries and, indeed, of all their neighbors. We must work together to stop them.

Both of our countries will also benefit from an effective global coalition against terrorists, international criminals, and drug traffickers. In his speech at the UN last September, President Clinton called on all nations to deny sanctuary to those global predators in the narcotics and terrorism field and to ratify the conventions that prevent and punish terrorism. In addition, China and the United States should forge strong ties between our law enforcement officials to fight common foes such as the drug lords in Burma whose traffic in heroin threatens citizens from Shanghai to San Francisco.

China and the United States have an immense stake in building an open global trading system for the 21st century. Together, our two nations account for almost one-third of the global trade and output. For both of our nations, exports are increasingly important to our economic growth. We can both profit by joining to establish and uphold rules that will open markets and will make trade fairer than it is now.

The United States actively supports China's entry into the World Trade Organization—WTO—on commercially meaningful terms. We welcome China's commitment not to introduce new laws or policies that would be inconsistent with its WTO obligations. We are prepared to negotiate intensively to achieve a WTO accession package on the basis of effective market access commitments by China and adherence to WTO rules.

Our economic growth and well-being are also dependent upon responsibly managing our natural resources. For the United States and China, choosing between economic growth and environmental protection is what President Clinton has called "a false choice, an unnecessary choice." Both are vitally important and both are mutually reinforcing.

Our nations must demonstrate global leadership on these critical environmental challenges; perhaps the most dangerous cur-

rent one is climate change. The United States and China are leading producers of greenhouse gases. These gases threaten to raise
disease levels, damage our crop production, and spread deadly
disease. As two nations at different stages of development, we
will shoulder our responsibilities in somewhat different ways,
but we should agree to act together and to act now—globally,
regionally, and bilaterally. That is why we are jointly promoting
renewable energy sources and energy efficiency. Most important
for the long term—and especially to great cities such as
Shanghai—we are exploring new energy technologies that are
less harmful to the world's atmosphere. On a wide range of environmental issues—saving fisheries, controlling toxic chemicals,
preserving forests—our two countries have recently expanded
our environmental dialogue. We do this to spur progress through
the Sustainable Development Forum which is led by Vice
President Gore and Premier Li Peng.

*"...the United
States will remain
a Pacific power in
the next century
no less than in
the last century."*

Let me now turn to the second broad area for cooperation
between the United States and China, namely, the important
regional interests that we share as great Pacific nations.

Across an ocean where terrible conflicts have given way now
to more peaceful relations between nations, today's hard-earned
security and prosperity depend upon maintaining and strengthening stability in this region. We have had significant successes.
We have joined together to ensure a non-nuclear Korean
Peninsula—and we are working with China to push forward
four-party talks to try to ensure permanent peace on the Korean
Peninsula. In Southeast Asia, our two countries have worked
together with the United Nations to promote peace and reconciliation in Cambodia.

Throughout the Asia-Pacific region, America's continuing military presence makes a vital contribution to stability. Some in
your country have suggested that our presence here in the Asia-
Pacific region is designed to contain China. They are simply
wrong about that. We believe that our security presence
advances the interests not only of the United States, but of China
and all the countries of the region. For this reason, the United
States will remain a Pacific power in the next century no less
than in the last century. In the wake of the Cold War, the United
States has taken steps to reinvigorate our relationships across the
Pacific. We believe that our five alliances in this region reinforce
peace and benefit all nations—including China. So do broader
contacts between the militaries of the United States and China.
My nation looks forward to increased exchanges between our
armed services, regular defense minister meetings such as the
one that will take place between Minister Chi and my colleague
Secretary Perry next month, and more port calls such as the one
paid by the *USS Fort McHenry to* Shanghai last February. The
United States and China also will gain from the success of new
regional security dialogues such as the ASEAN Regional Forum.
These dialogues encourage meaningful talks, they defuse ten-

sion, and they promote confidence-building measures.

The United States also is committed to working with China to promote regional economic growth and prosperity. When the original 12 members of APEC met in Canberra in 1989, they recognized that the best way to sustain Asia's dynamism was to ensure that the economies of the APEC countries would grow together. And now today's APEC members conduct almost 70% of their trade with each other. This week in the Philippines, the United States, China, and all the other APEC economies will set out plans that will lead to the elimination of all barriers to trade and investment in this region by the year 2020. We also will work on plans for economic and environmental cooperation throughout the region. China and the United States, as APEC's two largest members, have a special responsibility to turn these plans into forthright action.

Our ability to advance these regional and global goals ultimately rests on a strong U.S.-Chinese bilateral relationship—and that is the third matter that I want to touch on briefly today.

Here in Shanghai almost 25 years ago, the People's Republic of China and the United States of America—nations too long separated by mistrust and suspicion—took a historic step. We agreed to advance common strategic goals and broaden ties between our people. Since then, relations between our nations have been guided by the set of principles set out in the Shanghai Communique and the two communiques that followed in 1978 and 1982.

As I have said many times, the United States is firmly committed to expanding our relationship within the context of our "one China" policy as embodied in these three communiques. We believe that the P.R.C. and Taiwan must act to resolve their differences between themselves. At the same time, we have a strong interest in the peaceful resolution of the issues between Taipei and Beijing. We believe that the P.R.C. and Taiwan share that interest in a peaceful resolution of these issues. We have emphasized to both Taipei and Beijing the importance of avoiding provocative actions or unilateral measures that would alter the status quo or pose a threat to peaceful resolution of the outstanding issues. We are encouraged that both sides have taken steps to reduce tensions in the Taiwan Strait. We hope that the P.R.C. and Taiwan will soon resume a cross-Strait dialogue that can help build trust and settle differences.

Both China and the United States also have vital interests in a smooth and successful transition of Hong Kong from Britain to China. More than 40,000 U.S. citizens call Hong Kong home, and American investments total more than $13 billion in Hong Kong. We have welcomed China's pledge to maintain Hong Kong's unique autonomy, to allow its open economy to flourish, and to respect its traditions of law and individual freedoms. These guarantees are crucial to Hong Kong's continued dynamism—and to the prosperity of China as a whole. As that vital date approaches—as July 1, 1997 approaches—the world will look on with great interest and watch as China, we all hope, will respect its commitments to Hong Kong and to these important principles that will guide Hong Kong in the future.

China and the U.S. also stand to gain from the sustained economic growth that brings prosperity to every province of your nation. For two decades now, America's actions have reflected our deep interest in the success of China's efforts to lift the living standards of its people. The United States has supported multilateral assistance to help China meet basic human needs. American foundations have helped China promote education and health. And American universities have helped educate almost 200,000 Chinese students—some of whom, I'm sure, are here in the audience today.

Here in Shanghai, the economic benefits of our relationship are readily apparent. About 2,000 American companies have contracted to invest almost $4 billion in this city alone, more than anywhere else in China. From aerospace and computers to capital markets and life insurance, our businesses and workers are turning Shanghai into an engine of growth and innovation not just for China and the United States but for the world as a whole.

"...American universities have helped educate almost 200,000 Chinese students..."

These economic links have already made America your largest export market and China one of our most important customers. Now we can expand those links by cooperating to meet future needs in agriculture, energy, and infrastructure—areas where American know-how is unrivaled. We must work together to widen market access in China and open new opportunities for consumers and workers. We must consolidate the gains that we have already made, by strengthening the protection of intellectual property. Economic piracy poses a threat not just to American businesses but to China's software, film, and music industries as well. By upholding its commitments to protect intellectual property, China will enhance its ability to attract foreign investment in the future.

Our work in these and other areas is bringing together our business representatives, scientists, legal experts, and scholars—in person and on the Internet. Last year, more than 400,000 Americans came to China. Speaking of Americans in China, I am very pleased and proud to have with me today Ambassador James Sasser and his wife, Mary. Ambassador Sasser was a leading U.S. senator for 18 years, a member of the President's party, and now is our ambassador to China. Please join me in giving a hand to Ambassador Sasser. The flow of visitors has grown in both directions, and last year more than 160,000 Chinese visited the United States. From the Chinese officials who visit America's small towns to the Hollywood producers who flock to the Shanghai Film Festival, we are building a human bridge across the Pacific, enriching our countries and cultures with new ideas and new products. Strengthening these links will deepen our understanding and our trust and will enable our ties of friendship to grow even stronger.

In all the areas that I have discussed today—global, regional, and bilateral—one lesson stands out: Containment and confrontation will hurt both of our nations; cooperation and dialogue on the other hand will best advance our mutual interests. It is that spirit of cooperation and commitment that infuses my country's approach to our relationship. Cooperation, of course, is a two-way street: If we are to produce concrete results, China must also do its part.

The United States and China will continue to face profound differences, some rooted in history, others in tradition and circumstance. During my meetings yesterday in Beijing, we discussed our disagreements quite openly and quite candidly. We have a responsibility to ourselves and to the world to manage those differences constructively and to approach them in ways that do not undermine our ability to achieve our important common goals.

In recent years, our nations have had divergent views about democracy and the freedoms enshrined in the Universal Declaration of Human Rights. The United States tries to live up to these principles by fighting injustice at home and speaking up for all those who are persecuted for seeking to exercise universal rights-wherever they may live. While we recognize that each nation must find its own path consistent with its own history, we believe that these ideals of the Universal Declaration reflect the values not just of the United States but of countries and cultures all over the world.

Americans promote individual freedoms and the rule of law not only because they reflect our ideals but because we believe they advance our common interest in security and prosperity. History shows that nations with accountable governments and open societies make better neighbors. Nations that respect the rule of law and encourage the free flow of information provide a stable, predictable, and efficient climate for investment. Those that give their people a greater stake in their future are more likely to enjoy economic growth over the long term. China's recent efforts to invest authority in its people through legal and administrative reforms and village elections are a positive step in that direction.

For more than two centuries, Americans and Chinese have reached out to each other across a wide geographic and cultural divide. Many of my country's finest entrepreneurs, architects, scientists, and artists have come from your shores to shape our society and drive our economy. At times, the results have been nothing short of brilliant. Americans, in turn, have made contributions to China, whether building factories that provide jobs or bringing ideas that open new opportunities. Yet too often in our history, distance and difference have blinded us to our common hopes and interests, creating distorted images of each other that drive us apart.

Each of us still has much to learn. But technology has shrunk the miles between us and given us new insight into one another's lives. We know each other better now than ever before. In a world where barriers are falling and borders are blurring, our nations are united by increasingly shared opportunities and challenges.

The United States strongly supports China's development as a secure, open, and successful nation. We welcome its emergence as a strong and responsible member of the international community. Now, on the brink of a new century, our nations have a chance to establish a broad and durable set of ties for the new era.

As we meet together in this city "above the ocean" that links our great lands, let us rededicate ourselves to advancing shared goals. If we unite ourselves in common purpose, we can create a new era of promise. History has given us this priceless opportunity, and we must and will meet the challenge.

Cumulative Speaker Index:
1990-1997

A cumulative speaker index to the volumes of *Representative American Speeches* for the years 1937-1938 through 1959-1960 appears in the 1959-1960 volume; for the years 1960-1961 through 1969-1970, see the 1969-1970 volume; for the years 1970-1971 through 1979-1980, see the 1979-1980 volume; and for the years 1980-1981 through 1989-1990, see the 1989-1990 volume.

Abbas, Mahmoud, 1993-94, 100-110, Building Peace in the Middle East
Albright, Madeleine, 1995-96, 66-69, The United Nations at Fifty
Alexander, Jane, 1994-95, 143-149, The Arts and Education; 1996-97, 89-93, Identity through Art
Allen, Robert E., 1995-96, 157-165, Information Unbound
Anastaplo, George, 1996-97, 126-136, "Private" Gambling and Public Morality
Arafat, Yasir, 1993-94, 108-109, Building Peace in the Middle East
Archambault, David, 1992-93, 71-79 Whither the American Indian: Columbus Plus 500 Years?
Babbitt, Bruce, 1995-96, 70-79, To Protect the *Whole* of Creation
Barnes, M. Craig, 1996-97, 62-66, Choosing Good Government
Barone, Jeanne Tessier, 1996-97, 23-31, The Sky's No Limit at All
Beard, Daniel P., 1995-96, 63-66, The Myth About Public Servants
Bickel, K. R., 1991-92, 140-146, Forgive Mankind's Atrocities
Billington, J. H., 1991-92, 9-20, The Rebirth of Russia; 1993-94, 168-174, Preparing for Our Greatest Challenge
Black, Cathleen, 1995-96, 124-131, Observations and Opportunities in the 90's
Bok, Derek, 1991-92, 106-116, The Social Responsibilities of American Universities
Bradley, W. W. (Bill), 1991-92, 127-139, Race and the American City; 1993-94, 27-38, An Economic Security Platform
Branch, Taylor, 1992-93, 55-65, Democracy in an Age of Denial
Brindley, Amy Jo, 1995-96, 182-184, The Values of Unions
Burns, Kenneth Lauren, 1996-97, 94-99, Worth Defending
Bush, Barbara, 1990-91, 161-188, Choices and Change
Bush, George H. W., 1990-91, 37-43, Operation Desert Storm, 43-48, The War Is Over: A Framework for Peace; 1991-92, 91-98, America 2000: An Education Strategy; 1992-93, 15-24, Farewell Address: American Intervention
Byrd, Robert C., 1995-96, 31-41, Civility in the United States Senate
Cheney, L. V., 1991-92, 116-126, Political Correctness and Beyond
Chenoweth, Helen, 1995-96, 79-90, Preserving the Environment and Liberty
Christopher, Warren, 1992-93, 44-54, American Foreign Policy in a New Age; 196-97, 166-173, The U.S. and China: Building a New Era of Cooperation for a New Century
Church, F. Forrester, IV, 1992-93, 65-70, Shall We Overcome?; 1994-95, 71-78, Fear and Terror, 156-163, An American Creed
Clinton, Hillary Rodham, 1993-94, 48-62, Improving Health Care; 1995-96, 131-137, When Communities Flourish; 1996-97, 17-22, Our Global Family
Clinton, William J., 1991-92, 49-60, The New Covenant: Responsibility and Rebuilding the American Community; 1992-93, 9-14, Inaugural Address, 24-35,

State of the Union Address; 1993-94, 9-26, State of the Union Address, 100-110, Building Peace in the Middle East; 1994-95, 9-30, State of the Union; 1995-96, 42-57, A Government That Helps People Help Themselves, 107-120, Tearing at the Heart of America, 107-119; 1996-97, 32-41, Remarks to the American Legion Boys and Girls Nation, 43-47, Dedication of the Mt. Zion African Methodist Episcopal Church, 111-115, Second Inaugural Address

Cole, Johnnetta B., 1996-97, 83-88, A House Divided

Colson, C. W., 1991-92, 21-36, The Problem of Ethics; 1993-94, 63-72, The Enduring Revolution

Cuomo, Mario M., 1994-95, 50-65, A Farewell to Public Office

D'Alemberte, Talbot, 1991-92, 79-90, Civil Justice Reform

Danforth, John, 1992-93, 18-23, The Meaning of the Holocaust to Christians

Davidow, Jeffrey, 1996-97, 145-149, U.S. Policy Toward Latin America and the Caribbean: Building Upon a Solid Foundation

Dinkins, D. N., 1990-91, 129-143, In Praise of Cities

Dole, Robert, 1995-96, 152-157, Hollywood Violence

Edelman, M. W., 1990-91, 151-161, The Lessons of Life

Edwards, E. W., 1991-92, 60-70, Inaugural Address

Eitzen, D. S., 1991-92, 91-97, National Security: Children, Crime, and Cities; 1994-95, 78-87, Violent Crime: Myths, Facts, and Solutions

Ford, G. R., 1990-91, 184-196, Dwight D. Eisenhower: A Remembrance and Rededication

Frohnmayer, J. E., 1990-91, 143-150, Community and the Arts; 1991-92, 147-157, Free Expression and Human Rights

Geiger, K. B., 1991-92, 98-106, A Bill of Rights for Children

Gerbner, George, 1991-92, 169-181, Instant History in the Persian Gulf: Like Going to a Movie

Gerety, Tom, 1992-93, 98-102, Saving Our Cities

Gingrich, Newton L., 1994-95, 30-40, A Contract with America

Goizueta, Roberto C., 1995-96, 11-15, Remarks at Monticello

Gore, Albert, Jr., 1993-94, 82-87, Days of Remembrance

Gould, William B., IV, 1994-95, 111-120, Lincoln, Labor, and the Black Military

Grams, Rod, 1995-96, 57-63, Promises Kept: Controlling Government

Gronbeck, Bruce E., 1994-95, 95-110, Electric Rhetoric: The Transformation of American Political Talk

Hackney, Sheldon, 1993-94, 140-147, Beyond the Cultural Wars

Haiman, F. S., 1990-91, 93-105, Majorities versus the First Amendment

Hammer, Marion P., 1995-96, 188-193, Eddie Eagle Gun Safety Program

Heffner, Richard D., 1995-96, 24-31, The Essence of Free Speech

Hilliard, William A., 1993-94, 134-139, Values Deserving Our Attention

Hopkins, Claudia, 1996-97, 100-105, Learning Styles

Hyde, Henry J., 1994-95, 65-70, Congressional Term Limits

Jones, Ingrid Saunders, 1996-97, 106-110, Custodians of Our Culture

Jordan, Barbara, 1992-93, 111-117, The Arts and the American Dream

Jordan, Vernon E., Jr., 1994-95, 120-127, The Struggle Is Not Over; 1995-96, 101-107, Bridging the Racial Divide; 1996-97, 70-75, A Different Melody

Kagan, Donald, 1990-91, 167-174, E. Pluribus Unum

Kennedy, Edward M., 1994-95, 41-50, Commitment to Values; 1996-97, 51-55, The Issue of Prejudice

Kerman, George F., 1994-95, 128-132, Defining American Foreign Policy

Kindred, D. A., 1991-92, 182-192, Ninety Feet Is Perfection,

Lay, D. P., 1990-91, 105-111, Our Justice System, So-Called

Lewis, Bernard, 1990-91, 7-24, Western Civilization: A View from the East

Linowitz, Sol M., 1993-94, 175-178, Educating for National Security

Lyman, P. N., 1990-91, 74-81, Refugees in the 1990s

Mann, J. M., 1990-91, 82-92, Global AIDS: Revolution, Paradigm and Solidarity

Marier, Rebecca E., 1995-96, 120-124, Country Day Values

Mathews, J. T., 1990-91, 57-61, Man and Nature: The Future of Global Environment

McCullough, David, 1993-94, 148-160, A Sense of Proportion

Meneilly, Robert, 1993-94, 74-81, The Dangers of Religion

Minow, N. M., 1990-91, 111-125, Communication in Medicine; 1991-92, 158-169, How
    Vast the Wasteland Now?

Mitrovich, G. S., 1991-92, 36-48, Money and the Politics of Betrayal

Moseley-Braun, Carol, 1992-93, 123-127, Tribute to Thurgood Marshall; 1993-94,
    88-99, Getting Beyond Racism; 1996-97, 48-50, Church Burnings

Nolan, Joseph, 1992-93, 35-43, The Presidency and Public Opinion

Nunn, Sam, 1996-97, 56-61, The Whole World Is Watching

Paige, James H., 1995-96, 91-101, Dialogue, Interaction, and Commitment

Pelletreau, Robert H., 1996-97, 150-158, U.S. Policy Toward the Middle East: Steering
    a Steady Course

Perry, William J., 1996-97, 137-144, Completing Marshall's Plan in Europe

Peres, Shimon, 1993-94, 103-105, Building Peace in the Middle East

Perot, H. R., 1990-91, 25-36, First Commit the Nation, Then Commit the Troops

Powell, Colin, 1993-94, 179-192, American Military Leadership

Quayle, Dan, 1991-92, 71-79, The Most Litigious Society in the World

Rabin, Yitzhak, 1993-94, 106-108, Building Peace in the Middle East

Rather, Dan, 1993-94, 123-133, Call to Courage

Rawlings, H. R., 1992-93, 82-91, The University and the Public

Redford, Robert, 1990-91, 49-57, Saving the Environment

Reedy, G. E., 1990-91, 174-183, Changing Perspectives in Education

Reno, Janet, 1993-94, 39-47, Combating Crime; 1995-96, 15-24, Participating in the
    Process; 1996-97, 1-7, You Can Make a Difference

Roberts, Eugene L., Jr., 1993-94, 161-167, Writing for the Reader

Rogers, Britt, 1995-96, 184-188, Benefits and Responsibilities

Rooney, Andrew A., 1994-95, 88-95, Television News Reporting

Rudenstine, Neil L., 1995-96, 193-200, The Imagination of Prepared Minds

Sagan, Carl, 1992-93, 78-81, A Thousand Thomas Jeffersons

Saxon, Randall L., 1995-96, 172-178, A Better Country

Schindler, Alexander M., 1995-96, 166-172, The Value of Hospitality

Schlesinger, James R., 1994-95, 132-142, American Leadership, Isolationism, and
    Unilateralism

Schroeder, Patricia, 1996-97, 123-125, Proud of Liberal Accomplishments

Simon, Paul, 1993-94, 111-122, Violence on Television and Film: An Appeal for
    Responsibility; 1996-97, 67-69, Social Dynamite

Talbott, Strobe, 1996-97, 159-165, Ukraine at Five: A Progess Report on U.S. Policy

Tobias, R. L., 1992-93, 102-110, In Today Walks Tomorrow

Valenti, Jack J., 1994-95, 149-155, William Faulkner's Old Verities: It's Planting Time
    in America

Vazsonyi, Balint, 1996-97, 116-122, Four Points of the Compass: Restoring America's
    Sense of Direction

Wahls, Myron H., 1996-97, 76-82, The Moral Decay of America: Racism—Putting the American Dream Out of Reach

Watson, Courtney L., 1995-96, 178-181, Dreams: The Origin of Success

Wattleton, Faye, 1990-91, 125-128, Reproductive Freedom: Fundamental to All Human Rights

Wiesel, Elie, 1990-91, 69-73, The Shame of Hunger; 1994-95, 163-165, Close Your Eyes and Listen to the Silent Screams

Wireman, Billy O., 1996-97, 8-16, Productive Careers & Noble Lives: A New Mandate for Liberal Arts Education

Woo, William F., 1995-96, 138-152, As Old Gods Falter

Index

Adams, Abigail (quoted), 27
Adams, John (quoted), 27
Affirmative action
  benefits of, 67-68, 70-75
  Colin Powell as product of, 73
  criticism of, 67-68, 70-75, 85
African-American churches, burning of.
  See Church burnings
African Americans
  affirmative action and, 71-74
  first institution of higher education, 107
  preserving culture of, 106, 108
  racial discrimination. *See* Racism
African Methodist Episcopal Church, 106
Agency for International Development, 161
Air bag legislation, as accomplishment of
  liberals and Progressives, 124
America
  founding of, 116-17
  future of, 32, 35-41
  history, from perspective of inaugural
    address, 111-12
American Dream and racism, 79
American Indians, gambling houses run by, 126
American Legion, 33
American Legion Boys and Girls Nation, 32-33
Anthropological perspective on racism, 85-86
Anti-Semitism, 54, 85
APEC, 167, 170
Arab-Israeli conflict. *See* Middle East
Arafat, Yasir, 154
Arson, churches. *See* Church burnings
Art
  endurance of, 92
  as a human necessity, 90
  identity through, 89-93
  National Endowment for the Arts.
  See National Endowment for the Arts
ASEAN, 169
Asia
  China. *See* China
  economies of, 9, 170
  Korea. *See* Korea
  as leader in world progress, 12
  U.S-China relations and, 169
Asian Americans, affirmative action and,
  71-72, 74
A Way Out of No Way (Young), 109

B-2 Bomber, 97
Bakke decision, 68
Barkley, Charles, 60
Bartlett, Dewey, 61
Baseball, 95
Bazyluk, Teras, 159
Beat Generation, 91
Beethoven, 117
Belarus, 161
Bennett, Bob, 56
Berlin Wall, 9
Bernardin, Cardinal, 115
Bill of Rights, 35-36
Blacks. *See* African Americans
Blume, George, 33
Bosnia
  child's death in, 59
  ethnic hatred, 35
  Hungarian support for intervention, 139
  NATO involvement, 142-43
  Ron Brown, death in, 4
  Ukrainian soldiers in, 162
Botha, P.W., 64
Boys and Girls Nation, 32-33
Boys Nation, 33
Brady bill, 38
Brooklyn Bridge, 94
Brown, Morris, 106
Brown, Ron, 4
Budget deficit, 37
Bush, George (quoted), 9

Cambodia, 169
Campbell, Bill, 86
Campbell, Joan, 44
Caouette, Joe, 33
Caribbean, U.S. policy toward, 145-49
Carter, Jimmy, 153
Casino gambling, 126, 129-30
Cassidy, Michael, 64
Center for the American Founding, 116, 121
Central Europe
  Cold War. *See* Cold War, end of
    Marshall Plan, 137
  NATO expansion in, 139-40
Central European Free Trade Area, 163
Cervantes, Miguel de, Don Quixote, 24-25

Chace, Bill, 83
Champion v. *Ames* Supreme Court decision, 128
Character, 13-14
Chemical weapons, banning, 168
Chernobyl nuclear power plant explosion, 161-62
Children
    aspirations for, 17-18, 20, 22, 113-14
    poorest group of people in U.S., 21
    teacher's viewpoint of, 102-4
Chiles, Lawton, 61
China
    defense interests, 170
    economic growth, 170-71
    environmental destruction, 169
    as future superpower, 16
    global trading, 168
    Hong Kong, 170-71
    human rights in, 172
    law enforcement, 168
    nuclear weapons, halting spread of, 167-68
    relationship with United States, 166-73
    Taiwan, relation to, 170
"Choosing Good Government" (Barnes), 62-66
Christopher, Warren, 157, 163-64
Church Arson Protection Act of 1996, 51-55
Church burnings, 35, 43, 48-50
    Church Arson Protection Act of 1996, 51-55
    Matthews Murkland Presbyterian Church
      (Charlotte, NC), 44
    Mt. Zion African Methodist Episcopal
      Church (Greeleyville, SC), dedication of,
      43-47
    prosecution of, 46, 51-55
    synagogues, violence against, 54
"Church Burnings" (Moseley-Braun), 48-50
Churches, role in promoting unity, 45, 49
Civil Rights Act of 1964, 53
Civil Rights movement, 1-2, 9, 70-71, 87, 112
    as accomplishment of liberals and
      Progressives, 123
    church as civil rights bastion prior to, 45
    ongoing need for, 80-81
Civil War documentary films, 95-97
Clark, Johnny, 109
Clarke, John Henrik (quoted), 106
Clyburn, Congressman, 43
Coca-Cola Company, 106-7
Coe, Doug, 57, 60
Cohen v. *California* Supreme Court decision,
    131-32

Cold War, end of
    new opportunities for peace following, 138,
      153, 159, 167, 169
    new problems following, 9, 34, 57-58, 60,
      150-51
    peacefulness of, 57
College tuition, tax deduction for, 39
Communism, fall of. *See* Cold War, end of
Community, 13-14
    importance of art to, 90
Community Relations Service, 53
Compassion, need to teach value of, 15
"Completing Marshall's Plan in Europe" (Perry),
    137-144
Comprehensive Test Ban Treaty, 167
Connuck, Bruce, 160
Conscience, 13-14
Constitution
    First Amendment, 53
    racial unity and, 35-36
    return to principles of, 116, 118, 121-22
Conyers, John, 43, 46, 52
Corporation for Public Broadcasting, 97
Cosmetics industry, 28-29
Council of Europe, 163
Crime rate, 38
Crisis of the House Divided, The, 135
Cuba, 148
Culture, definition of, 107-8
"Custodians of Our Culture" (Jones), 106-110
Cynicism, 1-6

Dae Jung, Kim, 10
DeBois, W.E.B., 80
Declaration of Independence, 35-36, 118
"Dedication of the Mt. Zion African Methodist
    Episcopal Church" (Clinton, B.), 43-47
Defeatism, 1-2, 4-6
Deficit, budget, 37
Democracy. *See* also Cold War, end of
    complexity and, 3
    triumph of, 11
Department of Housing and Urban Development
    (HUD), 46, 52
Department of the Treasury, investigation of
    church burnings, 44, 53
Depression, Great
    libraries stayed open during, 98
    photographers of, 96

Deutch, John, 159
Dickerson, William F., 107
"Different Melody, A" (Jordan), 70-75
DNA of our civilization, libraries as, 96
Documentary films, importance of National Endowment for the Humanities funding of, 94-95
Domenici, Pete, 61
Domestic terrorism. *See* also Terrorism
  church burnings as, 48. *See* also Church burnings
  need to fight hatred and paranoia fueling, 3
  Oklahoma City Federal building bombing, 1, 6, 35
  World Trade Center bombing, 35
Domestic violence, 3
Don Quixote (Cervantes), 24-25
Dostoyevsky, 12
Douglass, Frederick, 80
Dove, Rita, 23-24, 30
  quoted, 23
Drug abuse, 78, 104
Drug safety laws, as accomplishment of liberals and Progressives, 124
Drug traffickers, 168
Duma (Russian parliament), 57

Eastern Europe
  Cold War. *See* Cold War, end of
  Marshall Plan, 138
  NATO expansion in, 137-40
Eban, Abba, 154
Eckerd College, 8
Economics as new master science, 11
Ecuador, 147
Edison, Harry "Sweets," 77-78
Educational documentaries, importance of National Endowment for the Humanities funding of, 94-95
Egypt, 152, 153, 155
Eisenhower, Dwight D., 142
Eliot, T.S. (quoted), 138
Emory University, 10
Energy technologies, new, 169
Engel, Ron, 33
Entitlements versus property, 120-21
Environment, improving, 37-38, 169
Ethnic hatred, 19, 35, 46-47, 71, 85, 151.
  See also Racism

end of Cold War and, 57
  "ethnic cleansing," 13
European Union, 163
Evans, Walker, 96
Extremism, 1-3, 5-6

Facism, 11
Faircloth, Lauch, 51
Faith and Humanity Award, 17-18
Family structure, 39, 57-59
Farm Securities Administration, 96
Federal Communications Commission, 40
Federal Emergency Management Agency, 48
Federalist Papers, 118
Feminist movement. *See* Women's movement
First Amendment, 53
First Things, 65
Florida Presbyterian College, 8
Flower Child era, 91
Food safety laws, as accomplishment of liberals and Progressives, 124
"Four Points of the Compass: Restoring America's Sense of Direction" (Vazsonyi), 116-122
France, NATO participation of, 144
Freedom versus authority, 62-64
Free Trade Area of the Americas (FTAA), 146-48
Fudan University (Shanghai, China), 166
Fukuyama, Francis, 11
Fuller, Millard, 46

Gaines, Wesley John, 107
Gambling, legalized, plea against, 126-36
Gangs, 38
Gates, Bill, *The Road from Here*, 34
General wealth, 14-15
Generation X, 91
Geyer, Georgie Anne, 29
Gingrich, Newt, 71
Girl Scouts of America, 23, 26, 29
Girls Nation, 32-33
Gore-Chernomyrdin Commission, 142
Government, vision of, 112-13
Grachev, Pavel, 142
Graham, Billy, 47
  quoted, 56
Great Depression

libraries stayed open during, 98
    photographers of, 96
Greenhouse effect, 169
Gregorian, Vartan, 96
    quoted, 96
Griffin v. Breckenridge, 55
Group of Seven major industrialized
    democracies, 162
Grunge, 91
Guatemala, 147
Gulf War, 153

Habitat for Humanity, 44, 46
Haiti, 147
Hamas, 154
Hamer, Fannie Lou, 87
Hands on Atlanta, 58
Han Nam University (South Korea), 8-10, 16
Harlan, John Marshall, 131
Harvard, Beverly, 109
Hate crimes, 49, 53
    church burnings. *See* Church burnings
Hate Crimes Statistics Act, 53
Hatfield, Mark, 61
Havel, Vaclav, 11, 13, 14
    quoted, 13
Head Start, as accomplishment of liberals and
    Progressives, 124
Hezbollah, 157
Higher education, growth in, 9
Hill, Larry, 44
Hippies, 91
Hispanics, affirmative action and, 71-72, 74
History, importance of (quotation by John
    Henrik Clarke), 107
Hollings, Senator, 43
Holmes, Gary, 109
Hong Kong, 170-71
Hopwood case, 67-68
Horbulyn, Volodymyr
"House Divided, A" (Cole), 83-88
Hubble telescope, 25
HUD (Department of Housing and Urban
    Development), 46, 52
Hughes, Harold, 61
Hungary, NATO aspirations of, 139
Hurricane Andrew, 6
Hussein, King, 19, 150
Hussein, Saddam, 151, 153

Hyde, Henry, 46, 52

"I care" generation, 91
"Identity Through Art" (Alexander), 89-93
Ideology, demise of, 10-11
IFOR (implementation force), 139, 143
Improvisation, 78-79
"Independence Day," 36
Indians, American, gambling houses run by, 126
Inglis, Congressman, 43
Internet, 2, 38, 90, 113
Interstate commerce, Church Arson Protection
    Act of 1996 and, 54-55
In the Beauty of the Lilies (Updike), 65
Intifada, 154
Iran, 152, 168
Iraq, 152
Iron Curtain, 1, 57. *See also* Cold War, end of
Islamic Jihad, 154
Israel
    peace in, 18-21, 35
    U.S. policy toward, 17-18, 150, 152-58
"Issue of Prejudice, The" (Kennedy), 51-55

Jackson, Jesse, 44, 70
Jaffa, Harry V., 135
James, Bishop, 44
James, William, 26
Japanese Americans, denied civil liberties in
    World War II, 68
Jefferson, Thomas, 95-96, 118, 120
Jiang Zemin, 167
Jim Crow, 45, 51, 71
Johnson, Ed, 44
Johnson, Lyndon, 9
    quoted, 72-73
Johnson, Pete, 33
Jolley, Samuel, 108-9
Jones, Mack, 44
Jones v. Alfred H. Mager Co., 55
Jordan, 150, 152, 153, 155
Joulwan, George, 142-43

Kempthorne, Dirk, 57
Kennedy, John, 9
Kennedy, Robert, 9
Kim, O-Bong, 9

King, B. B., 64
King, Martin Luther, Jr., 4, 6-7, 9, 77, 84
  quoted, 7, 45, 54, 108
Kluckhohn, Clyde, 87
Kokoshin, Andrey, 140, 142
Korea
  progress in, 9-10, 12, 16
  U.S.-China relations and, 169
Korean Herald, The, 9
Korematsu Supreme Court decision, 68
Ku Klux Klan, 51
Kuwait, 153

Lake, Tony, 164
Laney, James, 10
Lange, Dorthea, 96
Las Vegas, Nevada, 135-36
Latin America, U.S. policy toward, 145-49
  democracy, strengthening, 147-48
  economic reforms, 148-49
  poverty, 148
  resolution of disputes, 147
Leaders, selection of, religious perspective,
  62-66
Leadership, 109
"Learning Styles" (Hopkins), 100-105
Learning styles, uniqueness of, 101-2
Lebanon, 153, 157-58
Lee, Won Sul, 9
Lentsov, Alexandr, 142
Leonard, R.A., 44
Lewis, Bernard, 156
Lewis and Clark, government support of, 96
Liberal arts, origins of, 12
Liberals, accomplishments of, 123-25
Libraries
  as DNA of our civilization, 96
  New York Public Library, 96
  open during Great Depression, 98
Libya, 152
Likud, 155
Limits, challenging, 23-31
Lincoln, Abraham, 45, 84, 135
  quoted, 98
Li Peng, 167, 169
Locke, John, 120
Lohman, Patricia, 44
Long, Huey, 94
Lotteries, 128-29, 131

Low, Juliette Gordon, 26
Lowery, Joseph, 44
Lynchings, 45, 51

Mackey, Reverend, 43-44
Madison, James, 120
Madrid Middle East peace conference, 153
Magna Carta, 118
Malcolm X, 9
Mandela, Nelson, 14
Man of La Mancha (theater), 24
Maoz, Moshe, 150
Marshall, George C., 137, 144
Marshall Plan, 138-40, 144
  as accomplishment of liberals and
    Progressives, 123-24
Mather, Cotton (quoted), 131
Matthews Murkland Presbyterian Church
  (Charlotte, NC), burning of, 44
McCartan, Joyce, 19
McCarthy, Joe, 27
McCree, Mary, 107
McDonnell, John, 76
McGill, Ralph, 87
McKinley, William, 33
McVeigh, Timothy, 1
Mead, Margaret, 87
Medicare, as accomplishment of liberals and
  Progressives, 123
Me Generation, 91
Mercier, Jack, 33
Meshach, Shadrach, and Abednego, 44, 63
Middle East
  peace in, 18-21, 35
  U.S. policy toward, 17-18, 150, 152-58
Middleton, Merlissie, 106
Millenium change, differing ways to view, 92
"Moral Decay of America: Racism–Putting the
  American Dream Out of Reach, The" (Wahls),
  76-82
Morality, rebirth of, 76
Morocco, 155
Morris, Katherine, 33
Morris Brown College, 106-10
Mt. Zion African Methodist Episcopal Church
  (Greeleyville, SC), dedication of, 43-47
Mubarak, Muhammad Hosni, 19
Multiculturalism, 121

NAFTA (North American Free Trade Agreement), 148-49
Nash, William, 142
National Coalition Against Legalized Gambling, 126
National Council of Churches, 46-47
National Council of Jewish Women, 17-18, 21
National Endowment for the Arts (NEA), 89-91
  controversy concerning, 90-91
  funding of, 90-91
  importance of, 97
National Endowment for the Humanities (NEH)
  broad public support of, 97
  controversy concerning, 98
  importance of, 94-99
  proposal process, 95
National identity versus nationalism, 120
National Institute of Mental Health, 126
National Security and Defense Council, 164
NationsBank, 47
NATO (North Atlantic Treaty Organization), 137-44
  Russia and, 137, 140-43
  Ukraine and, 163-64
NEA. *See* National Endowment for the Arts
NEH. *See* National Endowment for the Humanities
Netanyahu, Prime Minister, 155-57
New world order, 151
New York Public Library, 96
Nichols, Terry L., 1
Nixon, Richard, 9
Non-Proliferation Treaty, 167
North American Free Trade Agreement (NAFTA), 148-49
North Atlantic Treaty Organization. *See* NATO
Northern Ireland, 35
Northern Michigan University, 77
Nuclear test ban, as accomplishment of liberals and Progressives, 124
Nuclear weapons, halting spread of, 167-68
Nunn, Michelle, 58

Offtrack betting, 126-27
Oil, Persian Gulf, access to, 152
Oklahoma City, bombing of federal building in, 1, 6, 35

Olympic Games, 83, 109
Oman, 155
Operation Uphold Democracy (Haiti), 147
Organization for Economic Cooperation and Development, 163
Organization on Security and Cooperation in Europe (OSCE), 163
Osborne, Randall, 44
"Our Global Family" (Clinton, H.), 17-22

Palestinian Authority, 156
Palestinians, 153, 154-56
Parks, Rosa, 87
Partnership for Peace (PFP), 138-41
  Ukraine and, 162-64
Pasqual, Carlos, 159
Paul, Apostle, 62-63
PBS (Public Broadcasting System), 95-97
Peace Now, 19
Perry Middle School Task Force, 5-6
Peru, 147
PFP. *See* Partnership for Peace
Phelan v. *Virginia* Supreme Court decision, 128-29
Philippines, end of dictatorship in, 57
Plesy v. *Ferguson* Supreme Court decision, 68
Poland, NATO aspirations of, 139
Potomac Foundation, 116
Powell, Colin, as product of affirmative action, 73
Prejudice. *See* Racism
"'Private' Gambling and Public Morality" (Anastaplo), 126-136
"Productive Careers & Noble Lives: A New Mandate for Liberal Arts Education" (Wireman), 8-16
Progressive Era, 33-34
Progressives, accomplishments of, 123
Prohibitionists, 126
Property versus entitlements, 120-21
Proposition 209
"Proud of Liberal Accomplishments" (Schroeder), 123-125
Public Broadcasting System (PBS), 95-97
Public television, 95-97

Qatar, 155
Qian Qichen, 167
Queens College (Charlotte, NC), 8, 15-16

Rabin, Yitzhak, 154
Racism, 35, 51, 67-76. *See* also Ethnic hatred
    affirmative action. *See* Affirmative action
    American Dream and, 79
    anthropological perspective on, 85-86
    anti-Semitism, 54, 85
    church burnings. *See* Church burnings
    church's role in fighting, 45
    cross burning, 49
    lynchings, 45, 51
    moving past, 50, 80, 113
    patterns of, 46
Reeves, Thomas, 65
Religious differences, 35
Religious vision, America and, 65-66
"Remarks to the American Legion Boys and Girls
    Nation" (Clinton, B.), 32-41
Rich, Nan, 17-18
Rodman, Dennis, 60
Rogue regimes, 152
Roosevelt, Franklin Delano, 111
Roosevelt, Theodore, 33-34
Rosensweig, Jeffrey, 10
Rule of Law versus social justice, 117-21
Rumania, NATO aspirations of, 139
Russia
    Cold War. *See* Cold War, end of
    Middle East peace process, 153
    NATO expansion and, 137, 140-43

Sadat, Anwar, 153
Sanger, Margaret (quoted), 27
Sappenfield, Peggy, 33
Sargent, John Singer, 33
Sasser, James, 171
Sasser, Mary, 171
Saudi Arabia, 152
Schlesinger, Arthur, Jr., 2
    quoted, 99
Schopenhauer, Arthur, 25
Schwartz, Hillel, 92
Science, endurance of, 92
"Second Inaugural Address" (Clinton, B.),
    111-115
Sexism, overcoming, 26-28. *See* also Women's
    movement
Shadrach, Meshach, and Abednego, 44, 63
Shakers, 95
Shakespeare, 24, 117

Shanghai, China, 169, 171
    Film Festival, 171
SHAPE (Supreme Headquarters Allied Powers
    Europe), 143
Shevtsov, Leontiy, 142
Simpson, Alan, 56
Simpson, O.J., 76
"Sky's No Limit at All, The" (Barone), 23-31
Slovakia, NATO aspirations of, 139
Smith, Adam, The Wealth of Nations, 14
Smith, Jerry, 68
Smith, Margaret Chase (quoted), 27-28
"Social Dynamite" (Simon), 67-69
Social justice
    need to struggle for, 80-81
    rule of law versus, 117-21
Social Security, as accomplishment of liberals
    and Progressives, 123
Solomon, Mary, 5-6
Somerville, John, 9
Soong Sil University (Seoul, South Korea), 10
Soviet Union, dissolution of, 159, 161. *See* also
    Cold War, end of
Spelman College, 83
Sperry, Lawrence, 33
St. Agnes Catholic Church (Kanawha City, WV),
    76
Stalin, Joseph, 138
Statue of Liberty documentary film, 94-95
Substance abuse, 78, 104
Supreme Court
    gambling-related decisions, 128-29, 131
    race-related decisions, 67-68
Supreme Headquarters Allied Powers Europe
    (SHAPE), 143
Surrell, Matt, 77
Sustainable Development, 146, 169
Synagogues, violence against, 54. *See* also
    Church burnings
Syria, 153, 157
Taiwan, 170
Taylor, Bill, 160
Teaching profession, 100-105
    children today, teacher's viewpoint, 102-4
    learning styles, uniques of, 101-2
Television
    public, 95-97
    V-chip for parental control, 40
Terrorism, 71, 151
    domestic, 1, 3, 6, 35, 48. *See* also

Church burnings
fighting, 3, 35-36, 168
Israel, 19-20
Northern Ireland, 19
Oklahoma City Federal building bombing,
   1, 6, 35
TWA flight 800, crash of, 32-33
U.S. troops, bombing of in Saudi Arabia,
   152
World Trade Center bombing, 35
The Road from Here (Gates), 34
Thomas, Annie, 107
"To Dream the Impossible Dream" (song), 25
Tokyo, poison gas in subway, 35
Toukan, Abdullah, 150
Treasury Department, investigation of church
   burnings by, 44, 53
Truman, Harry, 124
Trust, need to teach value of, 15
Truth, Sojourner (quoted), 27
Tunisia, 155
TWA flight 800, crash of, 32-33

Udovenko, Hennadiy, 164
Ukraine
   currency of, 161
   U.S. policy toward, 141, 159-66
"Ukraine at Five: A Progress Report on U.S.
   Policy" (Talbot), 159-165
United Board for Christian Higher Education in
   Asia, 10
United Nations, 151
Universal Declaration of Human Rights, 172
University of California at Berkeley, 72
University of Texas, 67-68
Updike, John, *In the Beauty of the Lilies*, 65
"U.S. and China: Buillding a New Era of
   Cooperation for a New Century, The"
   (Christopher), 166-173
U.S. Information Agency, 161
"U.S. Policy Toward Latin America and the
   Caribbean: Buidling Upon a Solid

Foundation" (Davidow), 145-149
"U.S. Policy Toward the Middle East: Steering a
   Steady Course" (Pelletreau), 150-158
Verveer, Melanne, 159
Vietnam War, 9
Violence in America
   domestic, 3
   reducing, 38
   terrorism. *See* Domestic terrorism
"Vital center" in politics, 2-3, 6
Voiko, Jaroslav, 159
Voting rights, as accomplishment of liberals and
   Progressives, 123

Washington, George, 117-18
Wealth of Nations (Smith), 14
Western Europe, Marshall Plan and, 138-40
West Virginia Council of Churches, 76
White, Randall, 90
"Whole World Is Watching, The" (Nunn),
   56-61
Wilson, Woodrow, 34
Wisdom, 12
Women's movement, 9, 26, 28, 91
   as accomplishment of liberals and
      Progressives, 123
   affirmative action and, 71, 73
Woodstock 2, 91
World Bank, 151
World Trade Center bombing, 35
World Trade Organization (WTO), 163, 168
World Wide Web, 91
"Worth Defending" (Burns), 94-99
Wylie, Steward, 107

"You Can Make a Difference" (Reno), 1-7
Young, Andrew, "A Way Out of No Way," 109
Yugoslavia, 19, 120
   Bosnia. *See* Bosnia
Yuppies, 91